manifestations of buddhas

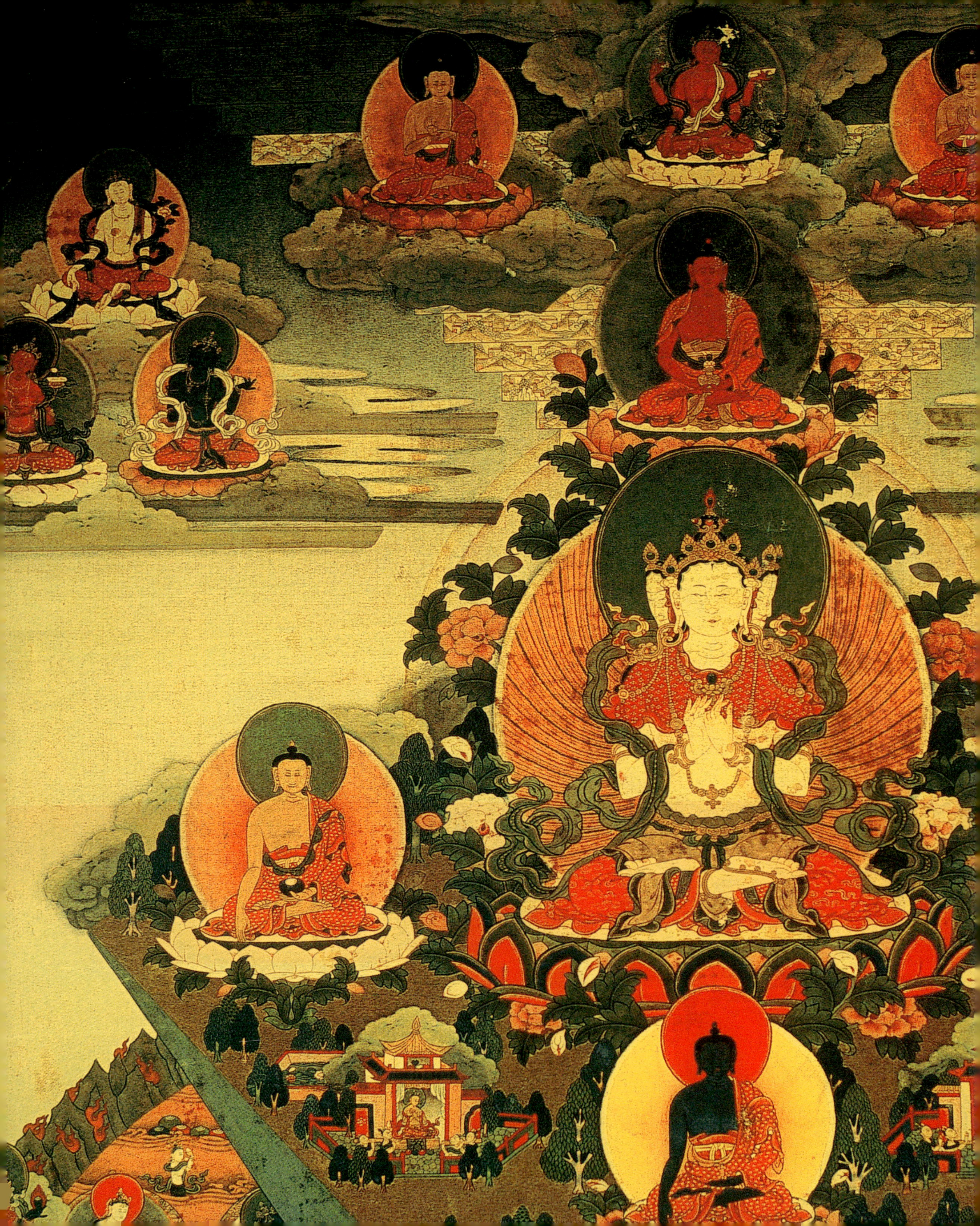

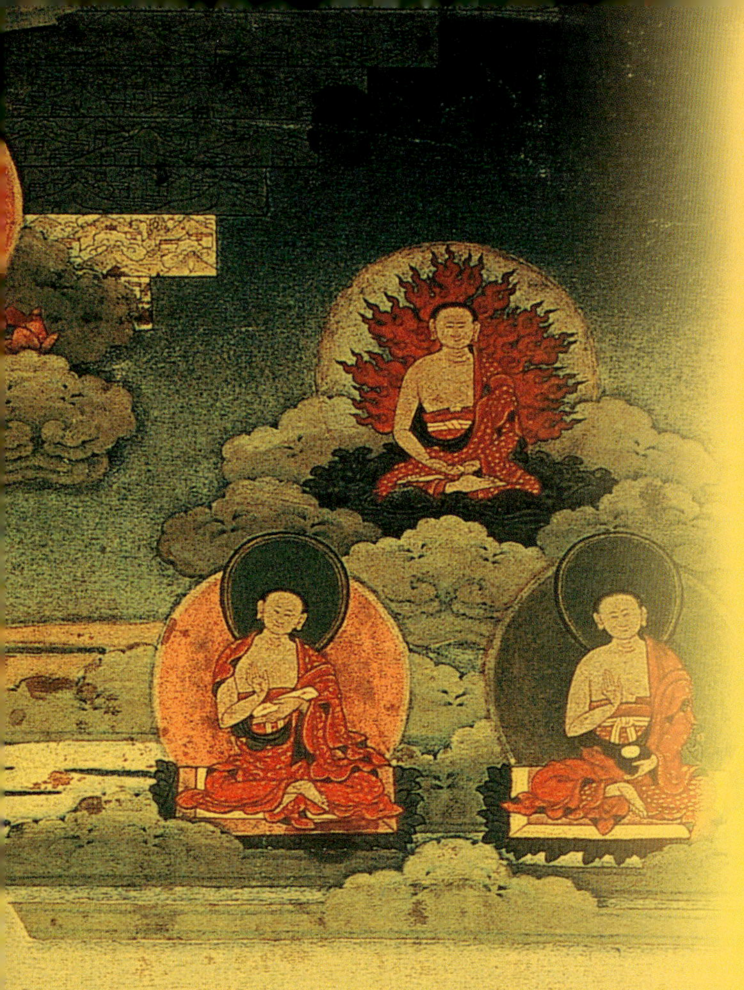

manifestations of buddhas

Shashibala

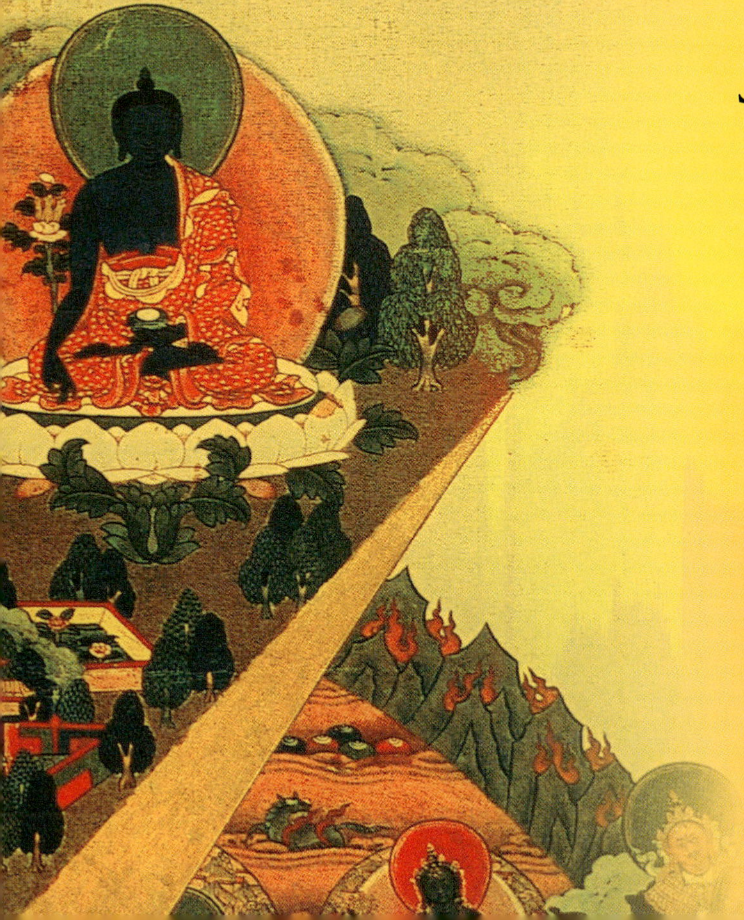

Lustre Press
Roli Books

ISBN: 978-81-7436-457-9

Published in India by
Roli Books arrangement with Roli & Janssen BV
M-75 Greater Kailash II Market
New Delhi 110 048 India.
Ph: ++91-11-29212782, 29210886
Fax: ++91-11-29217185
E-mail: roli@vsnl.com
Website: rolibooks.com

Editor: Neelam Narula
Design: Mukesh Singh
Layout: Narendra Kumar
Production: Kumar Raman & Naresh Nigam

Printed and bound in Singapore

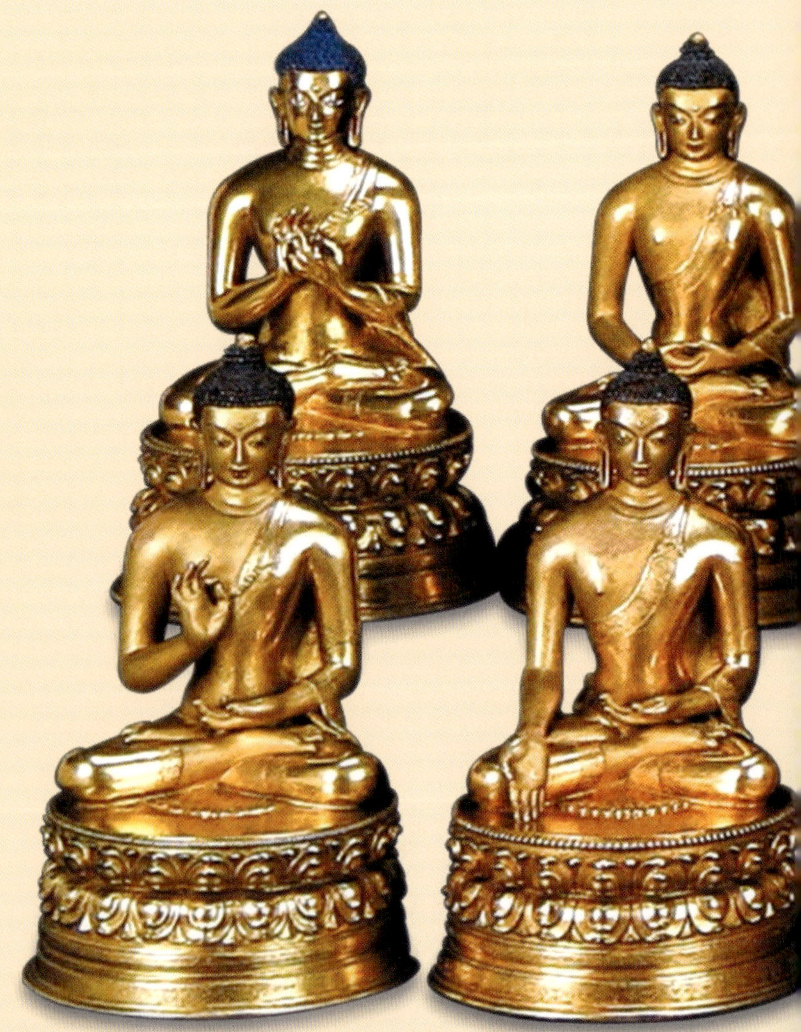

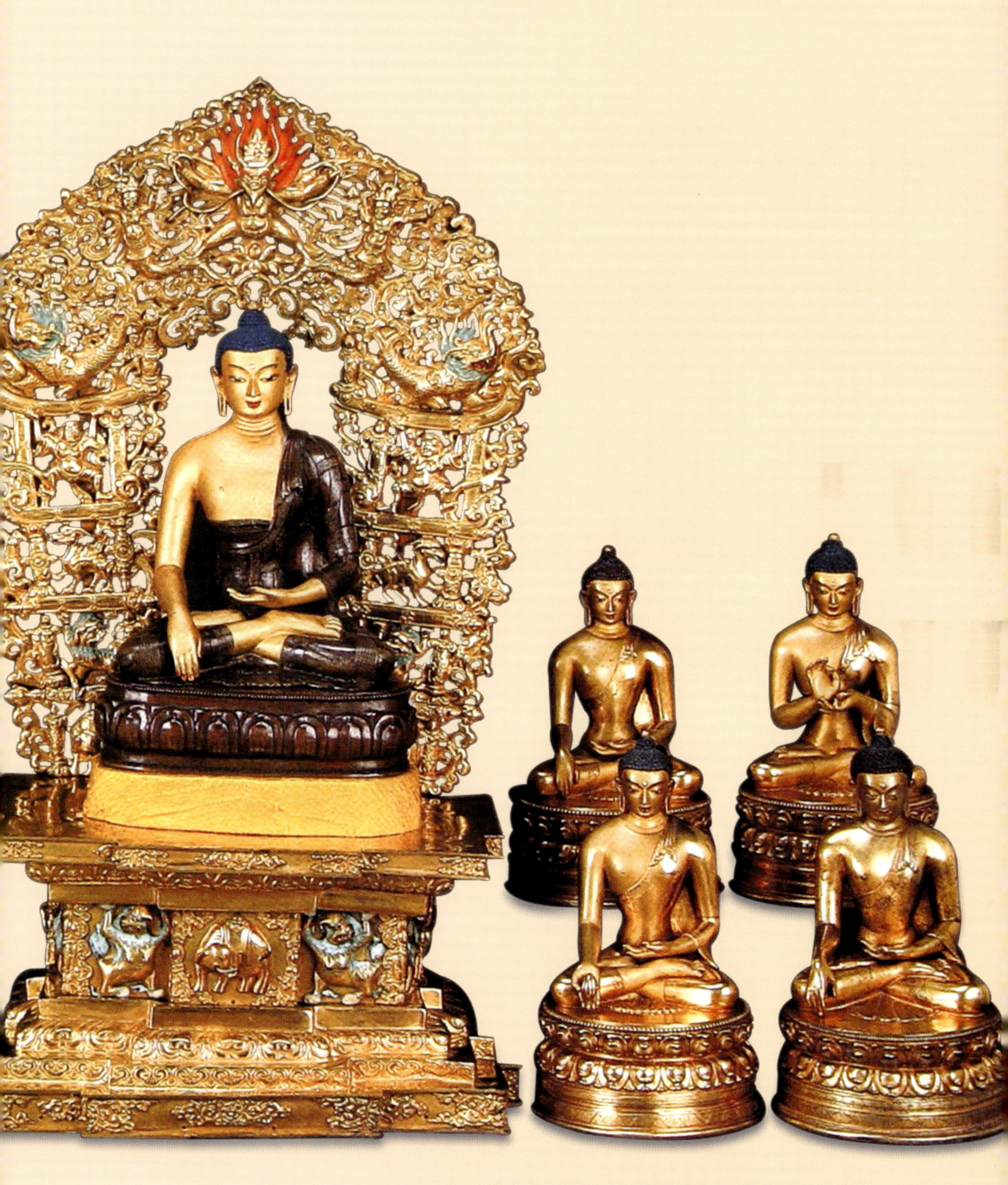

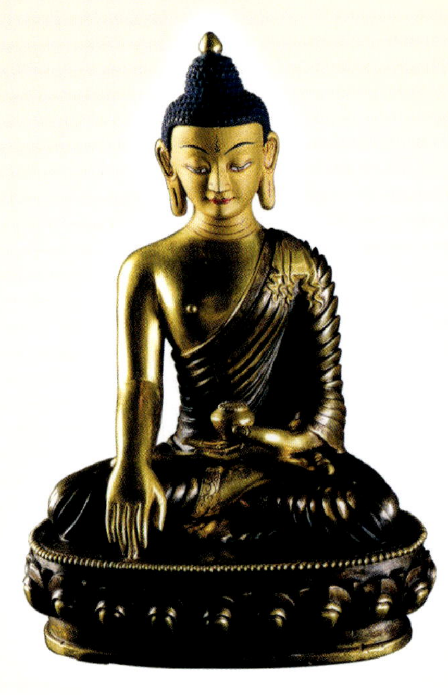

~

Dedicated to
Prof Lokesh Chandra

~

Contents

Introduction

There are several Buddhas, manifested in various forms and attitudes. 'Buddha', a philosophic term connoting an enlightened being, comes from the root in Sanskrit *'budh'* meaning 'to be enlightenend'. The term is not strictly used for Shakyamuni, the Historical Buddha. The Buddha has a multi-faceted personality – he is the Sage of the sages, the Divine Mendicant, a Yogi, a Teacher, a Prince, an Enlightened Being, a Compassionate Saviour, a Jina or the true conqueror, and a Healer. He is also depicted as a Universal Monarch, a Future Hope, the Transcendental Light, and Infinite Life.

When Shakyamuni became silent, and entered the unshackled state of existence or the final *nirvana*, the devotees wanted to adore and remember the Historical Buddha and this served as an inspiration for the creation of Buddha images. The followers could not accept that their teacher had completed his earthly sojourn and had departed forever. To venerate him in his absence, they distributed his relics and enshrined them in stupas. The Buddha, in his incarnation of a mortal being had assumed the most profound level of existence as *Dharmakaya*, or the Absolute. Thus the stupas began to serve as rememberances of the divine being. Symbolically, Buddha was represented in the form of footprints, an empty throne or other symbols. The ritualistic worship of the Buddha included placing garlands on these stupas, chanting mantras, and burning incense. But, the symbols were perceived to be inadequate for the expression of a devotee's *bhakti*. A suppressed yearning germinated in the hearts of the devotees for something more evocative and sensibly visual of the Supreme Lord.

Visualization of the Buddha initially began with formless, aniconic representations. Teachings and messages of the sutras were conveyed in consonance with symbols and shapes. The earliest known symbolic pictorial representations of the Buddhist art forms are found on the Ashokan pillars followed by the Jataka stories at Sanchi. Jatakas are a statement of the long evolution of the Dharma, or Buddhism, in hundreds of pre-incarnations of the Buddha. Earlier Dharma was eternalized through art, but gradually Buddhist iconography evolved from aniconic symbols like a cushioned throne, a tree of enlightenment, footprints, the wheel of law, amongst others, to anthropomorphic forms and complex mandalas containing different types of Buddhas.

Image of the Buddha in human likeness, in the iconic form began to appear in early red sandstone sculptures in Mathura. Seated and standing images in Indo-Hellenistic style sculpted in the northwestern region of ancient India during first-second century AD, became standardized in Indian art and was taken to other countries.

An intense debate arose within the monastic order as early as the first hundred years after the Mahaparinirvana of the Buddha. Some monks questioned the authenticity of the early scriptures and claimed to add new texts to them while others accepted the Pali Buddhist canon as the highest authority. Shortly before the beginning of the Christian era, a new form of Buddhism appeared in opposition to what is called Sravakayana or 'Vehicle of the Listeners' or Theravada, which was known as Mahayana. The Mahayana school of thought shifted focus from Arhatship, the aim of the followers of Shravakayana, to Bodhisattvahood. Shravakas sought entry into *nirvana* as quickly as possible while the Mahayanists aspired to become a Buddha and attain omniscience in order to devote themselves to welfare and happiness of all beings. The Bodhisattva concept also showed a way to venerate someone who could lead them to *nirvana* having postponed his own entry into it.

The Shravakas kept the Buddha on human plane. They claimed him to be the pre-eminent master endowed with knowledge and practice who became invisible after *nirvana*. But this could not satisfy the popular aspirations, which demanded a supreme spirit, and a pantheon. Thus Buddha was transformed into a 'God superior to the gods', and surrounding him were a host of other major and minor deities as well as powerful disciples. The followers of Mahayana increased the number of Buddhas and great Bodhisattvas.

Thus Buddhism started becoming a tradition of the visual, wherein images and murals translated the message of the sutras. And therefore buddhists started building their pantheon with multiplicity, which arose from meditation when mind is associated with *shunya* or

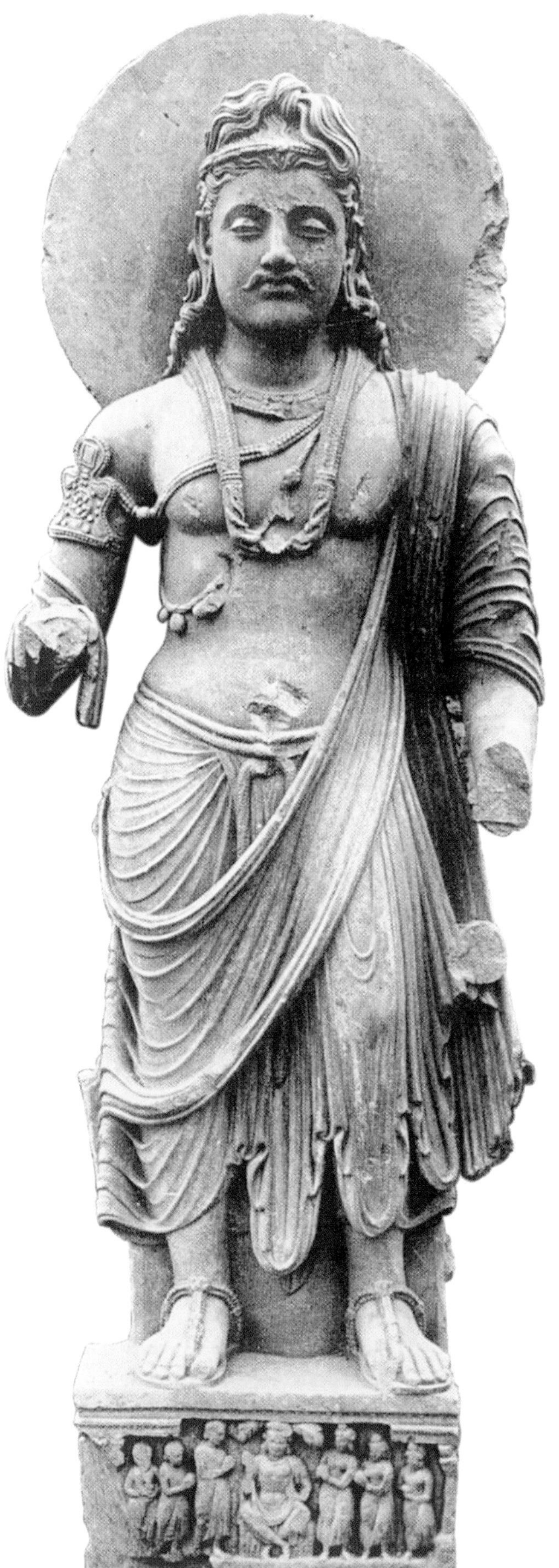

void at the highest state. Then the *bodhicitta* thought of enlightenment gets dissolved and visualizes spark-like innumerable visions, gradually assuming forms of various deities full of glory and divine beauty, adorned with ornaments and dressed in finery; while the deities who are worshipped to subdue the evil doers are violent in expression with disheveled hair, blood shot eyes, bare fangs, with ornaments made of human skulls and bones, and carrying terrifying weapons.

Greco-Buddhists are believed to have sculpted the first buddhist images. The *Guhya-samaja-tantra* is the first book to contain the idea of a well-classified pantheon with descriptions of Buddhas with their respective *mantra*s, *mandala*s and *prajnas* or female counterparts.

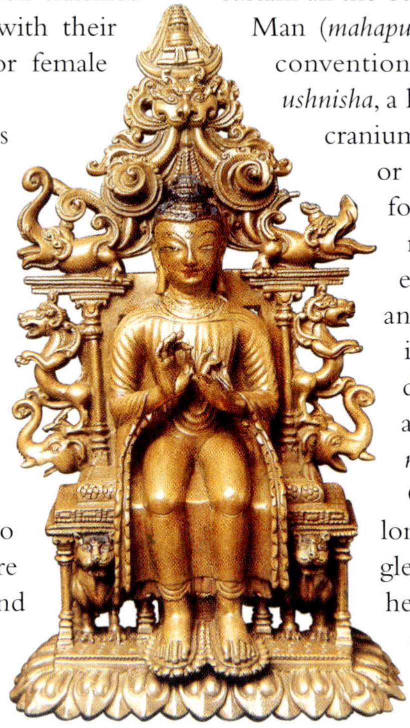

As the need for efficacious protectors grew more pressing, the devotees conceived a compassionate Buddha as Maitreya, and a universal monarch as Rocana. Amitabha, the Buddha of Infinite Light, and Amitayus the Buddha of Infinite Lifespan rule over the western paradise – Sukhavati. Akshobhya, the immovable, rules the eastern direction and resides in the Abhirati paradise. Bhaishajyaguru, the physician for the physical as well as spiritual illnesses also holds sway in the east. There are manifestations of Buddha's wisdom and compassion as well.

Devotion combined with needs and aspirations of people gave way to creation of a variety of Buddhas manifested in various forms in different countries across the world. The Mahayana pantheon infinitely increased the number of Buddhas, their respective abodes and the residents therein. For the devotees these images were supernatural beings who would lead them on their way to salvation. While making the Buddha images artists lent their own style and regional characteristics to their creations.

Buddhas in their *dharmakaya* forms constitute the transposition of the doctrine itself. They are enthroned in paradises in the midst of assemblies of gods and holy ones, whom they enchant with their *sambhogakaya*. Finally, they send into this world likeness of themselves called *niramanakaya* who expound the doctrine and show the path to *nirvana*. Images of the historical Buddha Shakyamuni serve as models for all the later manifestations. He is beyond all kinds of pain and pressures of the mortal world.

Varied conceptions regarding the Buddha gave rise to a kaleidoscopic iconography. Images of the Buddhas are primarily composed of symbolic and spiritual elements. The artistic considerations enhance and sustain all the other values. Thirty-two signs of a Great Man (*mahapurusha*) are seen in early iconographic conventions. For example Buddha, has an *ushnisha*, a lock of hair curled up at the top of his cranium. *Urna* is a small round bump of flesh or a tuft of hair in the middle of his forehead that emanates light. Three rings of flesh encircle his neck, his earlobes are exceptionally elongated, and a thousand-spoked wheel is imprinted on his soles. His soft skin does not hint at roughness. His fingers are webbed. Following the *mahapurusha lakshana*s or signs of a Great Man, his arms are exceptionally long and touch his knees. His body gleams, and there is a halo round his head. He is often shown taller than others while depicting narrative scenes. Apart from thirty-two auspicious signs, there are eighty subsidiary features of a superhuman that are added while portraying a Buddha through painting or sculpture.

Buddhas, as manifestations of the Absolute, are depicted in regal vestments more often than in the monk's robes. This tendency increased with the passage of time because one of the attributes of kingship is victory and Buddha is a jina, he who has won the great victory. Therefore Buddha images are usually adorned with regal robes, crowns, necklaces, and other jewels. He is a Universal Monarch, a *chakravartin*. Some Buddha statues are adored with flames at the shoulders and water flowing from his feet. As the Buddha of Healing, he is called Bhaishajyaguru. There are Buddhas who sit and preach in full majesty. Amitabha is one of them; he has risen to the paradise of beatitude, Sukhavati. Another Buddha form is Akshobhya, who is surrounded by the choirs of the blessed in Abhirati heaven, and Maitreya, the Future Buddha in Tushita heaven.

Buddha images can be identified through their attributes and characteristic features, such as Amitayus holds a vase containing the nectar of longevity, Shakyamuni often sits in dharma-chakra-pravartana-, bhumisparsha-, or varada-mudra. But attributes and mudras differ in different traditions and texts, and symbolise various aspects. Preaching of the Law alludes to the revelation and availability of truth to man. Protection or assurance signifies that only Truth can free man from the cycle of rebirth. Touching the Earth, bhumi-sparsha mudra, for example, refers to the certainty of possessing the Truth. The mudra of meditation recalls that without concentration Truth will not shine.

Each Buddha has his own throne or vehicle – Akshobhya rides an elephant, Vairocana a dragon, Amitabha a peacock, Ratnasambhava a horse, and Amoghasiddhi a Garuda. They can also be distinguished through their colours: Akshobhya and his family are blue, Vairocana is white, Amitabha is red, Ratnasambhava is yellow, and Amoghasiddhi green. Colour as an essential element in mystic symbolism replaces the splendour of gold. Buddha was of golden colour, and all the images were gilded because gold was the sign of resplendent spiritual luminosity.

Thus Buddha images became symbolic representations of the Absolute. A deep spiritual significance is attached to their characteristic features. For example, white and yellow colours are prescribed for *shantikavidhi* or propitiatory rites, for protective rites yellow is used and for bewitching and attraction, that is *vashyavidhi* and *akarsana*, yellow, green or red are prescribed. Blue is meant for the terrific ones. All thirty-two signs of greatness and eighty subsidiary signs should be exhibited in a Buddha image. An image should carry symbols of Buddha nature in his hands, and these attributes are supposed to confer Buddhahood or success in rites. This led to complex iconography described in texts. Major literary works on iconography are *Nishpannayogavali* by Mahapandita Abhayakara and *Sadhanamala*. Buddhist icons in painting and sculpture are different aspects of religious beliefs and they function as an aid in meditation and comprehension of spiritual truths. An icon should be regarded as a reflected image or shadow of a supreme being, the creator, the preserver and the destroyer of the world.

Sutras, the canonical scriptures of the teachings of Buddha developed and constantly introduced new forms of Buddhas. While Avatamsaka sutras refer to Buddha as colossus, the Lotus Sutra represents him as being flanked by Samantabhadra and Manjushri, Amitayurdhyan-sutra as Amitayus, Sukhavativyuha-sutra as Amitabha. They provide lists of Buddhas such as Seven Historical Buddhas, Buddhas of Three Times, Buddhas of Ten Directions, Thirty-five Buddhas of Confession, Tathagatas are contributed by Mahavairocana-sutra and Sarvatathataga-tattva-sangraha.

Therefore, from the second century BC to the modern times, iconographically and stylistically different images, from tiny amulets to colossi, from the simplest to the most sophisticated and well-defined forms, from a mendicant to bejeweled and crowned Buddha, wearing rich garments have been created by devoted artistes.

Pantheons were drawn and painted using iconographical details prescribed by the sutras and tantras. These iconographic treasures correlate to the texts, which were unique to aid in creating iconographically varied forms. Tibetans and Mongols create the divine in statues and scrolls to visualize the ineffable, the immeasurable in the immense network of monasteries, hermitages, and other sacred places. The deities of heaven merge into icons in the cave temples in China, painted on the walls or carved out of rocks. Hundreds of thousands of bronze, wood and clay images brought forth a combination of artistic skills and devotion, material splendour and state power to the visual representation.

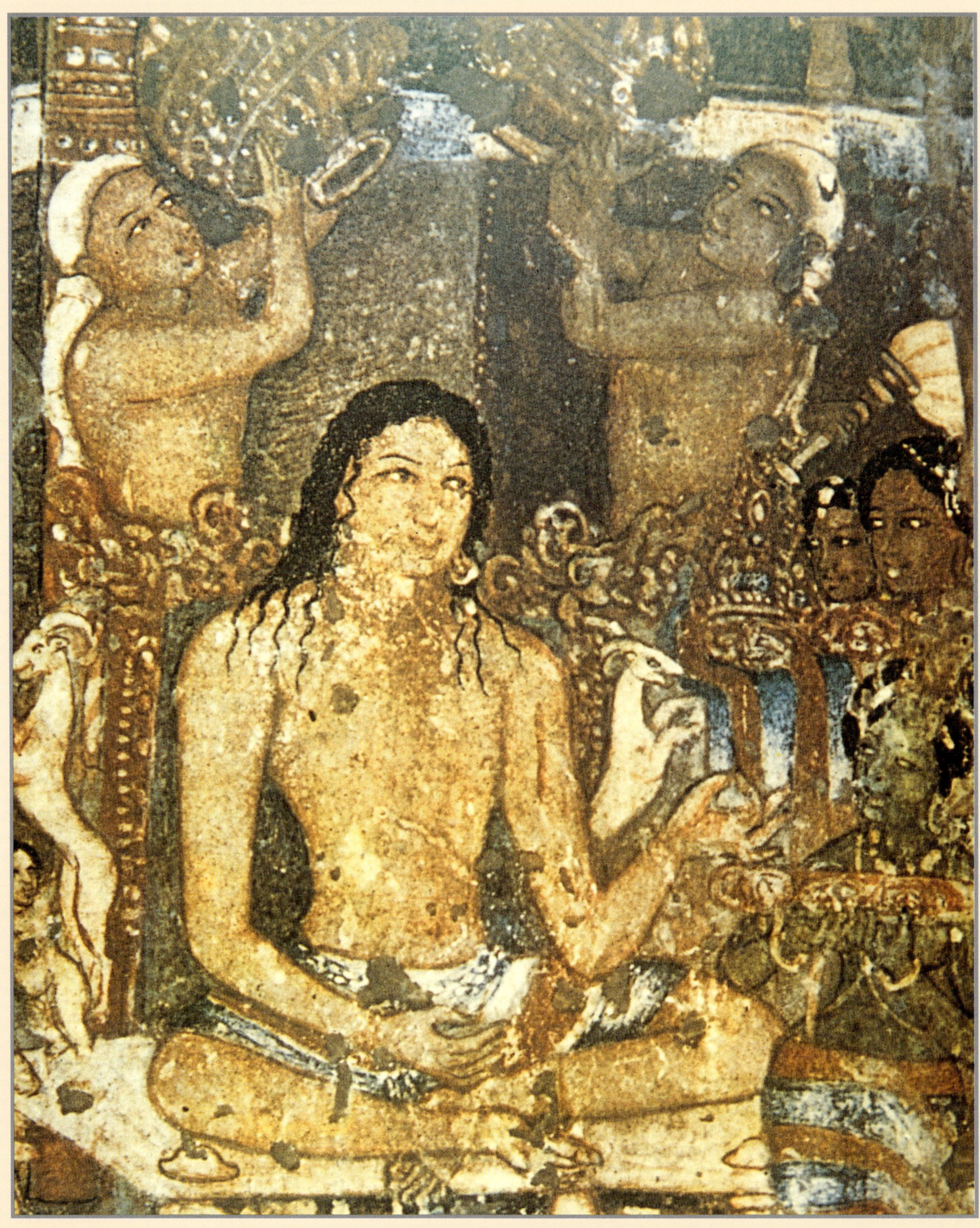

Before the Earthly Sojourn

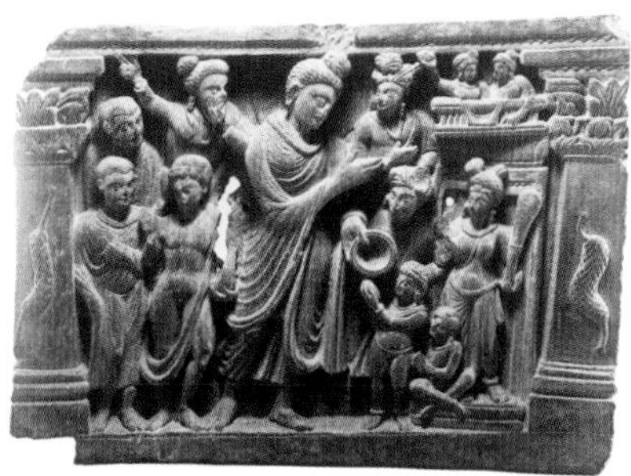

Lord Buddha traversed this earth a number of times before taking birth as a prince, born as the son of King Shuddhodana. As a prince he renounced the world, meditated hard, got enlightenment, and became a Buddha. His previous births as a man, a deity, or as one of the higher animals, are detailed in the form of stories called Jatakas. Most of these stories portray him as an exemplary figure highlighting his qualities such as wisdom, compassion and ascetic detachment. Jataka has been used as a term for denoting a particular genre of Buddhist literature. Buddha attained a recollection of all his previous lives on the day he attained *bodhi* or enlightenment. He used to talk and quote from these recollections during his sermons whenever he found it necessary to relate a point or shed light on some aspects of his teachings. Sometimes these stories were quoted for giving moral or social lessons to the followers. Buddha is depicted as a Bodhisattva in the Jatakas. During his career as a Bodhisattva he makes a vow, a *pranidhana*, to become a Buddha. A Bodhisattva has *bodhi*, or perfect wisdom as essence, or he is said to be a being who is seeking for *bodhi* or is destined to attain enlightenment.

Thus stories in the Jatakas illustrate that Buddha in his previous lives cultivated various virtues and qualities, which finally contributed to his attainment of Buddhahood. *Jatakatthakatha*, Explanation of Birth Stories is a massive collection of 547 prose and verse Jatakas. The Jatakas do not only exist in Sanskrit and Pali literature but also in the Chinese and Tibetan canons including several vernacular languages and texts. Many of the Jatakas are intended to illustrate the Bodhisattva's cultivation of one of the ten perfections known as Paramitas, necessary for attaining Buddhahood. Stories of the Jatakas are arranged according to the perfections, which are ten in the Theravada tradition, and six in the Mahayana tradition. In

ABOVE: *Presentation of dust, told in Divyavadana, recounts how two kulaputras, Jaya and Vijaya, were playing in dust and saw Buddha on his alms round. Jaya gave him a handful of dust calling it coarsely ground meal while Vijaya expressed approval by joining his hands. On Jaya's pronouncing an aspiration (pranidhana) to universal monarchy, the Buddha predicted his rebirth one day as the Emperor Ashoka.*

FACING PAGE: *A cave painting from Ajanta depicting the story of a prince who was banished from his homeland, is crowned king in the land of Videha by having water poured on his head by two servants while the royal insignia, fly whisk and crown are in readiness in the background.*

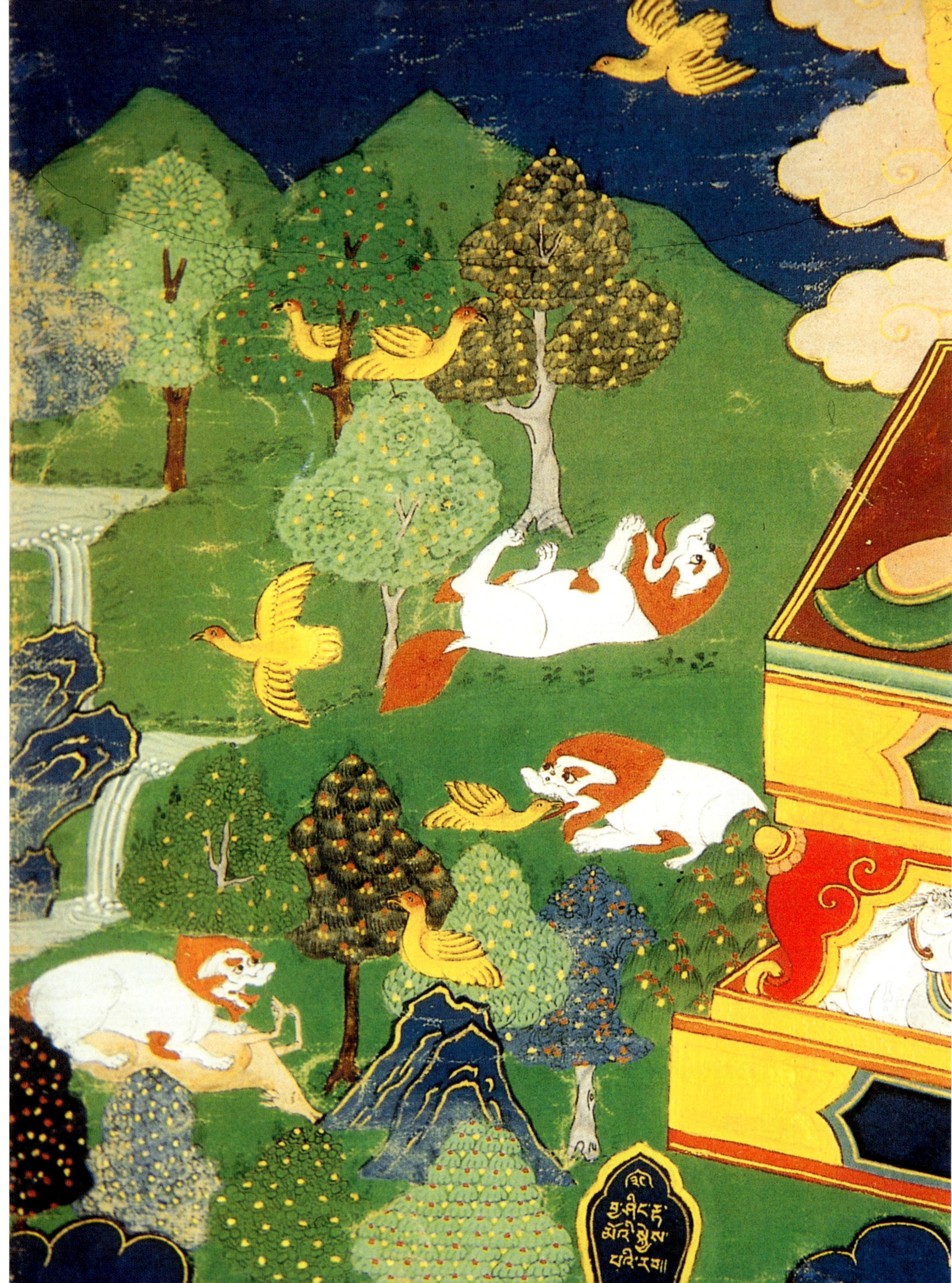

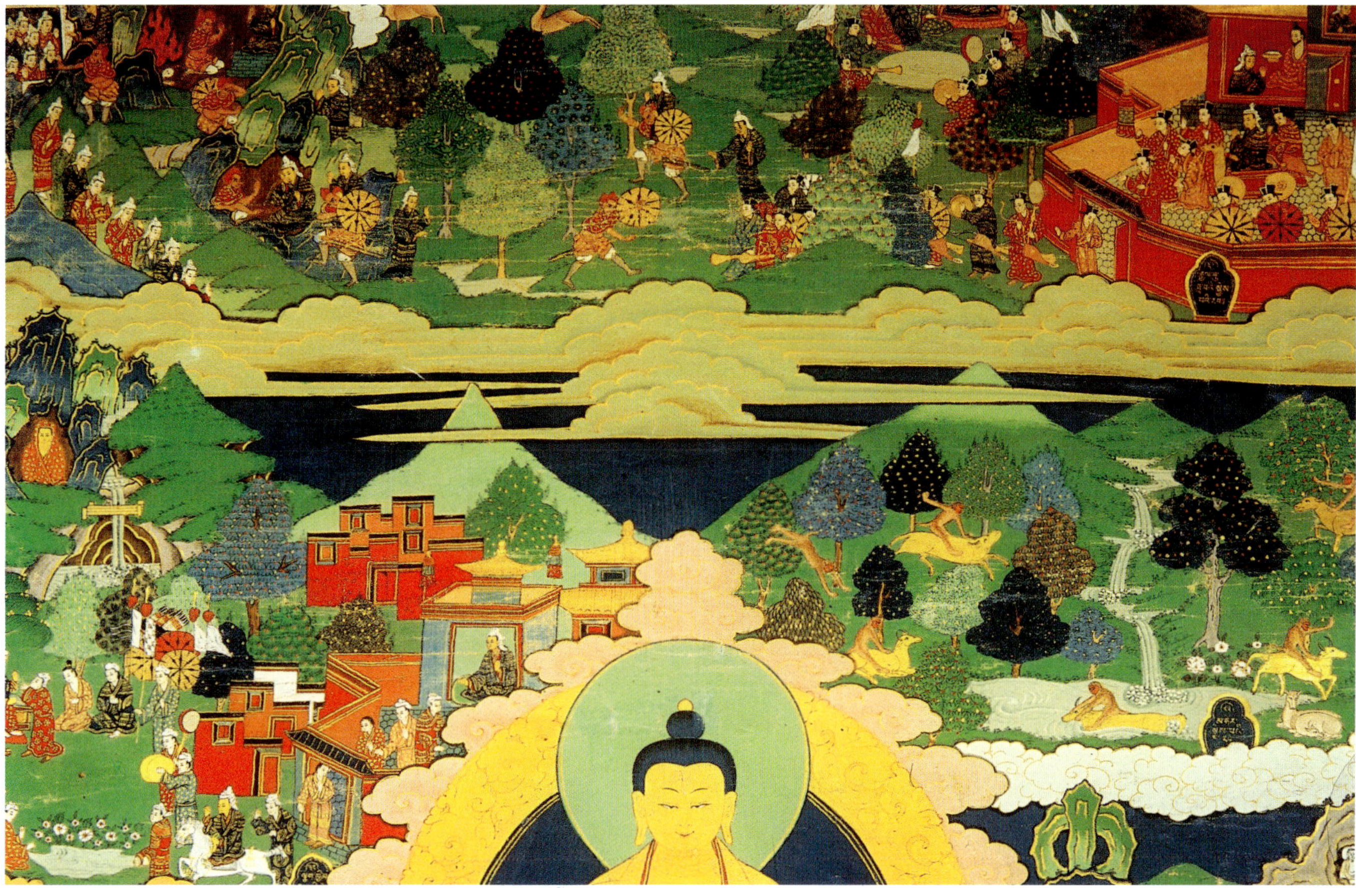

Jatakamala, a collection of Jatakas by Aryashura, written in Sanskrit in around fourth century, the bulk of thirty-four stories is arranged in accordance with the six perfections, while in *Chariyapitaka*, a collection of conducts in Pali canon, the stories are arranged in accordance with the Theravada list of ten perfections.

In the Shasha Jataka, the Bodhisattva offers his body to a traveller cultivating the perfection of generosity; in Brahmana Jataka he refuses to steal, cultivating the perfection of morality; in Kshanti Jataka he is an ascetic who calmly tolerates the mutilation inflicted on him by an angry king, cultivating the perfection of forbearance. Buddha offers his body by jumping down a cliff, to a hungry tigress who had just given birth to seven cubs. The genre assimilated an enormous amount of Indian folklore into the Buddhist fold. One such example is Ramayana rendered as a Jataka into Chinese in the third century AD.

Jataka stories were painted on walls of stupas, temples and monasteries to instil a feeling of reverence

ABOVE: *Sutasoma Jataka – The Buddha was once born as Prince Sutasoma in the royal family. One day he was about to listen to a brahmana poet that a dreaded Prince Kalmashapada arrived who had a taste for human flesh. Sutasoma offered himself to avoid further violence. But he requested Kalmashapada to let him go to listen to the brahmana poet promising that he would soon return. He went off, rewarded the poet and came back. Kalmashpada was amazed and inquired about the message by the poet. On hearing him he abandoned his former ways and devoted himself to virtue.*

FACING PAGE: *Once the Buddha was a woodpecker adorned with beautiful feathers. Rambling through forest once he came upon a lion who had a bone stuck in his throat. The woodpecker found a piece of wood, placed it between the lion's jaws and pulled out the bone. Later the woodpecker was looking unsuccessfully for food when he encountered the same lion feasting on a freshly killed young antelope. The woodpecker asked for a morsel but the lion curtly replied, 'Is it not enough that you are still alive after entering the mouth of a creature like me?' A forest spirit witnessed the scene and prompted the woodpecker to retaliate but it rejected and pointed out that one should grant aid without any expectation of return. Forbearance, after all has its own reward.*

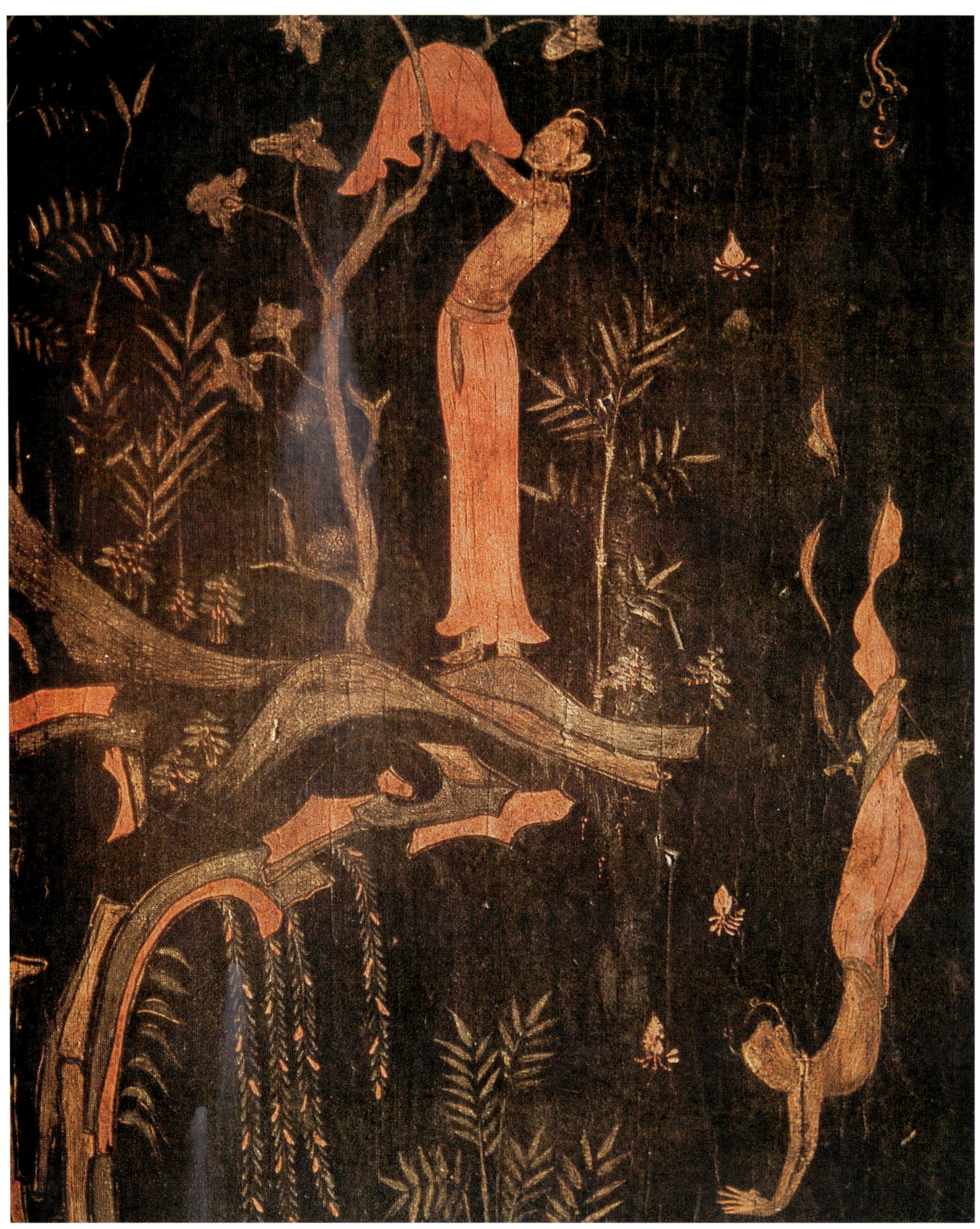

for the divine teacher and dissemination of Buddhist teachings. The earliest visualization of these stories in India goes back to second to first century BC. Pictorial representation of these stories indicate that Shakyamuni and devotion to him are the focus of Buddhist practice and belief. Their visual representation re-create the Bodhisattva's marvelous deeds as models to be imitated and as transcendental actions to be worshipped. Jataka cycles allow Buddhist pilgrims to follow the Buddha's steps by walking through his previous lives. In Theravada cultures of Southeast Asia a number of Jatakas of Pali tradition are widely known and frequently alluded to in everyday life.

The pictorial representations of the Jatakas embellished the monastic interiors. As has been narrated in the Buddhist text of Vinaya that once Anathapindada wanted to decorate the walls of the Jetavana monastery which he wanted to offer to the Buddha. But the monks did not know what to do. The Buddha suggested that instead of using a single colour, all the four kinds of colours should be used. The painters asked the Buddha 'what should we represent'. The Buddha said, 'At the entrance portal a *yaksa* holding a *danda*, in the vestibule the grand miracle and the Wheel of Existence ... and in the cloister the garland of Jatakas.'

Caves built for the monastic purpose had quarters for the monks and passage ways. Jataka stories were painted on the inner walls of these caves. The murals at the caves of Ajanta depict scenes from the Jatakas chosen to illustrate the frozen moments to put forth a message for transcendence. Scenes based on the stories continue without leaving any unfilled space blending into each other without any indication of division of scenes. Minor figures and patterns skillfully lead the eyes of an onlooker towards the focal point in every scene.

Shibi Jataka, Mahajanaka, Champeya, Shankhapala, Shasha, and Mahakapi are some of the famous stories in Ajanta murals in which Buddha had sacrificed himself in his previous births through and by acquisition of virtues like charity, wisdom, morality and forebearance. In the account of the Shasha Jataka, Buddha was born as a hare that jumped into fire so that his roasted body could serve as meal for Indra, and as a monkey in Mahakapi Jataka. In another Jataka, Shakyamuni is born as a learned brahmana who on hearing of the Buddha Dipankara's visit to Dipavati tried hard to gather some flowers to adore him. But all the flowers of the city had already been collected for the visit of the king's orders. Fortunately, Shakyamuni could get five flowers out of the seven that a girl had secretly kept. She gave him the flowers but with a promise that he would marry her. He was overjoyed and went to offer them to Dipankara. As he threw the flowers they became immobilized around the head of Dipankara. Dipankara showered rain and the crowd dispersed but the Bodhisattva did not move. He spread his hair on the muddy road so that Dipankara's feet may not get soiled. Dipankara perceived the young man's spiritual perfections and predicted that he would be a Buddha in future.

A Buddhist monument in Indonesia, Borobudur displays sculpted examples of a unified Jataka cycle, which is possibly an extended biography of the Buddha. Similar cycles proliferate in the mural paintings on the walls of the cave monasteries on the Silk Road in Kyzil and Kucha. Burma has the longest and the most prolific tradition of visual Jatakas, which ceramists, painters and wood carvers narrate individually in small groups or in cycles. Circumambulatory terraces of Ananda temple compose a cycle of 554 Jatakas. Their origin in the stupas and monastries of Burma and especially Pagan, can be traced back to the eleventh century.

Buddhist monks relate stories from the Jatakas, Avadanas and Nidanas so that sophisticated concepts are made apprehensible and palatable, becoming enjoyable and memorable. The tradition of telling unforgettable tales was transmitted to China and Japan through Central Asia from India, by the monks who carried the message of Shakyamuni to distant lands.

FACING PAGE: *In order to save a tigress and her cubs from starving to death, the Buddha-to-be offered himself to the mother who could then feed her young. In the illustration, first he puts his clothes on tree, then dives off the cliff towards a bamboo grove, the gruesome conclusion is painted at the bottom.*

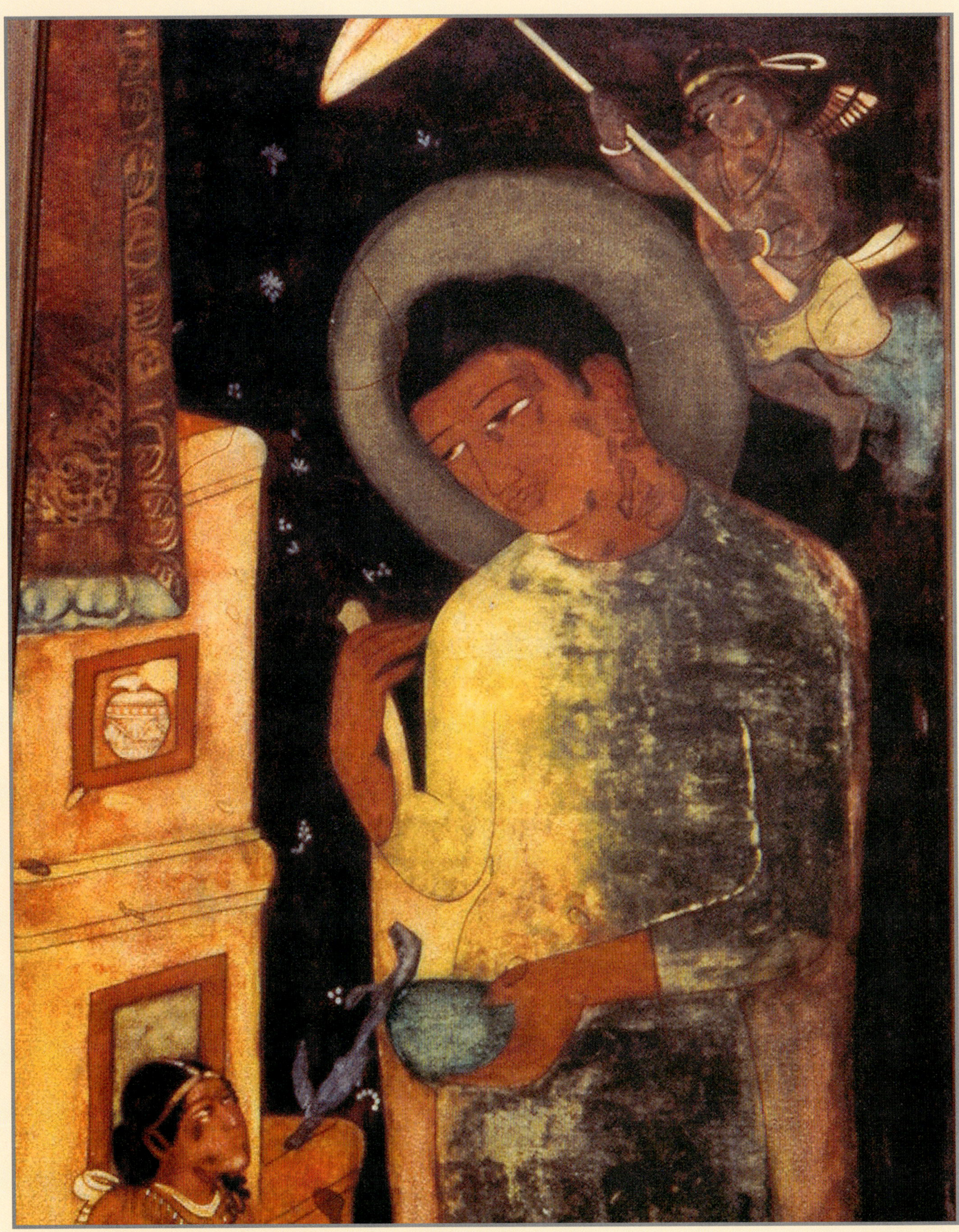

Historical Manifestation as a Mortal Being

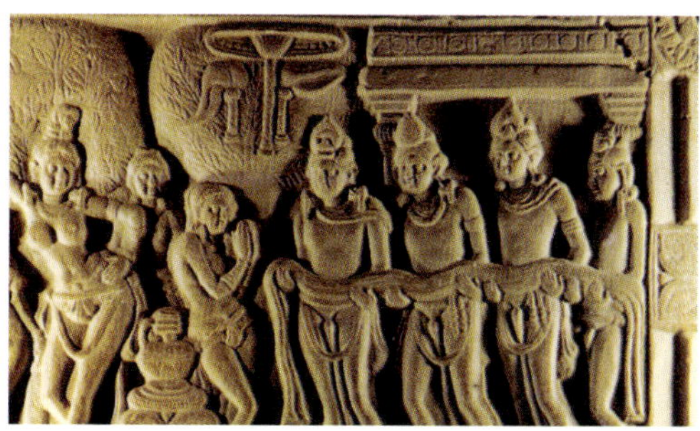

Buddha appeared on this earth two and a half millennia ago to show the path, a way to salvation to the humanity through transcendence of the self, and moral and psychological methods in this very life. Siddhartha is his childhood name, meaning one who has achieved his purpose or accomplished righteousness, but later he became famous as Buddha because of being enlightened; Shakyamuni because he was the sage of the Shakya tribe; Gautama because of the clan name; and Tathagata because he is the person who had attained the essence of the Dharma. As a divine teacher he was addressed by his followers as Lord, Bhagavan, the Blessed One, etc. Shakyasimha, an epithet given to Shakyamuni means that he is lion among the Shakyas. Buddhist scriptures describe the king or emperor as a lion; at his accession he roars like a lion; he sits on a lion throne and dies on a lion couch. The Buddha inherits all royal attitudes, and thus is hailed as Shakyasimha. The Buddha as Jina, the true conqueror, defeats the fearsome enemies of attachment, anger, pride, and ignorance, etc.

Lumbini, situated on the Nepal side of the Indo-Nepalese border became a sacred land where Siddhartha was born to Queen Maya. Shuddhodana, his father, ruler of the Shakya tribe and Gautama clan with his capital at Kapilavastu, brought him up in the sheltered luxury of the royal palace but he was obsessed by the tribulations of the mortal life. Legends around the events preceding the birth of Siddhartha mention that he had descended from the Tushita heaven. One day his would-be mother, the queen had a dream where she saw herself being taken to the Himalayas by the Divine Guardians. There she was bathed to remove human contamination, anointed with perfumes,

FACING PAGE: *After a long sojourn Buddha came to Kapilavastu. Buddha's wife Yashodhara presented Rahula, their son, to him so that he assumes his father's inheritance. But the Buddha was resolved that he should obtain a much greater treasure, namely enlightenment and nirvana.*

ABOVE: *Queen Maya, the would-be mother of the Buddha-to-be holds a branch of a tree in the garden at Lumbini, while giving birth to the Prince and the Four Divine Beings stand with a golden net to receive the newly born.*

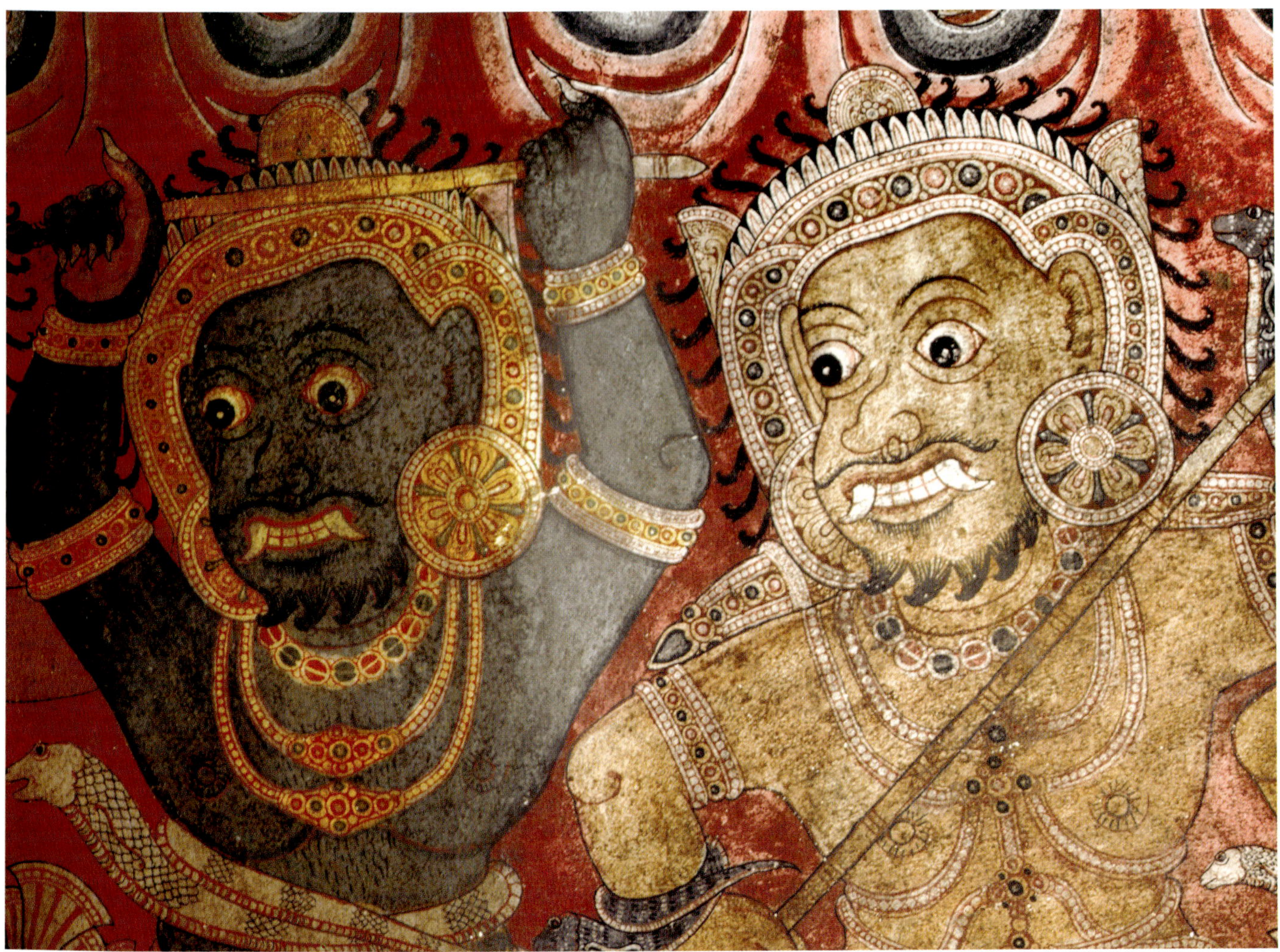

clothed in heavenly robes and decked with heavenly flowers. The Bodhisattva-to-be was roaming there on a golden mountain in the form of a white elephant, a symbol of good omen. It entered the womb of the queen. Thus the queen conceived on the full moon night. The next morning she got up and related the story of her dream to the king. He summoned sixty-four eminent brahmanas to decipher the meaning of the queen's dream. The brahmanas declared, 'Do not worry, great King, a male child is conceived. He will be a *cakravartin*, a monarch, if he leads a settled life, but he will be a Buddha, to remove the illusions from the world, if he retires.'

The queen at her full term of ten lunar months, wished to visit Devadaha, the place of her parents. The queen left in a golden palanquin attended by a thousand courtiers. On her way she saw the beautiful garden at Lumbini and decided to spend some time in the grove of *sala* trees. Suddenly as the time of the impending birth came closer; her labour pains started; a curtain was hung around her; she took hold of a branch of Ashoka

ABOVE: *The demons sent by Mara tried to tempt and threaten the Buddha by agitating his mind, but they were unable to drive him away from his path. The Buddha overcame inner conflicts due to the merits accrued in his practice of Ten Perfections.*

FACING PAGE: *Shakyamuni devoted himself to strict asceticism for six years in quest of enlightenment. His golden body emaciated and he was wrecked with severe pain. He realized that such austerities served no purpose and the way to enlightenment is the middle path.*

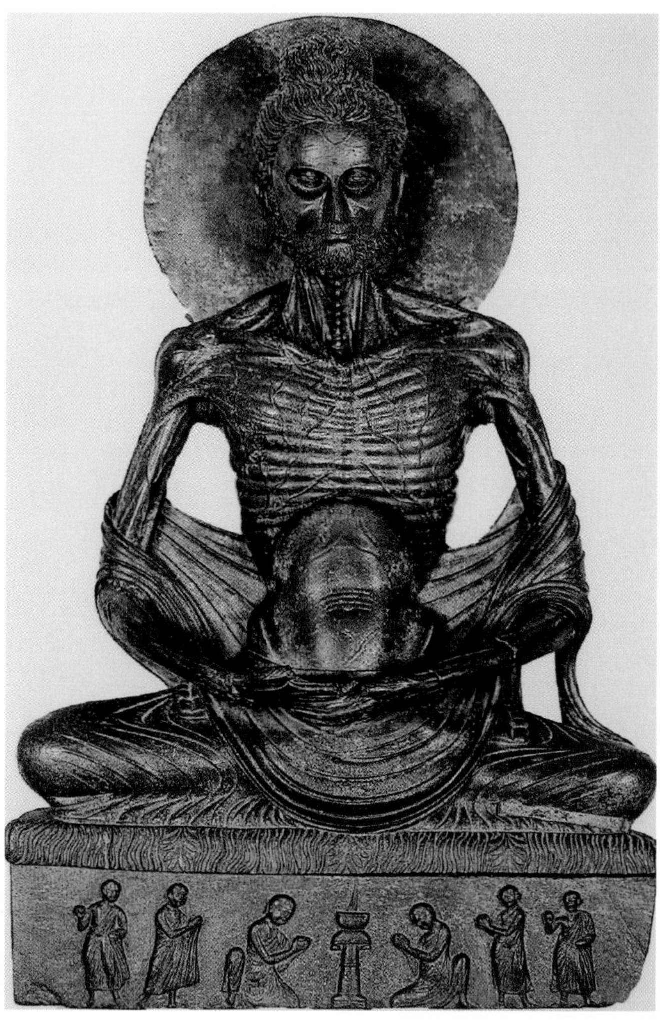

tree stretching out luxuriantly; and while standing, she gave birth to the Bodhisattva from her right side. Four divinities with a golden net received the baby and placed him before the queen.

Brahmanas prophesied the child becoming a Universal Monarch, a *cakravartin* or a Buddha to retire from the world to remove the veil of ignorance. The king desired his son to be a *cakravartin*, and not an ascetic. But somehow the stars were not in favour of the prince. The father was concerned about his son's unworldly and unmilitary ways. He decided to bind his son more firmly by arranging his marriage at the age of sixteen (547 BC) with the beautiful princess Yashodhara. Yashodhara bore Siddhartha a son, Rahula.

The Bodhisattva was sad but determined. The luxurious confines of the palace, joys of the married life could not save him from depression. He was entertained by beautiful heavenly maidens singing and dancing in the palace full of beauty and splendour, but he grew weary obsessed by the problems of human life. At the age of twenty-nine he found a way out of the palace to seek the truth and find a solution to end sufferings of human existence. Life of a wandering mendicant was the only option to satisfy him. He left the palace gates and reached a grove. It was full moon of the month of Asadha (May-June). The Prince took off his robes and jewels, handed them to Channa, the head charioteer and his royal servant, to take them back. Kanthaka, Siddhartha's horse could not bear the grief of the departing Prince, his heart broke and he died. Channa had to return weeping and wailing. In order to be an ascetic, the Prince cut off his *ushnisha* and shaved his head. King Suddhodhana sent a minister and a court priest to persuade the Prince to come back but to no avail. As a truth seeker Siddhartha walked from place to place to seek the Ultimate Truth.

Siddhartha sat on the path of a series of ascetic practices in the company of five brahmanas who ultimately became his first disciples. He, with his disciples went to mount Gaya, where on the peak they sat under a tree and entered into contemplation. From Gaya they went to the east bank of Uruvela pond and saw the Niranjana River. And Siddhartha underwent religious training at Uruvela, later known as Bodhgaya.

Siddhartha sat under the tree and made a firm resolution, 'Let my skin sinews and bones become dry and the flesh and blood of my body dry up, but I will not break the cross-legged position until I attain perfect enlightenment.' He was assailed by a band of demons. An army of Mara tried to tempt and threaten by agitating his mind. The army shouted, made a whirlwind, caused a rain of rocks, blades, swords, daggers, live coals, hot ashes, sand and mud, and finally darkness, but Mara was unable to drive away the Bodhisattva from his path. The Bodhisattva could overcome the attack of Mara due to the

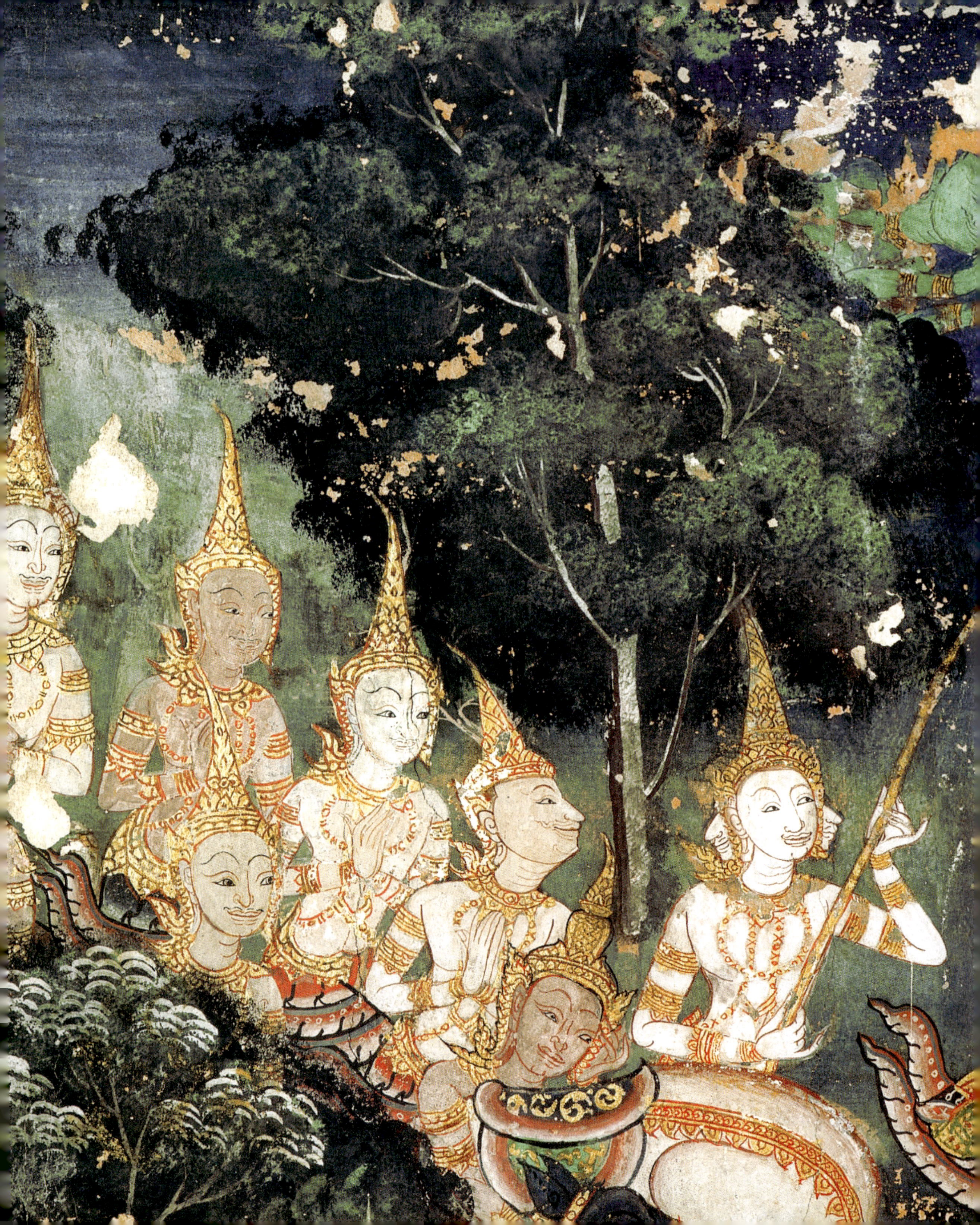

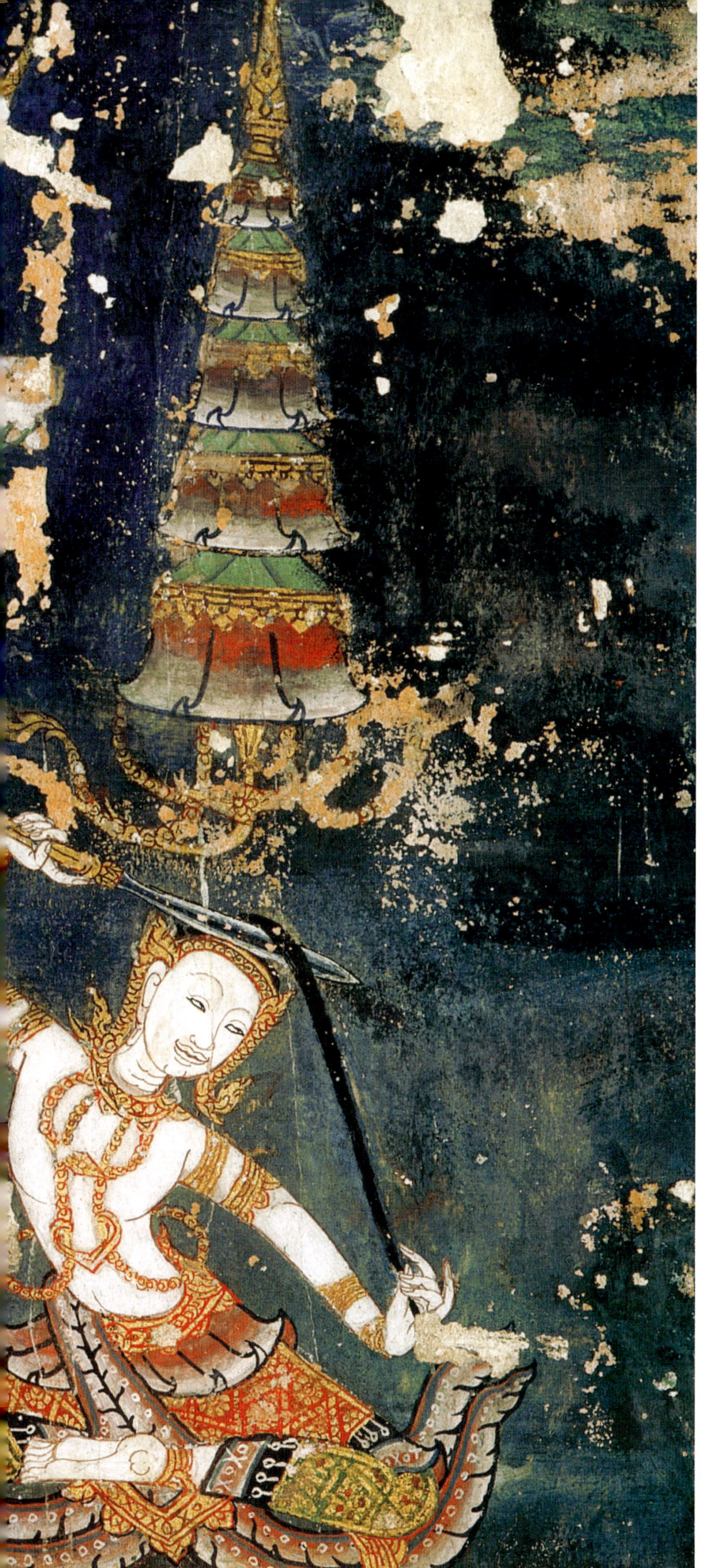

Siddhartha, the Buddha-to-be, determined to renounce the world, made his way to the stables, asked Channa to saddle his horse Kanthaka, and bring to him. Channa brought Kanthaka and also his own horse. They led the horses out of the palace, rode to the edge of a forest near the Anoma River, undisturbed by men. Siddhartha pulled out a sword, grasped his long princely hair in his left hand, and cut them off with the right and then handed Channa the hair and the sword.

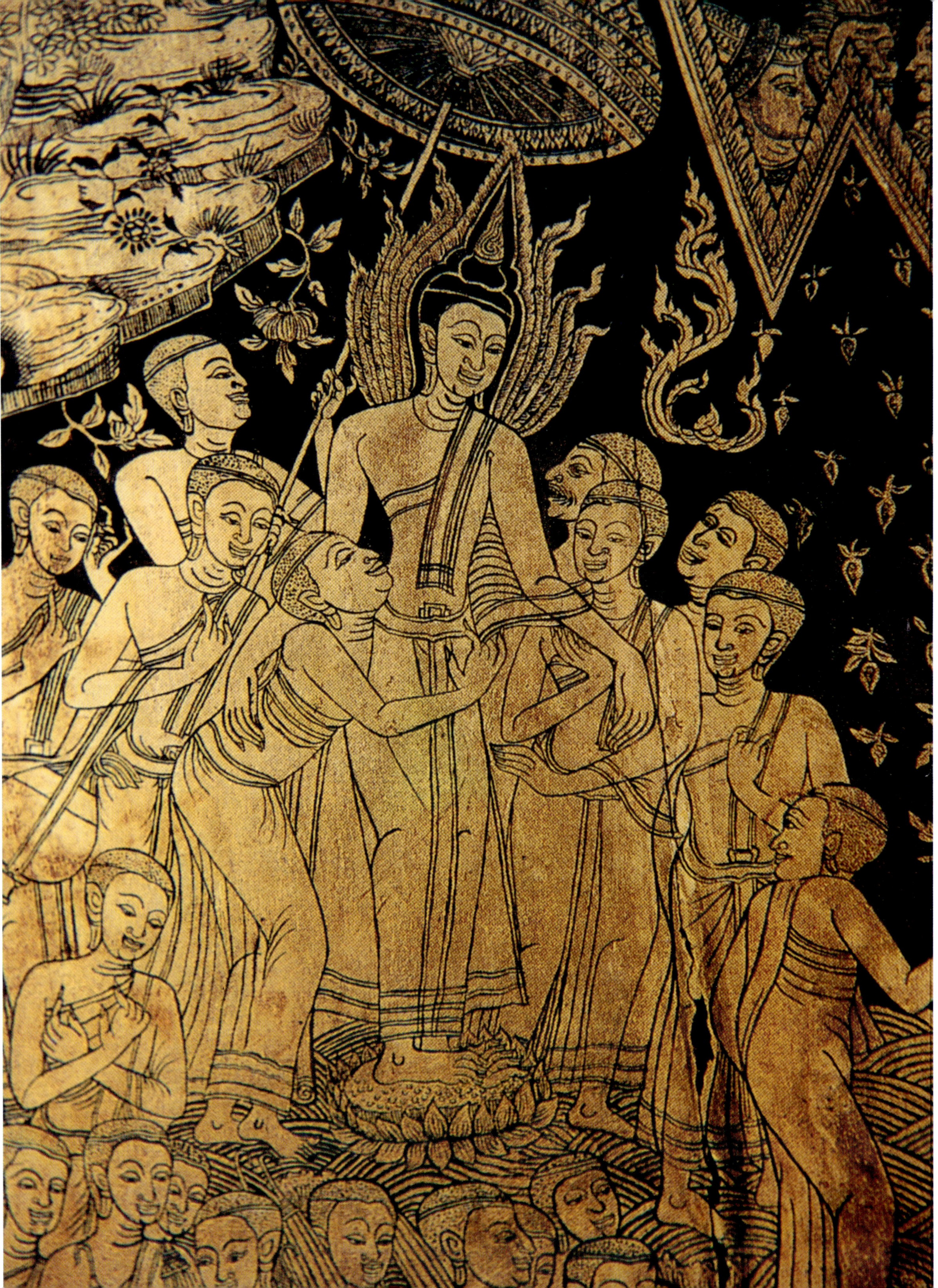

merits accrued in his practice of Ten Perfections. The army of Mara fled, leaving their head ornaments and even robes.

Practices of Gautama were severe; he fasted until his body turned into a skeleton. Some times he lived on just one grain of rice or a sesame seed. His golden body turned black and emaciated, thirty-two marks of a great man were concealed. At times he was wrecked with severe pain and even lost consciousness. The great being spent six years undergoing austerities, but finally realized them to be meaningless like trying to tie a knot in the air. When he realized the Truth that this was not the way to enlightenment, he gave up austerities and went out to seek alms moving among the people again. One day a young girl Sujata offered him *kheer* (rice cooked with milk) on the full moon day of Vaishakha. The Bodhisattva rose and went to the bank of Niranjana that flows near Bodhgaya, bathed and ate the *kheer*. His disciples at this sight thought that he was not able to attain wisdom and so they deserted him.

Early morning he went to the foot of the nigrodha (peepala) tree, sat there illuminating the whole tree with the radiance of his body. For seven weeks he stayed at the throne of enlightenment. During those forty-nine days he did not bathe or eat, just spent his time enjoying the pleasure of meditation, its ways and its fruits. Gods lauded, the day of enlightenment had arrived. The tree under which he was practicing was illuminated with the radiance of the body of the Buddha, the enlightened one. It was the most important event of his life. He was thirty-five at that time.

Among men he became a suprememan, from a Bodhisattava he became a Buddha. The Truth that he had discovered was beyond impermanence, unreality and emptiness of appearances.

'To whom should I first teach the Dhamma,' was the question for the Buddha. He wanted a worthy disciple to whom he could pass on the truth. Alara Kalama and Uddaka Ramaputta, the two teachers came to his mind, but they had already died. Then, he began walking towards Varanasi. On his way he met an Ajivaka named Upaka. Impressed by Gautama's appearance, Upaka asked, 'Venerable One, what do you seek in leaving the world? Who is your teacher and whose teachings do you profess?' Buddha replied, 'I am the Victor over all, omniscient, free from defilements. I have abandoned everything and have become liberated, free from craving, ...' For him there was no teacher. He was the most venerable, the supreme teacher. The Buddha passed through several villages on his way to Varanasi. People offered him food and drinks. Eventually, he reached the bank of the Ganges and flew across the river as he had no money to pay to the ferryman.

The two extremes in practice, which should not be followed to seek the way are – the way of pleasures and desires, which is the way of ordinary ignorant people. The other is that of self-torture, or inflicting pain on one's own body. None of these is adequate, or the way of the wise to seek the dhamma. It is the way in the middle that leads to perfection of concentration, knowledge, awakening and *nirvana*. And that is the Noble Eightfold Path – the path of right understanding, right thought, right speech, action, livelihood, effort, mindfulness and concentration.

Buddha turned the Wheel of Law, delivered sermons, travelled from place to place, through the regions of the middle Ganges for forty-five years preaching the doctrines and founding a religious community, called Sangha. At the age of eighty, the flame went out and the time for *nirvana* came. It was not a death as it is for other mortal beings, it was not the final point to depart, it was a release from the cycle of innumerable existences in divine, human and animal forms. As the monks agree, *nirvana* is experienced as a state of ineffable calm – a joyous tranquility.

He ordered the monks, 'Go forth, O Bhikshus, for the good of the many, for the happiness of the many, out of compassion for the world, for the good, benefit, and happiness of gods and men. Let not two go by one way: Preach, O Bhikshus, the Dharma, excellent in the

FACING PAGE: *A scene from a Buddhist legend from Thailand illustrating miraculous powers of the Buddha crossing the waters of a flowing river, standing on a lotus.*

beginning, the middle and the end, both in the spirit and in the letter.' He laid emphasis on virtue and wisdom – 'Wisdom is purified by virtue, and virtue is purified by wisdom.' Where one is, so is the other. The virtuous person has wisdom, and the wise person has virtue. The combination of virtue and wisdom is called the highest thing in the world. He talked at length about suffering in life but also accepted that, '… suffering is only one face of life. Life has another face, the face of wonder. If we can see that face of life, we will have happiness, peace and joy. When our hearts are unfettered we can make direct contact with the wonders of life. When we have truly grasped the truth of impermanence, emptiness of self, and dependent co-arising, we see how wondrous our hearts and minds are.' Answering to a question like – 'Do all religions teach the same dhamma?' He said, 'No, they do not desire the same or pursue the same. And why? This world is made up of many and various elements, and people adhere to one or another of these elements, and become tenaciously addicted to them, saying – this alone is true, all else is false.'

Buddha spoke his last words in Kushinagar and closed his eyes. The earth shook, sal blossoms fell and bhikshus flung themselves on the ground. The eyes of the world were no more.

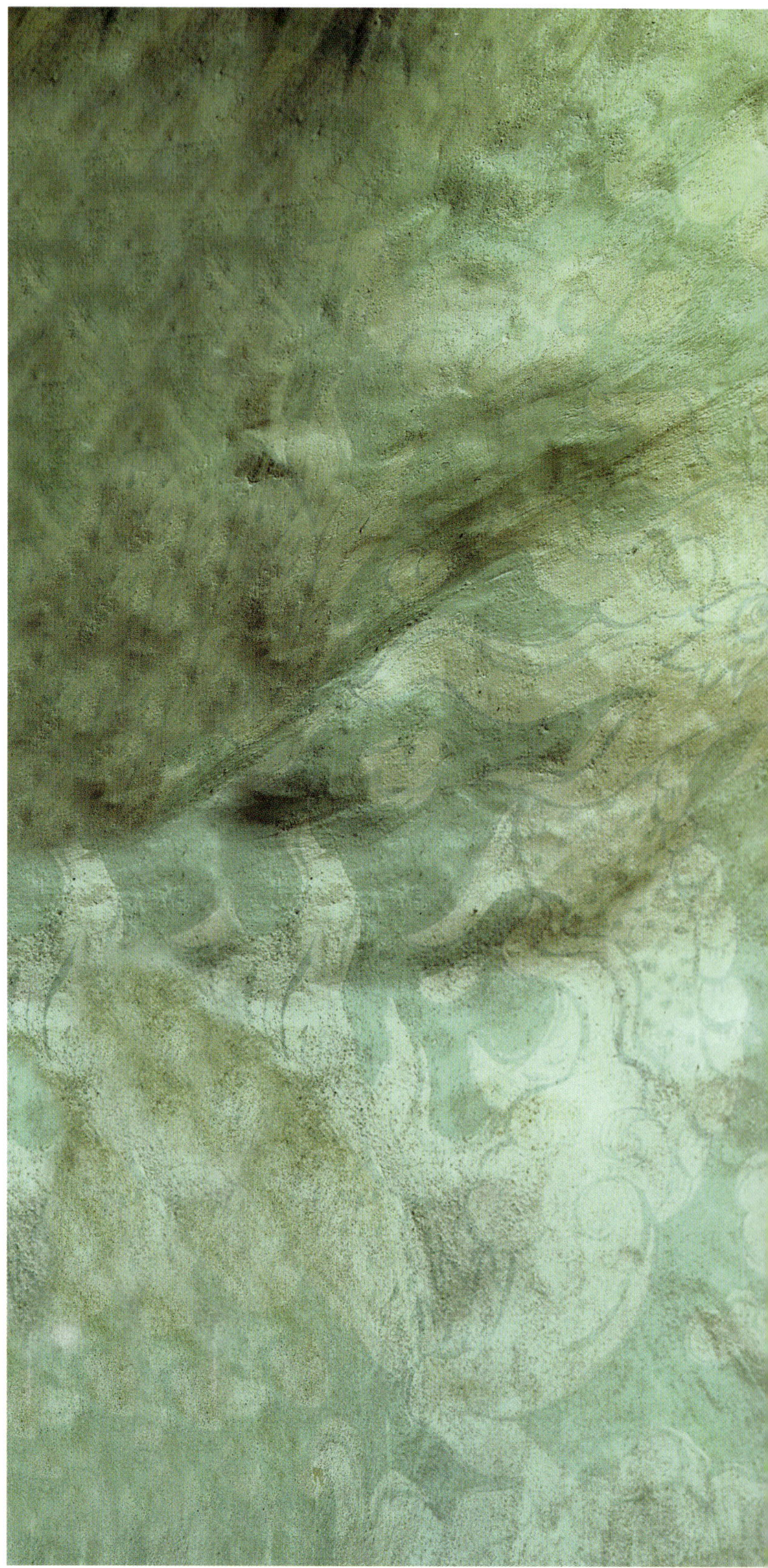

Buddha statue at Quoc Tu Pagoda, Ho Chi Minh City, Vietnam.

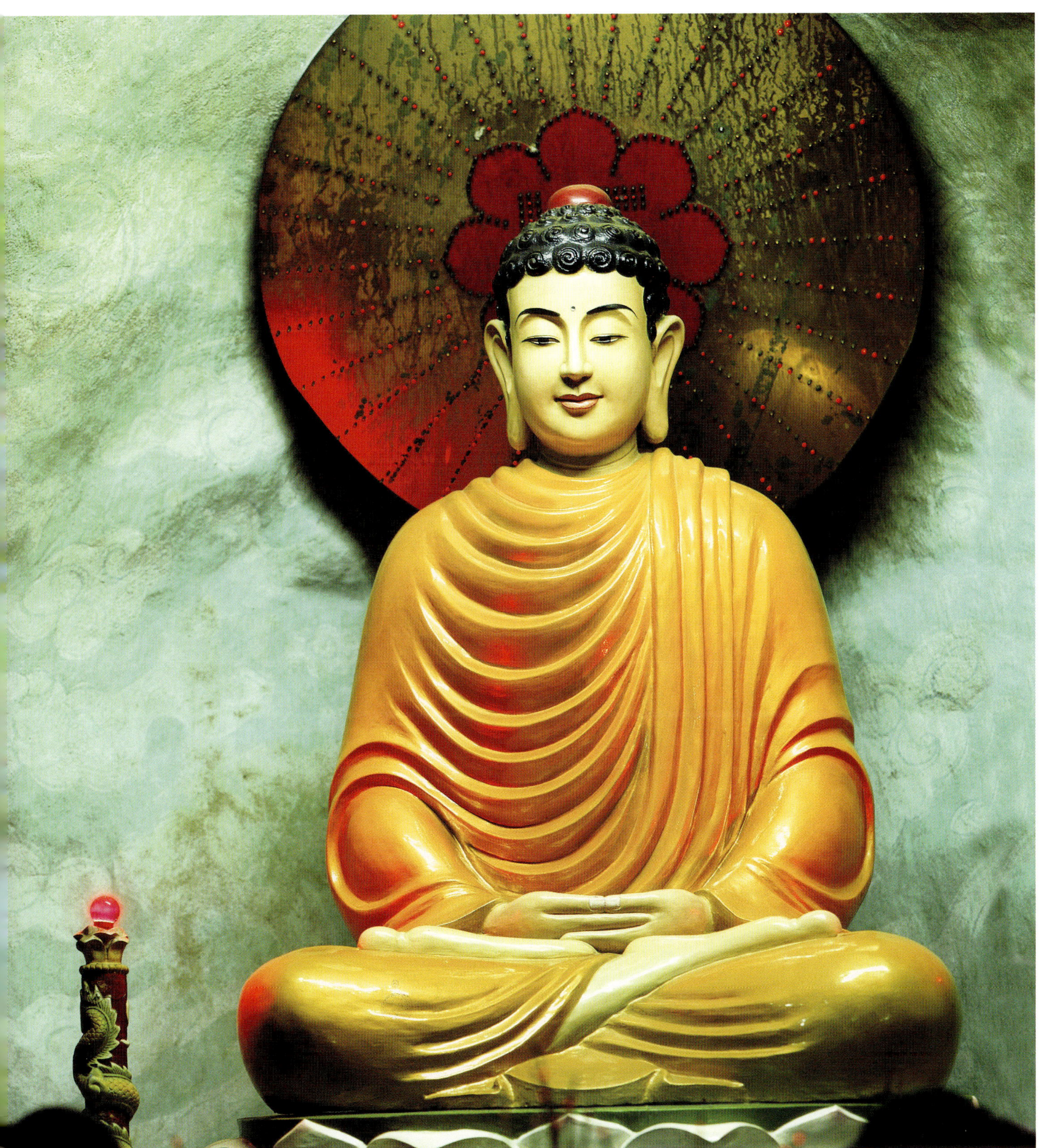

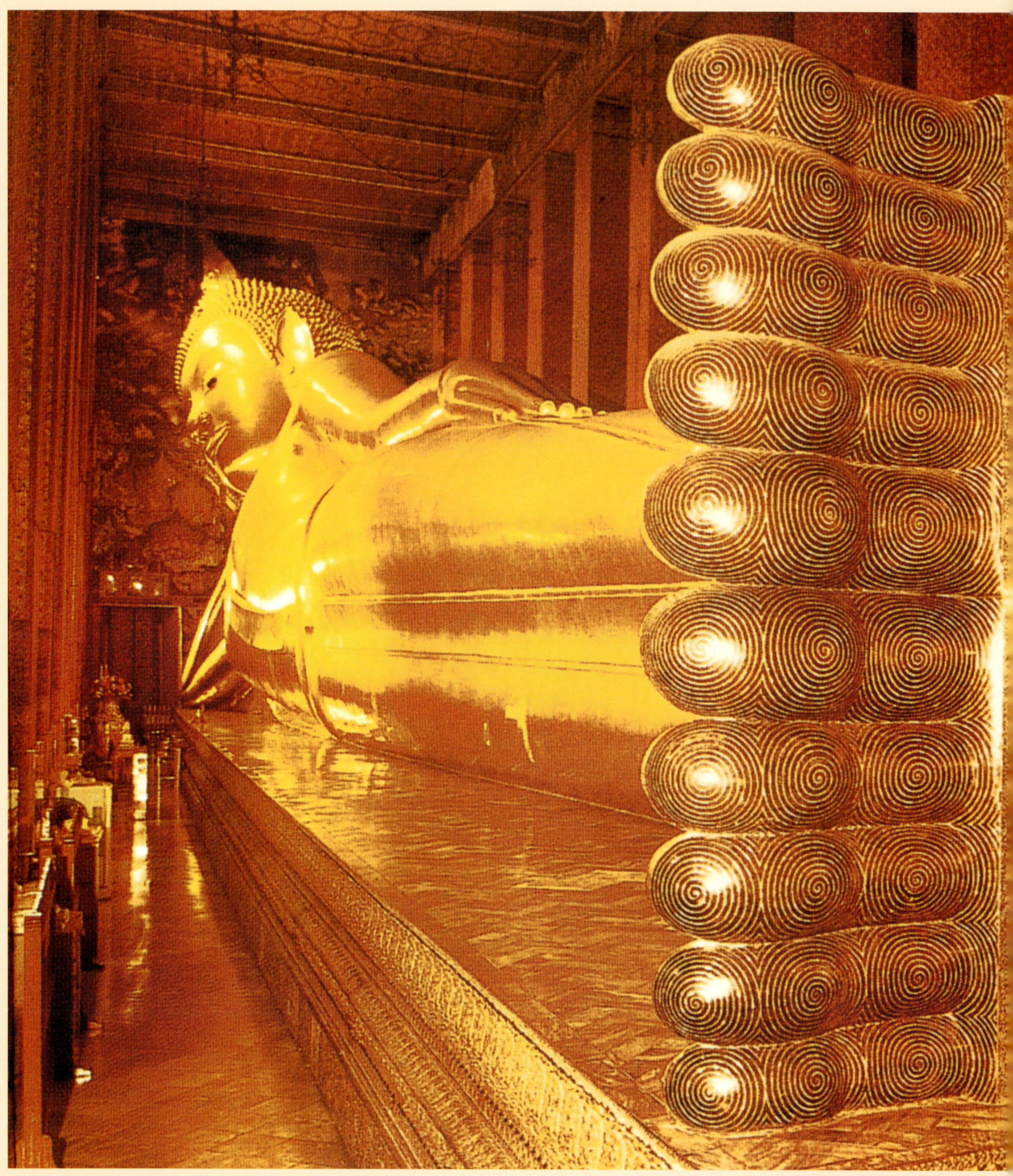

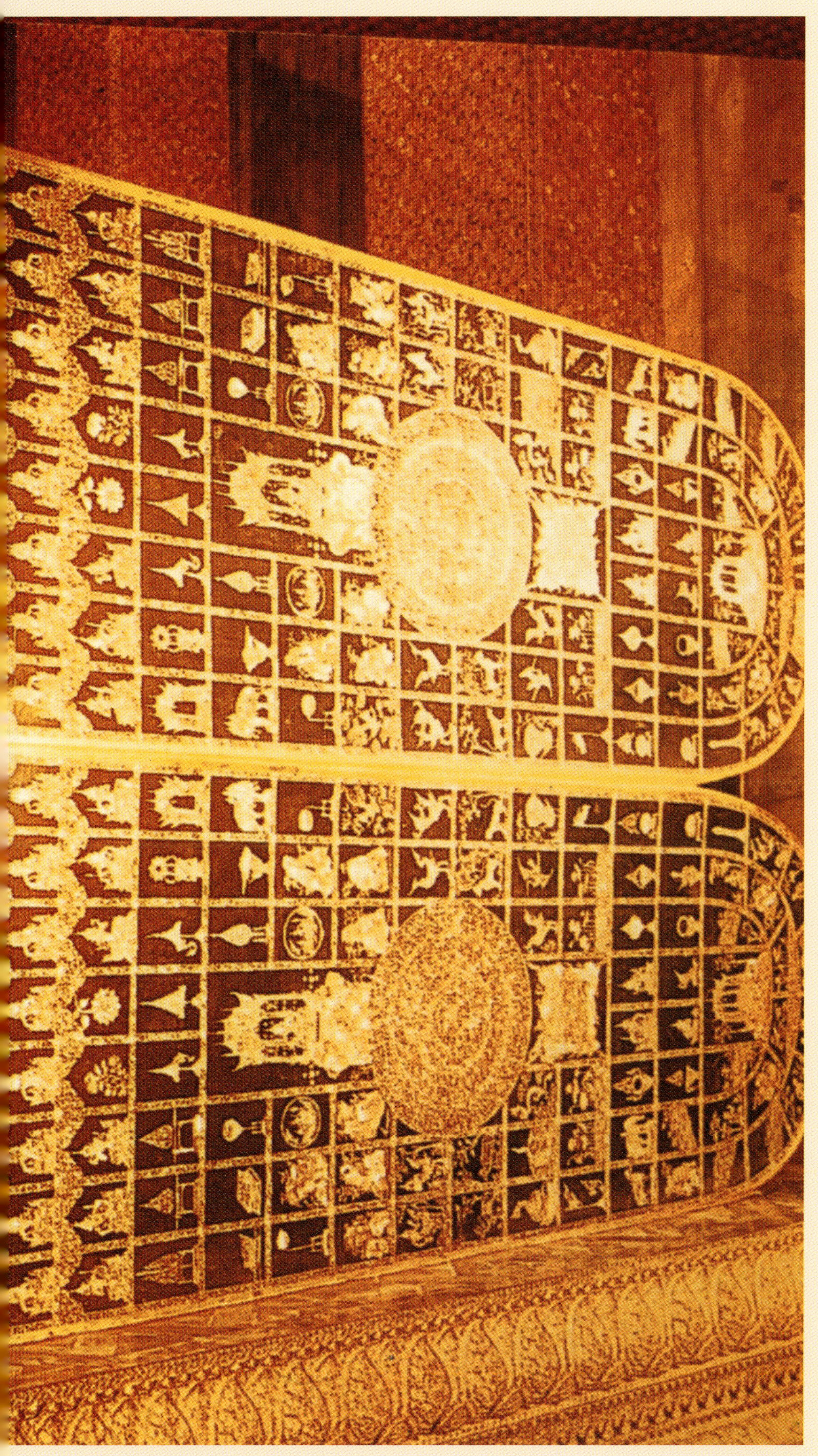

Thirty-two Auspicious Marks on the Buddha's Body

His feet have level tread, on the soles of his feet are wheels with a thousand spokes, complete with felloe and hub. He has projecting heels, long fingers and toes, soft and tender hands and feet. His hands and feet are net-like. He has high-raised ankles and his legs are like an antelope's, standing and without bending, he can touch and rub his knees with either hand. His male organs are enclosed in a sheath and his complexion is bright, the colour of gold, skin is delicate and so smooth that no dust can adhere to his body. His body-hairs are separate, one to each pore, and body-hairs grow upwards, each one bluish-black like collyrium, curling in rings to the right. His body is divinely straight and has the seven convex surfaces. The front of his body is like a lion's. There is no hollow between his shoulders and he is proportioned like a banyan-tree. His height is the same as the span of his out-stretched arms, and conversely, his chest is evenly rounded. He has a perfect sense of taste, his jaws are like a lion's, with forty bright teeth, which are even with no spaces between. His tongue is very long, his voice like Brahma's, like that of the karavika-bird. His eyes are deep blue, with eyelashes like that of a cow. The hair between his eyes are white and soft like cotton-down and his head is like a royal turban.

The Buddha lived in this world for eighty years and finally travelled to Kushinagar accompanied by his disciples. Time for his final rest had arrived, he laid down, put his right hand beneath his head and crossed his feet like a lion king. Such images with auspicious signs engraved on the soles, commemorating the event of mahaparinirvana are found all over the Buddhist world.

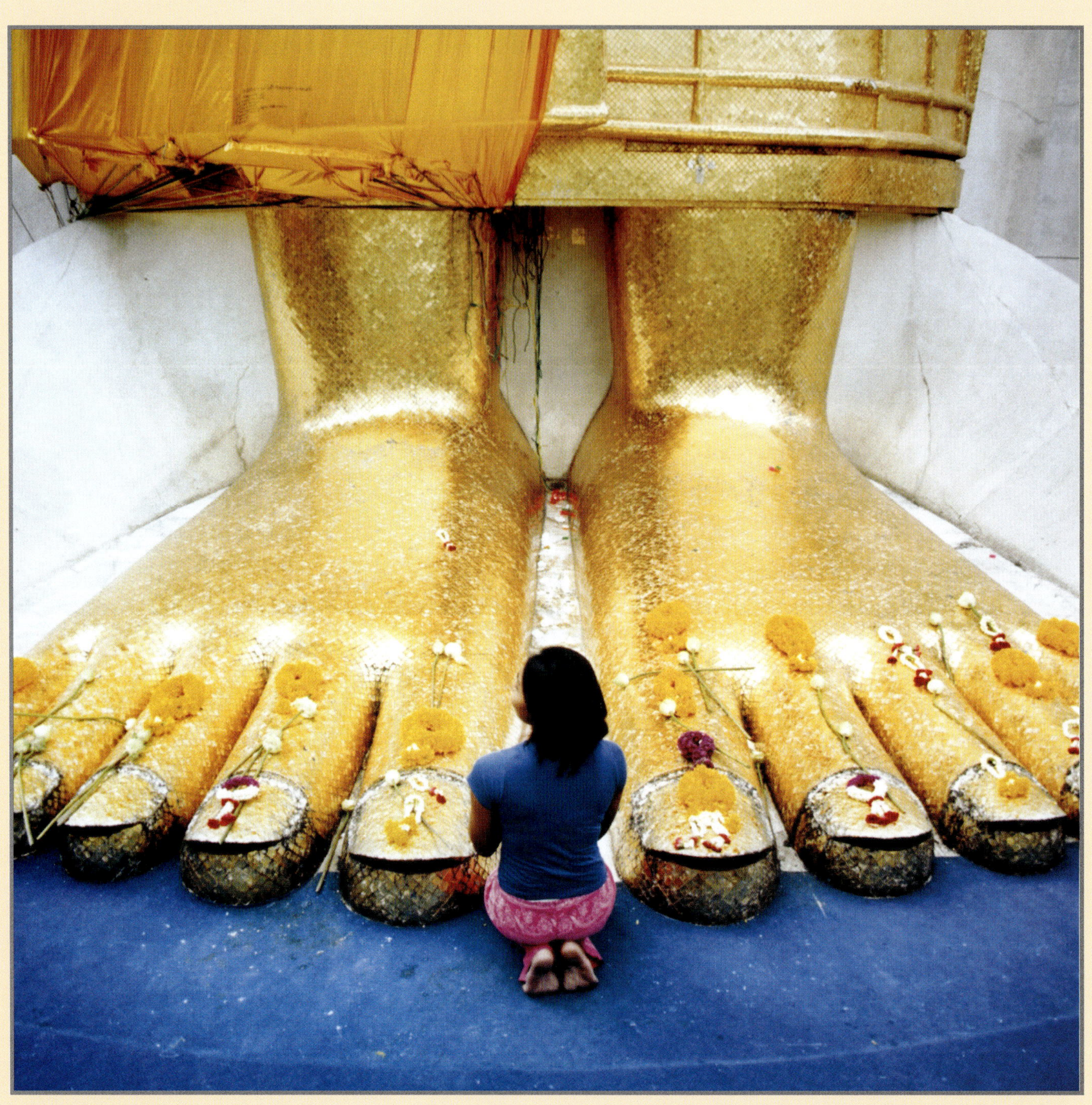

Buddha in Absence

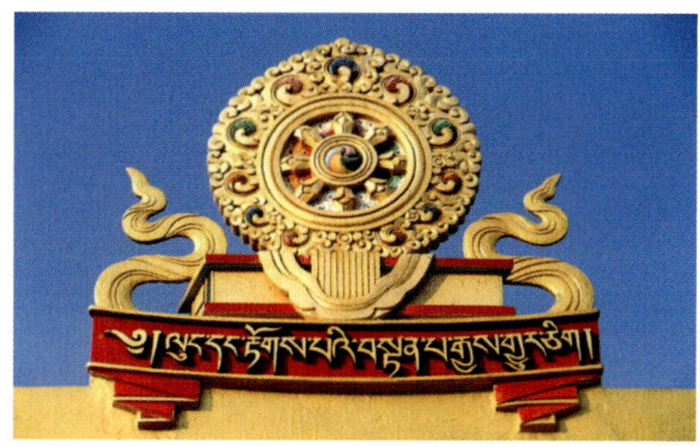

Devotion to Buddha began soon after his *nirvana* but his images began to be created only around the first century AD. Prior to that, he was worshipped in aniconic forms because it was thought to be impossible to represent him once he had passed into *nirvana*, a state of being inconceivable in human and this-worldly terms. Thus Buddha was represented only through symbols. Moments of crucial importance in his life were suggested by symbols like a bodhi tree under which he attained enlightenment; a Wheel of Doctrine suggesting his delivering the first sermon; a stupa representing his presence in absence. Footprints were carved to indicate his presence, an empty throne, the pillar encircled by flames etc., were some of the other prominent symbolic references. Sometimes they were also combined to form an imaginary body of the Buddha. Many of the symbols related to some important events in his life – birth, enlightenment, his decision to take up preaching, or *nirvana*. Thus these symbols served three types of function – historical, biographical and narrative.

An abstention from pictorial representation was by no means the result of an actual ban, as was the case in Islam or in Old Testament times. It was, in fact, a continuation of the Hindu practice of worshipping the divine beings in formless forms, called *nishakala* or *nirakar*. Stupa worship began with adoring the Buddha in his absence after *nirvana*. Stupas were therefore the first monuments built by the Buddhists, symbolizing presence of the Lord in Absence. From massive monuments to tiny votive offerings they can have many levels of meaning. At the deepest level they are symbols of *Dharmakaya*, attributing three main functions: as reliquaries they contain ashes of the Awakened Ones, as memorials they mark important events in the life of the Buddha,

ABOVE: *Buddha's teachings were initially called 'turning the wheel of the dharma'. Thus a wheel has become a symbol of Buddhist teachings and the first sermon given by the Buddha. It is often carved or painted on the entrance gates of the Buddhist monasteries and temples.*

FACING PAGE: *Buddhism crossed the boundaries of India and became thoroughly integrated into the cultures of several Asian countries. Its deep rooted spirit and the teachings of the Buddha inspire people to attain a higher goal in their lives. Millions of Buddhist devotees are scattered throughout the world.*

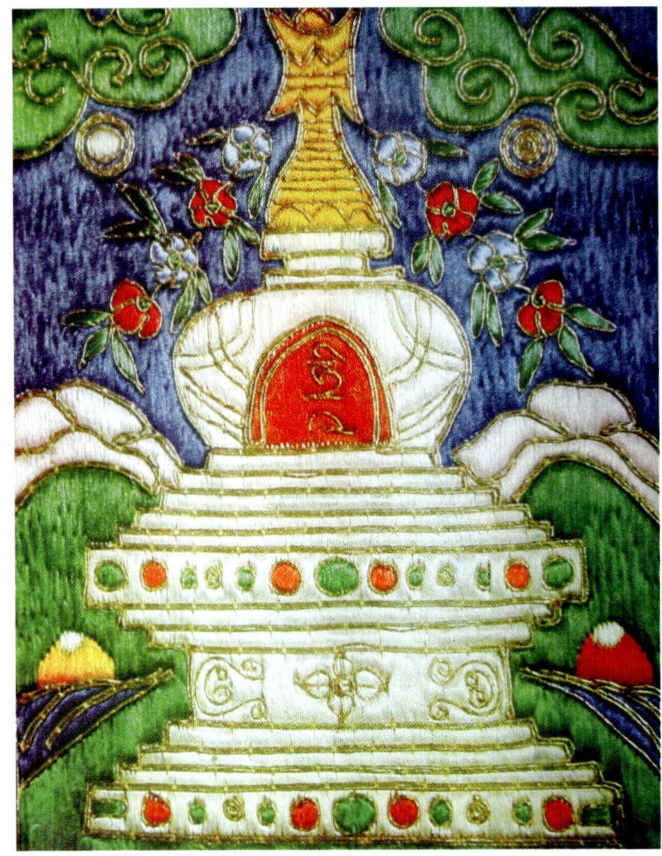

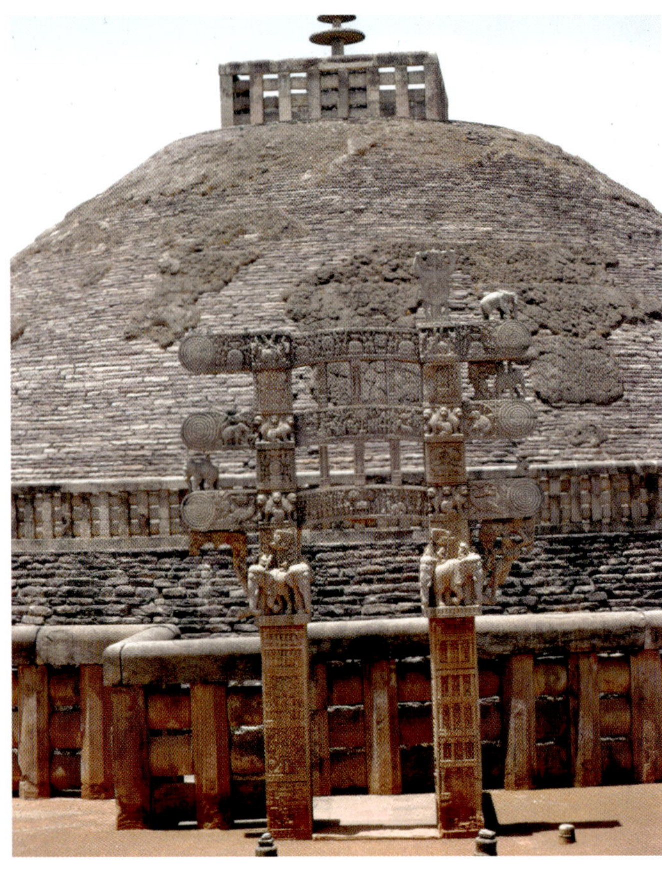

and as votive stupas they are symbols of meritorious acts. They were originally erected as relics holding monuments of the Buddha himself and later for the eminent saints. In ancient times eight stupas were constructed to honour the major events in Lord Buddha's life, namely – birth in the garden of Lumbini, enlightenment at the Bodhi tree at Bodhgaya, first sermon at Varanasi, manifestation of the grand miracle at Shravasti, descent from the Tushita heaven at Kanyakubja, preaching at Rajgriha, and *nirvana* at Vaishali. Gradually they assumed a philosophic meaning and became central symbols of the Dharma.

Stupas were also carved as focal points in chaitya halls inside caves. Bharhut is the first classical example of the use of non-iconic symbolism as it does not represent Buddha in figural form. However, the symbols invoke his presence. There is a second century relief from Amaravati in which the central stupa stands for Buddha's final *nirvana*. Two intertwined snakes are coiled around the dome and the umbrellas on either side are signs of honour. Two elephants kneel in worship on both the sides. Normally they symbolize royalty or supremacy and are a conventional sign of good fortune.

Buddha as Shakyasimha, symbolized through lions is the earliest example of symbolic representation. As a sign of devotion to the teachings of the Buddha, Emperor Ashoka got them engraved on stone columns and set them up at points associated with important events of his life. The column discovered from Sarnath, the best preserved among the so far discovered, is surmounted by a plinth with four animals and four wheels in relief

LEFT: *The stupa with the letter 'hrih' written on the rotund cupola represents perfect enlightenment. Rays of light streaming forth out of the letter purify the sins and ignorance of all.*

RIGHT: *The stupa at Sanchi in central India is topped by a three part umbrella symbolizing three aspects of Buddhism – the Buddha, the dharma and the sangha. The stupa, a large solid mass is used as an image itself.*

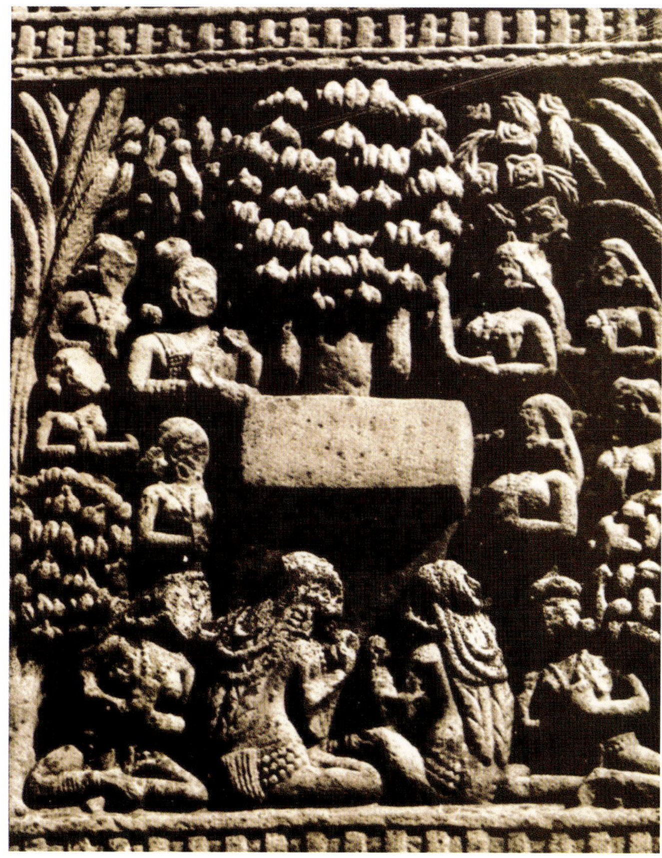

which in turn is surmounted by four lions. Lion is a symbol of royalty and the Buddha is described in the texts as the Lion of the Shakya clan, who himself was of royal blood.

Aniconic scenes from the life of the Buddha are carved on medallions on the railings of the stupa at Bharhut. For example, Buddha coming to the womb is represented through the dream of Queen Maya when she sees a white elephant in her dream. On a medallion from a railing of a stupa from Amaravati one can see Rahula before his father, the Buddha. The scene represented took place when the Enlightened One visited his family, whom he had earlier deserted; his wife Yashodhara, also called Gopa, presents to him their son Rahula so that he may assume his father's inheritance; but the Buddha resolved that he should obtain a much greater treasure, namely enlightenment and *nirvana*. Thus, his son becomes one of his disciples. On the medallion in the midst of a lively scene with an abundance of figures the Buddha is represented in non-iconic form by means of symbols, like the empty throne, the footprints with the Wheel of the Doctrine, and the blazing pillar, symbolizing the world axis, topped by the Wheel of Doctrine and the trident representing the three jewels. On the left, Rahula is being led in raising his hands to his father in veneration; around this central group are worshippers. The relief itself is encircled by a stylized lotus.

Sanchi is the greatest monument of the early Andhra period. A three-part umbrella atop the stupa symbolizes three aspects of Buddhism – the Buddha, the Dharma, and the Sangha. Tridents as symbols of the Buddhist triad supported by lotus wheels of the law are carved on the topmost architrave of the gateways at Sanchi. *Jatakas* are also visualized on the three architraves in which Buddha is sometimes a human being while at others he incarnates as an animal.

A cushioned throne topped by a bodhi tree, from the second century AD, representing enlightenment of the Buddha is kept at Musee Guimet in Paris. The throne visualizes the assault of Mara. Sculptured slabs from Amaravati sometimes combine both iconic and non-iconic forms. The lower registers visualize the usual symbols while Buddha in person sits on the top.

Such symbols stood in the midst of panels containing reliefs representing scenes from the life of the Buddha. The earliest such examples are from the stupas at Bharhut and Sanchi built around two to three centuries after the reign of Ashoka. Thus in the early phase of Buddhist art Buddha is manifested as impersonal symbols on one hand and in narrative legends on the other.

ABOVE: *There are sculptured slabs and engravings on the railings and gateways surrounding stupas representing Buddha both in iconic and aniconic forms. The usual symbols are often used to represent and visualize activities of the Buddha – an empty seat under a tree symbolizes enlightenment, the wheel of law – the teachings of the Buddha, footprints to indicate his presence in absence.*

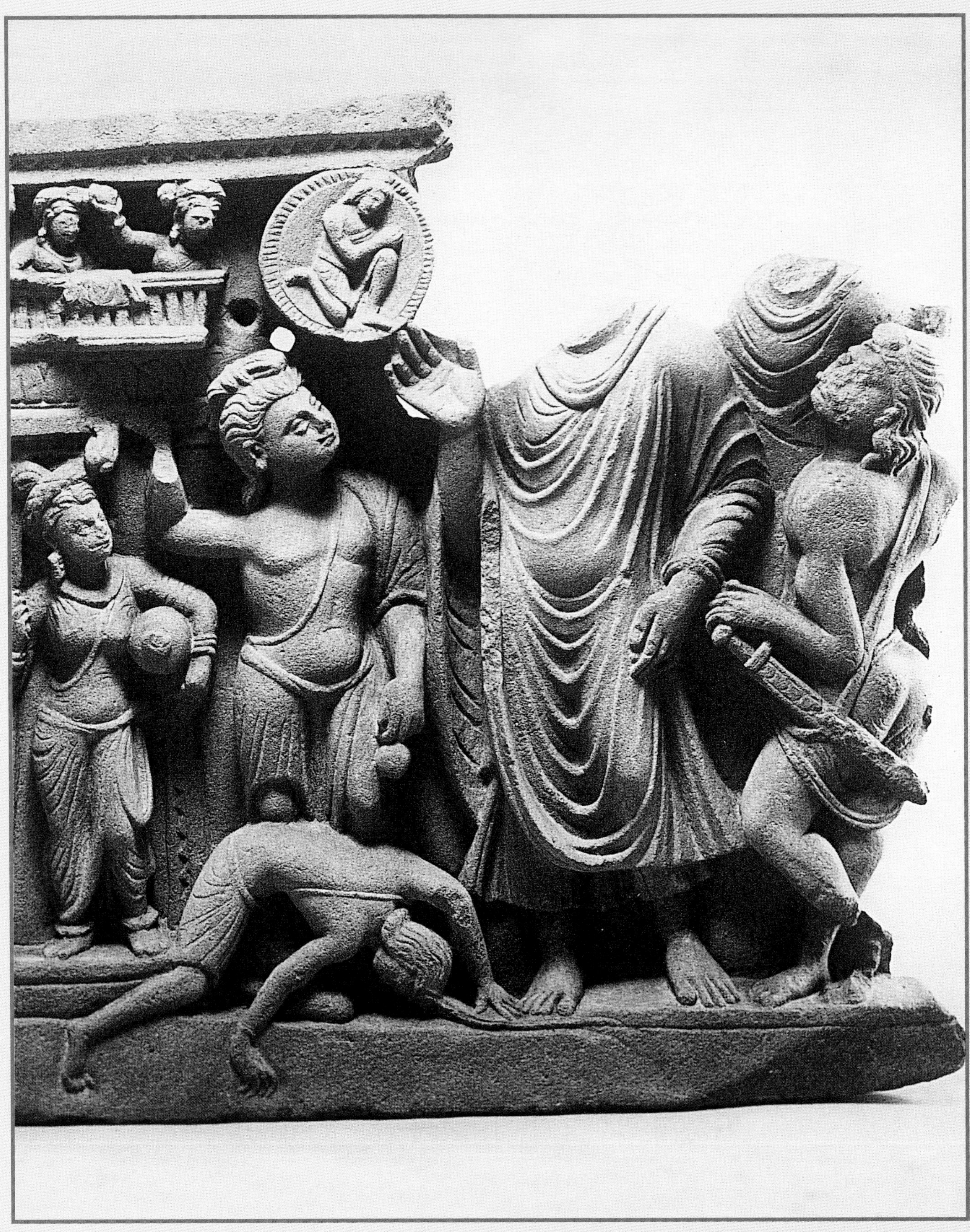

Buddhas of Three Times

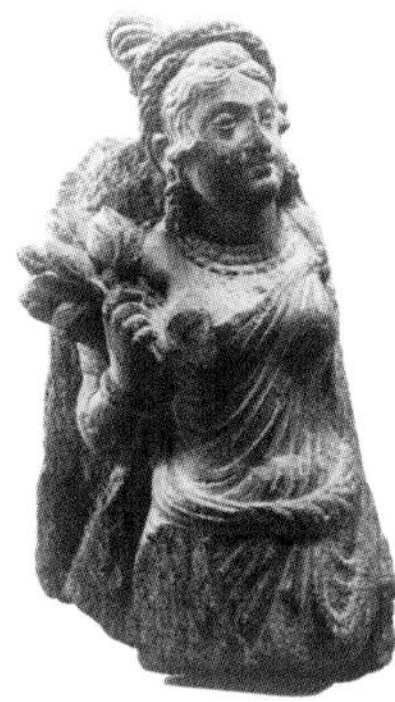

DIPANKARA: THE BUDDHA OF PAST: Dipankara is one of the Buddhas of three times – past, present and future, one of the twenty-four Buddhas and as one among the group of nine Buddhas. As a Buddha among twenty-four, he was born in Ramavati, to King Sudeva and Queen Sumedha. He lived a princely life, but abandoned his home and practiced austerities. He delivered his first sermon at Nandarama to his followers. At eighty cubits he is described as colossal in height. A tradition says that it was during the time of Dipankara that the ascetic Sumedha, who later became Gautama Buddha, first declared his intention of becoming an aspirant for enlightenment.

'Dipankara' comes from *'deepa',* meaning lamp. He is the most celebrated and the first of twenty-four Buddhas. Dipavati is the name of his capital city. In a past *kalpa*, King Arcishtra lived there. Dipankara was a Bodhisattva in Tushita heaven during the same *kalpa*. When the time came for him to descend he entered the womb of one of the spouses of the king, as he was thought most suitable to be his father. When the queen was in the throes of childbirth, she asked the king to send her to a lotus pond. As soon as she reached the spot, an island sprung up in the middle of the pond for the Bodhisattva to take birth. And a large number of bright lamps manifested miraculously.

There are other legends also about his birth and life. According to *Mahavastu,* a Buddhist text, Dipankara was born as the son of King Arcimat and Queen Sudipa in the royal city of Dipavati, as a resplendent light. Hence he was named Dipankara. He sat on lotus with petals as large as chariot wheels, appeared in yellow robes of a recluse and entered in meditation. Megha, who was learned in the Vedas offered him five lotus flowers and asked him to become a Buddha in one of the future existences. He was foretold that he would become Shakyamuni Buddha of Kapilavastu.

ABOVE: *Megha had obtained flowers from a brahmana girl Prakriti, to honour Dipankara. Plausibly this is the girl bearing flowers from a panel from Gandhara, kept at the British Museum.*

FACING PAGE: *The picture illustrates Dipanakara jataka. According to the story given in Mahavastu, Megha, a brahmana student, spreads his robe on the ground, throws himself at Dipankara's feet and wipes his sole with his hair. In the Divyavadana he is Sumati and in the Pali account he is Sumedha.*

Another Buddhist treatise *Bodhisattv-avadna-kalpalata* calls him 'maker of an island' for he was born on an island. Different versions of the legend are found in various sutras, which have been translated several times. Illustration of the legend in art began with the Gandharan style where he was often represented in narrative reliefs. A number of stele reflect the special place given to Dipankara by making Him as an oversized icon, against whose colossal size the other figures, even Shakyamuni are dwarfed. Buddha images at Shotorak have flames bursting from shoulders. The painting of the scholar-youth spreading out his hair before Dipankara was executed in the 420s at a mountain hermitage near Canton by just-arrived missionary from Kashmir. Frequent representations in Chinese art show a typical respect for Him as a First Ancestor. At caves of Kanheri in India, jataka of Dipankara has been depicted in relief. Moreover, portrayal of Dipankara on gilt copper plates, panels in stucco, murals and free-standing images found from Sri Lanka, Indonesia, Thailand, China, India, Afghanistan, Central Asia, Mongolia, and Nepal witness a wide range of his popularity.

Dipankara as one of the Buddhas of past, present and future sits performing the mudra of fearlessness with the right hand and a *karana* or the mudra of benediction with the left. The three are honoured as a triad in Lamaism whom the Mongols call 'Three White Buddhas'. The earliest manuscript of *Ashtasahasrika-prajna-paramita* from Nepal bears a depiction of Dipankara sitting on a chair with both legs pendant. He is also found at Svayambhunath temple at Kathmandu, Nepal, as one of the nine Buddhas of the treatise *Dharmakosasangraha.*

The Japanese make thirty images of thirty Buddhas, sacred for each day of the month. Among them Dipankara comes as sacred to the seventh day and is called Nento Butsu. In this form he sits in dhyana mudra.

Dipankara Buddha is believed to have lived on this earth for 100,000 years. He kept on finding someone worthy of hearing the divine truth. Then he decided to convert the world and caused a miracle, which appeared in the form of a great city that materialized from his lamp and became stationary in space. Fierce flames emitted from the four walls while the people of Jambudvipa gazed upon the miracle. Their hearts were filled with fear and they looked for Buddha to save them. Dipankara came forth from the burning city, descended, and seated himself on a lion to teach the law.

Like all other Buddhas, Dipankara has short curly hair, *ushnisha, urna*, and long earlobes. Sometimes his right hand is in abhaya mudra. When a triad is formed he is flanked by two Bodhisattvas. Dipankara has always been popular in China. Several examples of Dipankara can be seen in the cave temples of Yun-kang and Lung-men.

SHAKYAMUNI: THE BUDDHA OF PRESENT

Buddha is a teacher in Hinayana Buddhism; his life is an example that everyone must follow. In the Mahayana path, he is a manifestation of the Truth and the Absolute. His word is the self-revelation of truth. He has an infinite number of colleagues, all reflections of the same truth. The concept underwent profound changes, and as a manifestation of self-revealing Supreme Existence, he became Shakyamuni. He was considered as the Buddha who is seen on celestial planes. Finally, he was seen as the Supreme Buddha.

With an increasing popularity of Buddhism, Shakyamuni attained various manifestations and was given a variety of meaningful appellation – Bhagavan, Tathagata, Sattha, Jina and Buddha. In the legends his name Gautama, is put into the mouths of those outside the rank of his followers. He is Bhagavan, the one who is endowed with divine riches, to the devotees. His followers call him with another name Sattha, as he is not merely an instructor or a teacher, he was able to remove barrenness of heart. One could rely on the teacher, on his system, his sect and teachings. Sattha is a dynamic expression of his personality. Buddha was frequently refered to by himself and also by others by the name Tathagata, because he is the person who has experienced and realized the culmination of the Dharma himself. And he is the Buddha who has attained *sambodhi*, the supreme enlightenment. He bears the attributes that place him as a *mahapurusha* in his followers' eyes, on his person as marks of a suprememan. He emits supernatural light from his body and can see into the past and the future. A conqueror of all imperfections, he transcended life, hence his alternative name is Jina. He had lotus-like qualities – born and dwelling in the world but remained unstained by it.

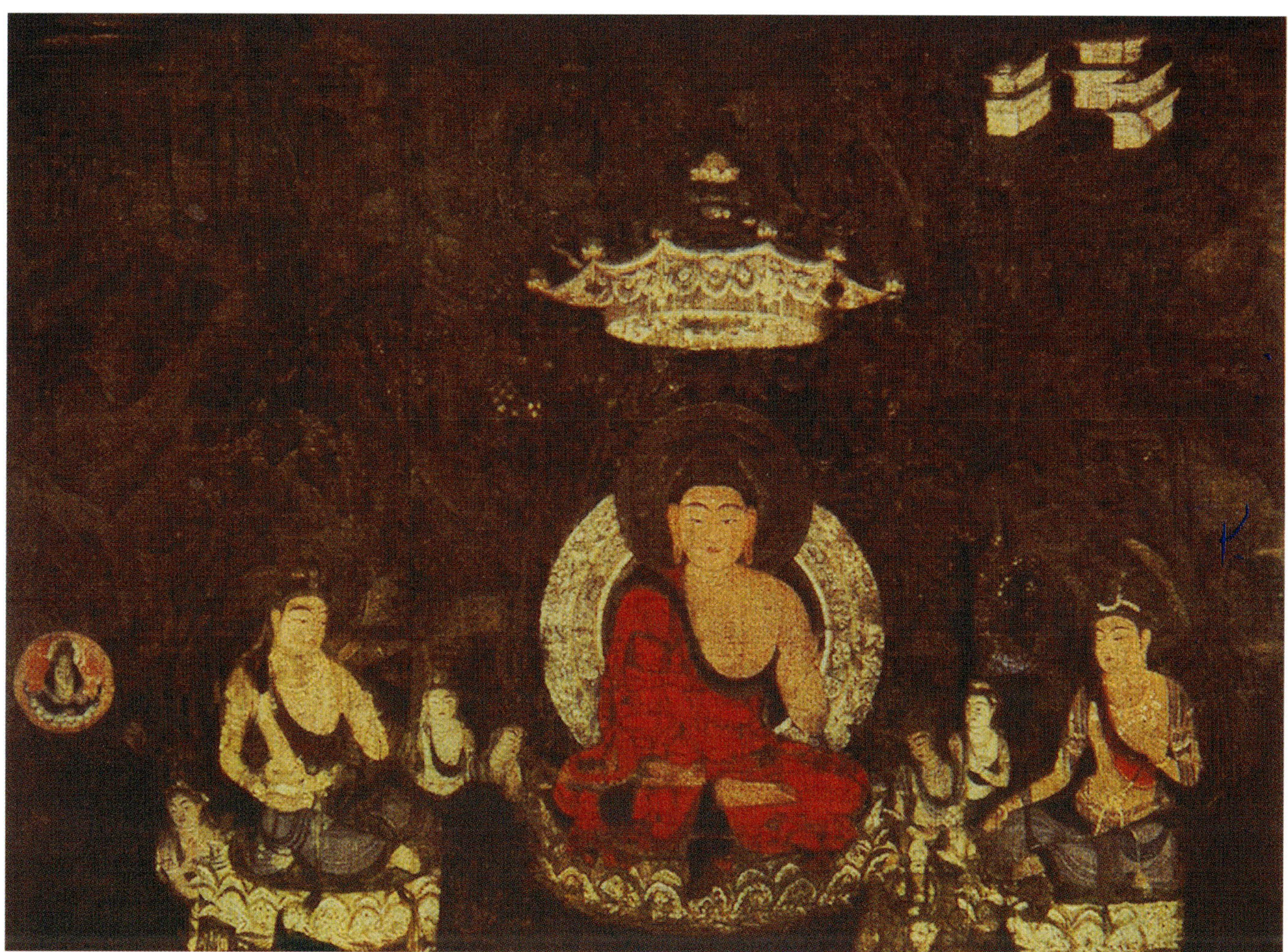

During the earthly sojourn Shakyamuni sought a way of life beyond all pains and pressures overcoming innumerable temptations. He taught the causes of suffering and ways to eliminate them.

AS AN INFANT

Buddha as a newly born was given bath and consecrated with nectar, *amrta*. Soon he took seven steps unaided in all the directions, pointed towards the worlds, nether and above and proclaimed to be the ruler of the world. Sculptures from Gandhara, Nagarjunakonda and Nalanda depict the legend of Buddha taking the seven steps. In Japan an annual festival is celebrated to commemorate the birthday of the Buddha. An image of the newborn pointing towards heaven and earth is placed in a basin. For the annual celebration of the birth of the Buddha on the eighth day of the fourth month every year, sweet tea is poured over and distributed among the devotees as sacred. In this type of sculptures Buddha is an infant but looks mature to denote his inner wisdom. The earliest known image of Shakyamuni in this form from Japan is at the Todaiji Monastery in Nara.

AS A YOGI

After renouncing the world as Siddhartha, the Buddha had taken the path of extreme asceticism. In order to be an

ABOVE: *Lord Buddha delivering a sermon from the Vulture Peak, Gridhrakuta mountain. Buddha is seated on a seat surrounded by Bodhisattvas and angels above him honour him with music, and monks and laymen standing below listen to the law.*

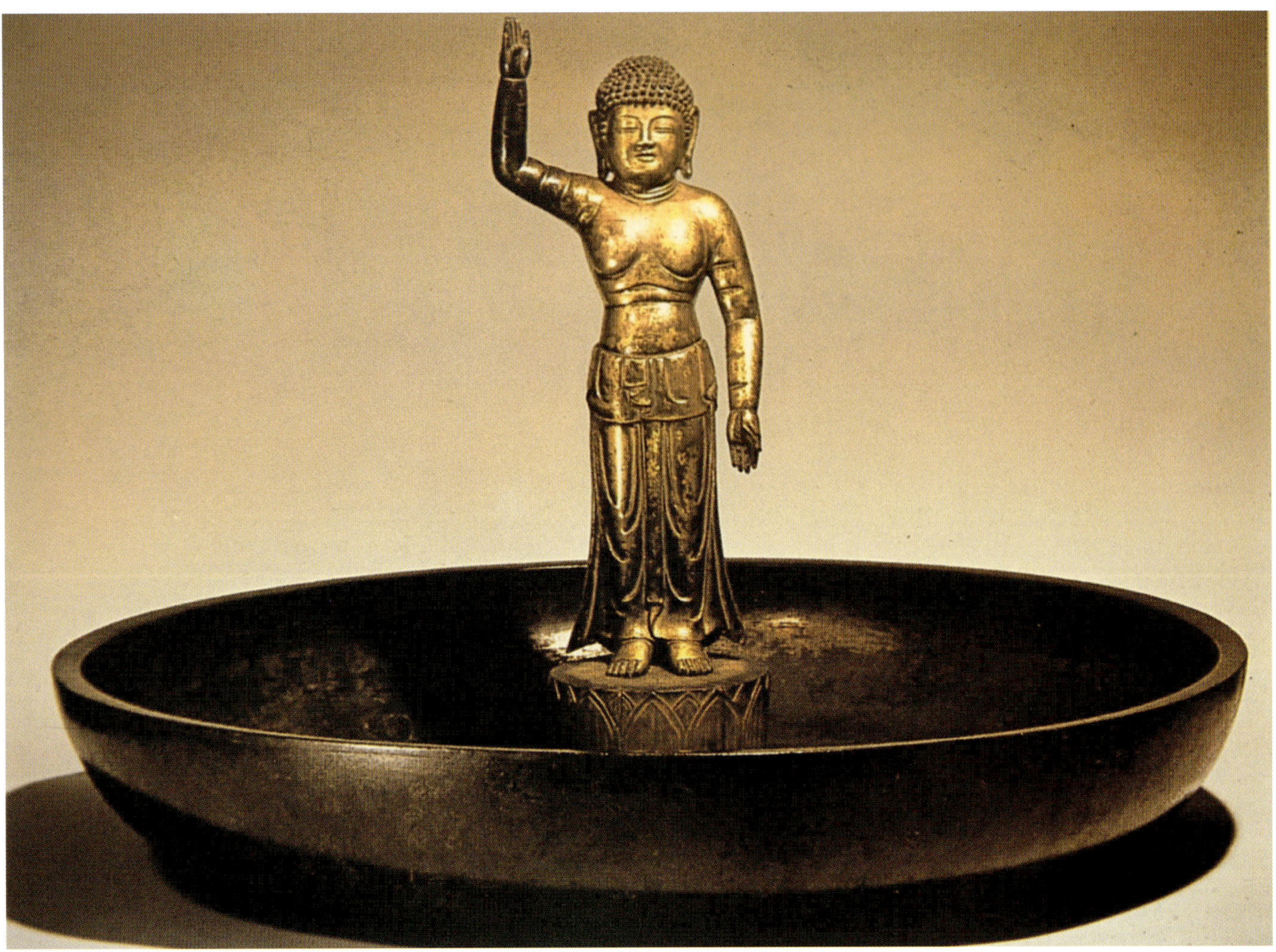

ascetic, he cut off his *ushnisha* and shaved his head. Mahabrahma Ghatikara offered him eight requisites of a *bhikshu*, which are – three robes, a bowl, a razor, a needle, a sash and a water strainer. As a *bhikshu*, sometimes Gautama lived on just one grain of rice or a seasame seed. His golden body turned black and emaciated, the thirty-two auspicious marks of a great man were concealed. At times he was wrecked with severe pain and even lost consciousness.

As a yogi Buddha sat under the Bodhi tree. He was a Buddha, an enlightened being who had overcome the temptations of Mara to lead the world beyond all kinds of pains and pressures, toil and tears, transcending the barriers of love and hate. He had to struggle intensely to save the mankind from darkness of ignorance. He discovered the causes of sufferings and the ultimate way to liberation. Buddha in this form is a Jina who defeats the fearsome enemies of attachment, anger, pride, and ignorance. Such an image of Shakyamuni, the suprememan among men, the supra divine being, is an inspiration to overcome the overwhelming craving for life and lust.

IN BHUMISPARSHA MUDRA

Shakyamuni is often seen with his right hand in touching the earth posture and with the left he holds an alms bowl. His palm is turned inward and the fingers are straight. If he performs the posture of fearlessness or benediction with the right hand then the left may hold robes, rest in lap or perform the posture of benediction. His posture of sitting cross-legged on lotus, feeling serene and motionless, signifies the supreme moment of enlightenment. Buddha had touched the earth as witness to his enlightenment as he had no other to confirm because he meditated in total isolation. The Earth Goddess emerged from the ground near him and said, 'It is as you say and I am the eyewitness.' The gesture also signifies destruction of all the enemies.

IN DHYANA MUDRA

Buddha was determined to gain enlightenment through meditation. He believed that one should pay attention to one's breathing, meditate on body, feelings, mental formations, consciousness and objects of consciousness. Look deeply in order to see the process of birth, growth, and fading of every phenomenon, from your own body, emotions, mind, and objects of mind. The statues of Shakyamuni sitting in dhyana mudra are not so many as there are in the posture of dharma-cakra-pravartana or bhumisparsha. A few examples come from the Korean and Japanese tradition. For example there is an image at the National Museum of Korea at Seoul from sixth century and drawings from Japan from twelfth century AD.

SETTING THE WHEEL OF DHARMA IN MOTION

After enlightenment, Brahma and Indra, the lords of earth and heaven standing on the right and left of the Buddha requested him to set the Wheel of Dharma in motion. Buddha sitting in dharma-cakra-pravartana-mudra represents delivering his first sermon at Sarnath. He brings both his hands to the chest level, the left hand forms a lotus bud-like shape while with the right he opens its petals one by one. The images of Shakyamuni sitting in the posture of turning the Wheel of Law can be found engraved in stone, or free sitting images in various materials, paintings and even in illustrated manuscripts. While in this mudra he may sit on a white lotus called *pundarika* in Sanskrit, or a throne, and the throne can be of different styles and designs. It can be a lion throne or a lion throne with four elephants paying homage. He may be attended by five acolytes – Avalokiteshvara, Manjushri, Maitreya, Vajrapani and Samantabhadra. The colour of his body is shining gold.

Buddha turning the Wheel of Law is the eleventh episode among the twelve in his life. When he was enlightened, he decided to impart his teachings to the five ascetics whom he found in a garden in Sarnath. This is known as the first sermon or Turning of the Wheel of

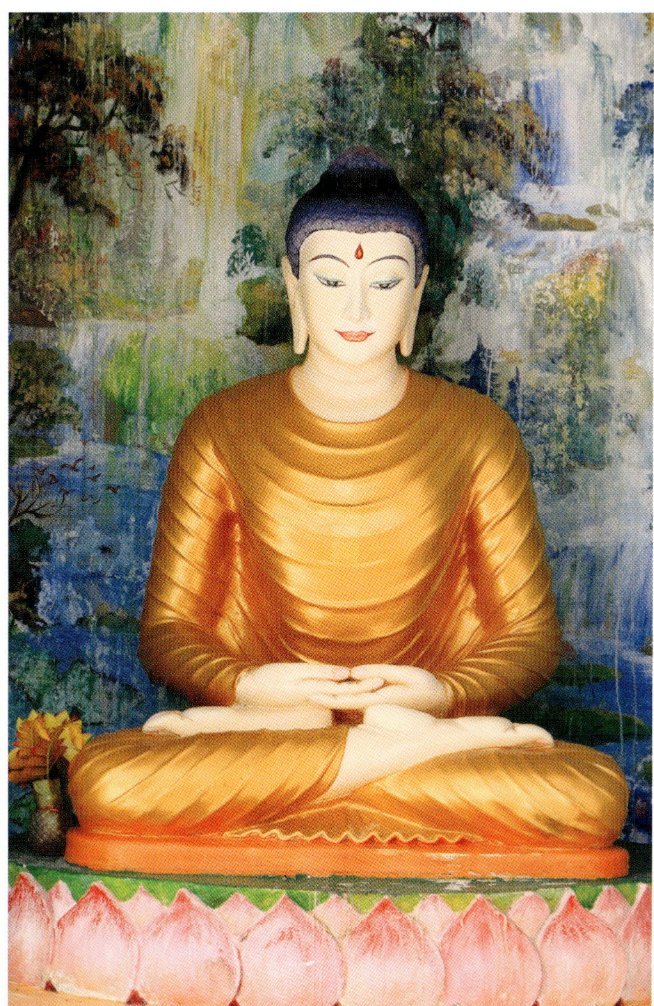

ABOVE: *Shakyamuni Buddha sitting cross legged in dhyana mudra to meditate. The position symbolizes qualities of tranquility and impassivity. This is the mudra of mind at work, perseverance in meditation and also dispersing the disorders of heart.*

FACING PAGE: *Images of Buddha as an infant are enshrined in Buddhist temples to celebrate his birthday on the eighth day of the fourth month (Hindu calendar) each year. He raises his right hand and points down with the left proclaiming his domain.*

Dharma. The Buddha sat on a pedestal flanked by Brahma and Indra and the five disciples listened to him. Hence on, for forty-five years he was constantly on the move with his disciples and his worshippers increasing by the day. Richly coloured wall hangings were made for the temples that depict such scenes. Shakyamuni sits on the sacred throne

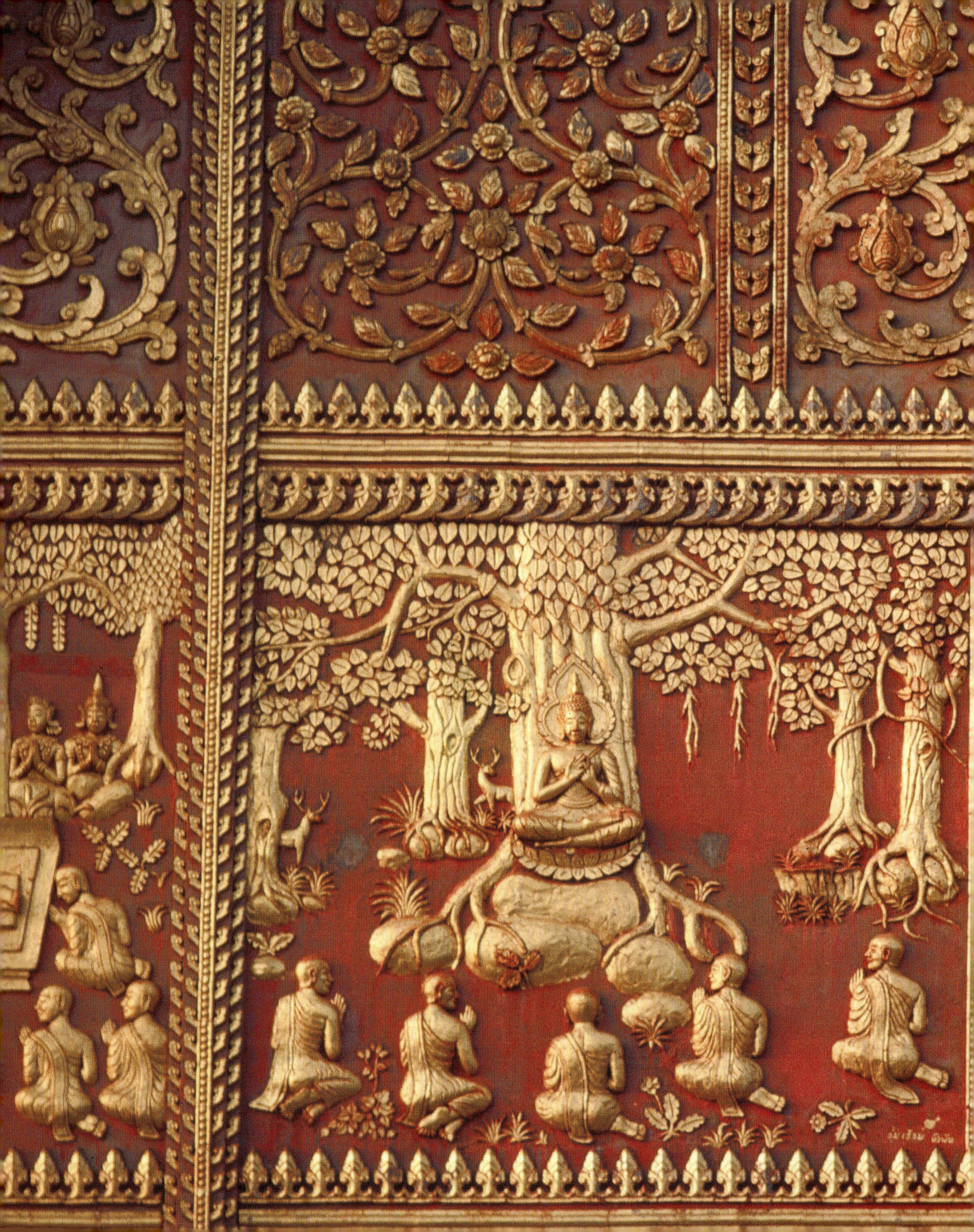

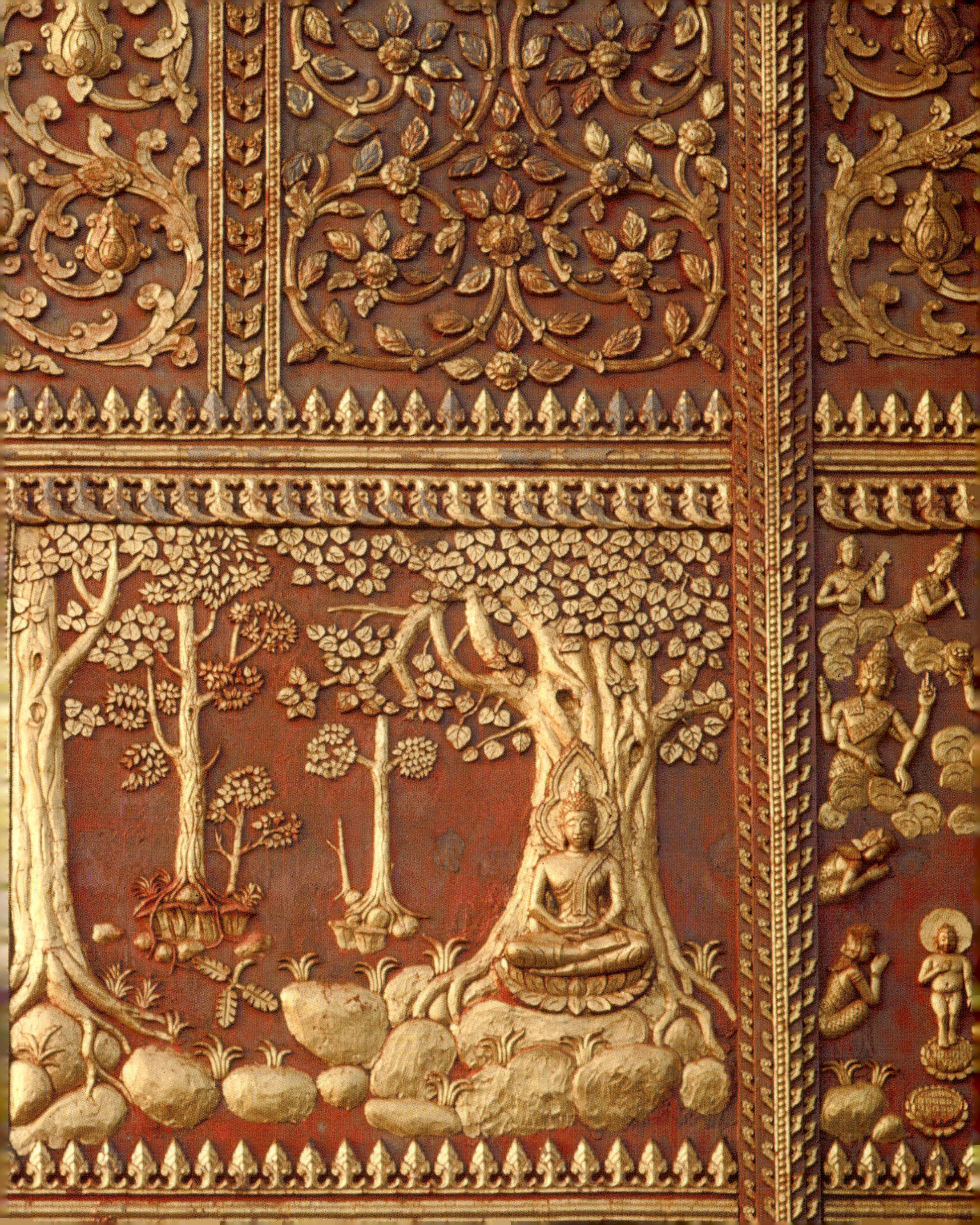

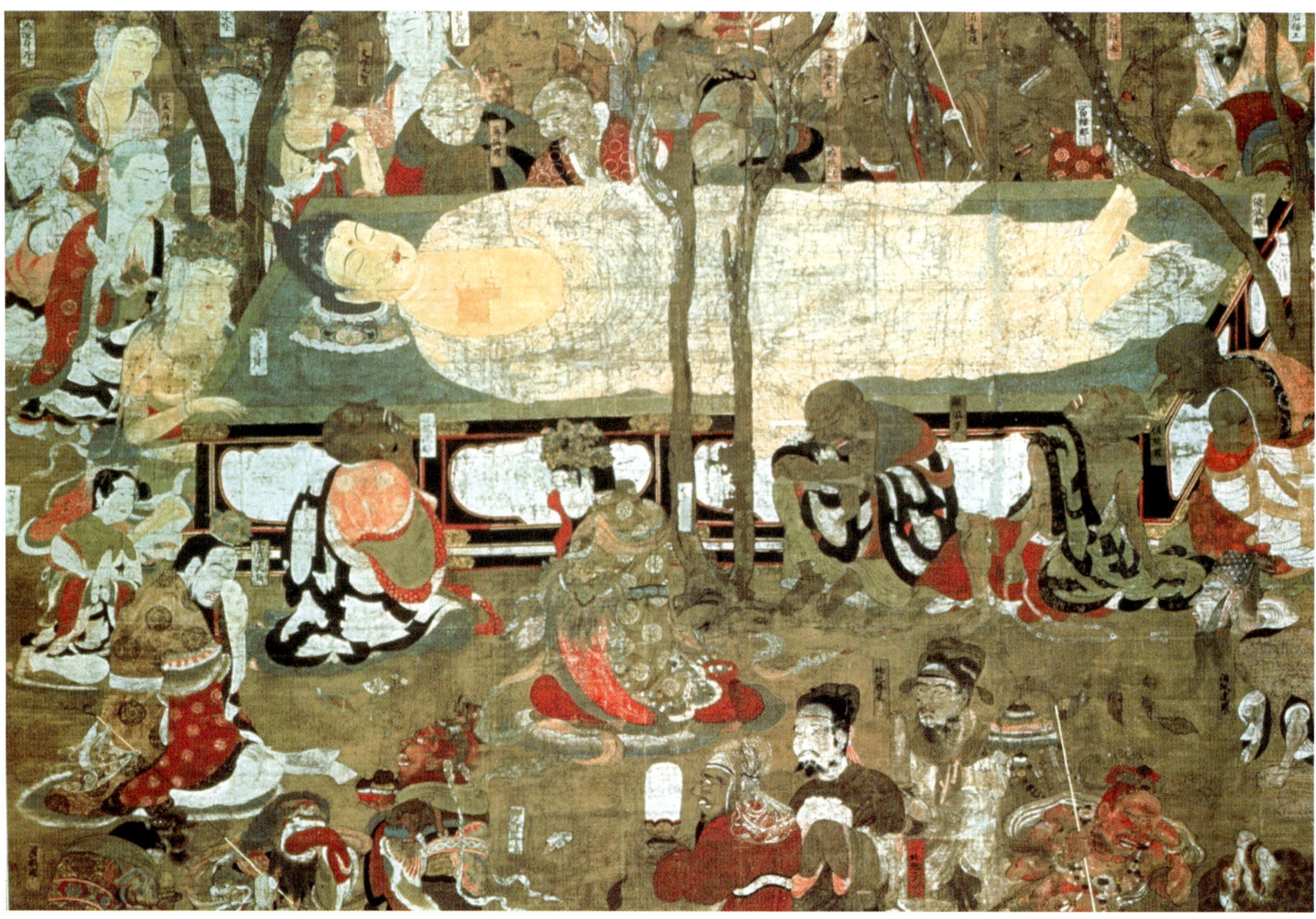

surrounded by Bodhisattvas and disciples. Heavenly angels fly on clouds. Embroideries based on the theme were also produced.

Shakyamuni's sermon from the Gridhrakuta Mountain is another important theme for pictorial representation. In this representation, the Buddha sits in dharma-chakra-pravartana-mudra flanked by Bodhisattvas Samantabhadra and Manjushri and is surrounded by his disciples.

BUDDHA RECLINES FOR THE FINAL REST

The theme of *parinirvana* of the Buddha has inspired a large number of masterpieces throughout the Buddhist world. It is the final episode of his life, which occured when the Buddha reached Kushinagar accompanied by his disciple Ananda and others. He sat between two sala trees and directed Ananda to prepare his couch. Ananda wept but obeyed his orders. The Tathagata laid down with his head towards the north, put his right hand beneath his head, and crossed his feet like a monarch. His followers gathered around, the wind hushed, the forest streams were

ABOVE: *Buddha entered the state of nirvana, the great earth quacked, the sun and moon withdrew their shine, the wind hushed, birds and beasts became silent, trees shed their flowers and leaves mournfully, Bodhisattvas sat impassively but the disciples mourned, prayed, cried, and even shouted raising their heads to the sky with distorted faces in agony.*

FACING PAGE: *Buddha as Shakyasimha in the mandala of Durgatiparishodhana, remover of misfortunes is a form of Mahavairocana. He sits inside a white stupa, performing dharmacakrapravartana mudra – turning the wheel of law. This is also identified as the wheel of universal law govering all events and phenomena.*

PRECEDING PAGES: *Details of Buddha's sermons from Gilded Relief, Wat That Luang Neua, Laos.*

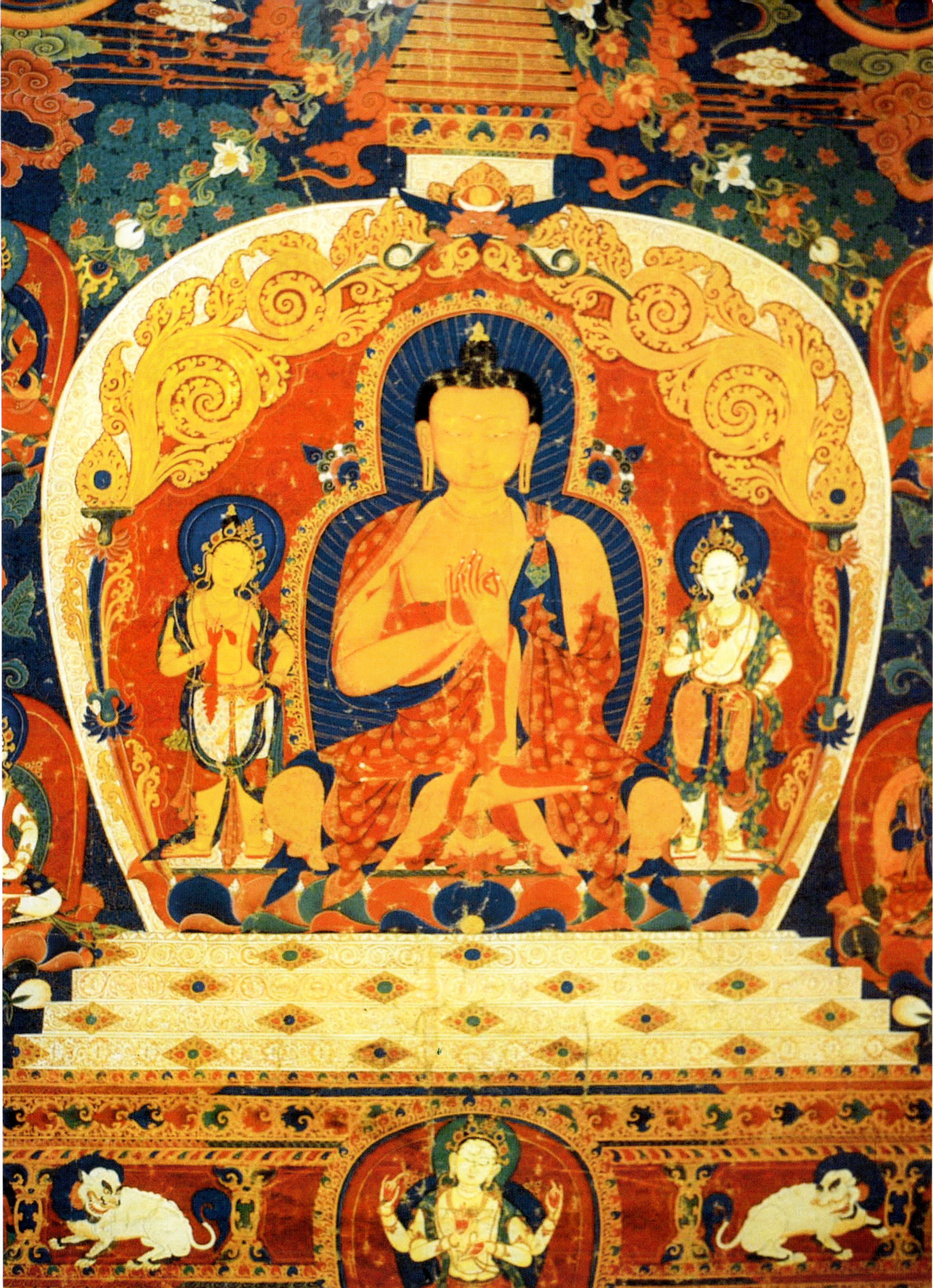

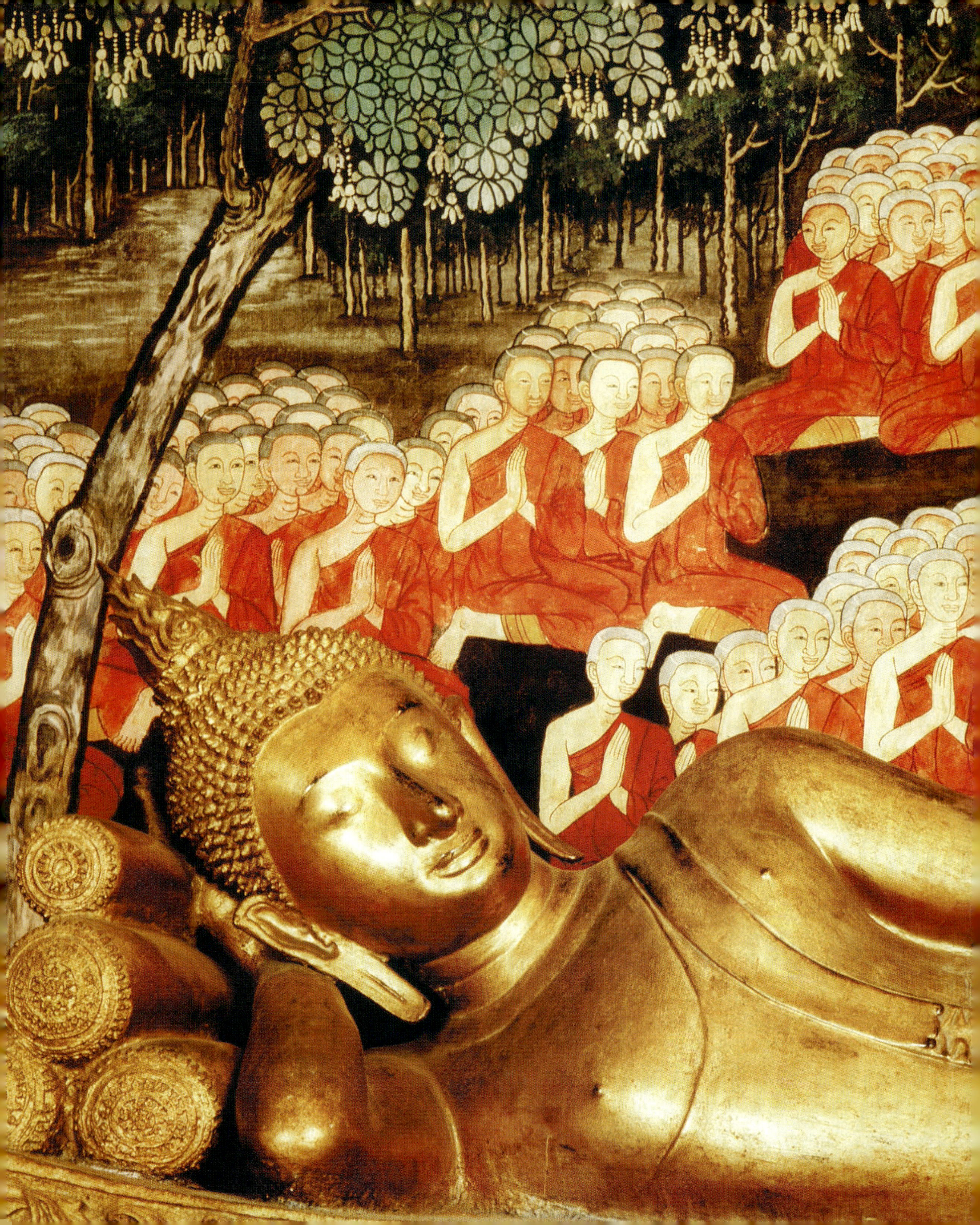

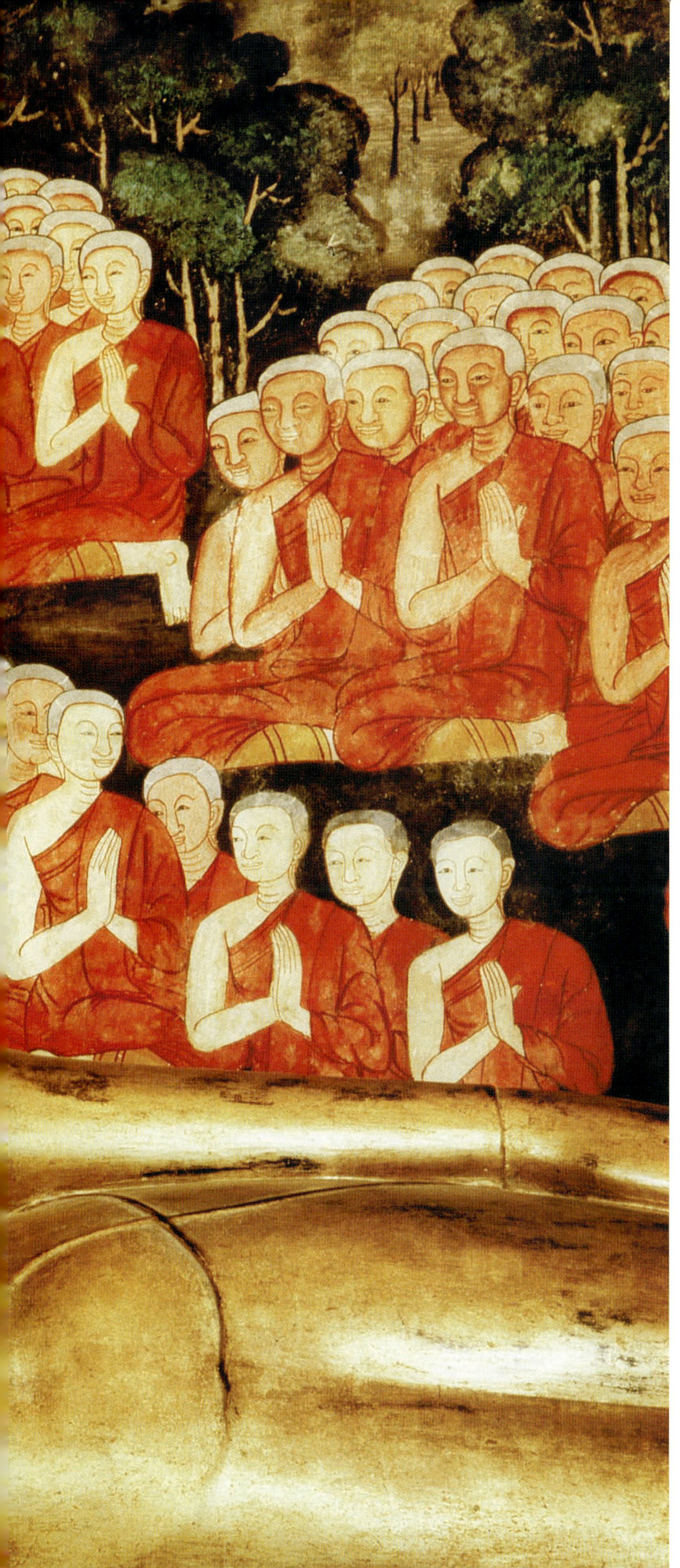

When Buddha reached the forest of sal trees at the entrance of Kushinagar, he asked Ananda to prepare a place for him to lie down. The Buddha laid on his side facing north. Ananda was sad as he knew that the time for nirvana of the teacher was approaching. His disciples and all people gathered around and he spoke the last words on enlightenment, eight-fold path, birth, death, and impermanence etc.

silent, no sound was heard, trees sweat out large flowing drops, flowers and leaves fell mournfully. And he passed away. The great Earth quaked, the Sun and the Moon forgot to shine. The *parinirvana* of the Buddha is famous all over the Hinayana as well as Mahayana countries. Colossal reclining images depicting this stage were carved out of rocks in Bamiyan and other parts of Asia. In Bangkok an image of the Reclining Buddha is housed in Wat Pho.

SITTING ON LION SEAT

In several images Shakyamuni can be seen sitting on a throne supported by two leaping lions on the sides which indicate his being Shakyasimha, lion among the Shakyas. He is the one who vanquishes all but cannot be vanquished by anyone. Lions signify steadfast pursuit of wholesome striving.

AS A MONARCH

Relics of the Buddha were ordered to be deposited like that of a *chakravartin* as he was fit to be a Universal Monarch as has been said in Buddhist literature:

> 'You are a bhikkhu of lovely appearance and your skin is like gold. What is the use of being a samana who possesses the highest beauty?' 'You deserve to be a king, a cakkavatti, king of kings, having conquered the four corners (of the earth), a lord of India.' 'Wealthy khattiyas and kings are devoted to you. So, Gotama, rule as a king of kings, a leader of men.'

WALKING BUDDHA

The best-known examples of images of Walking Buddha are found in Thailand from the Sukhothai period. Walking Buddhas are freestanding images derived from representations in relief depicting the Buddha as he descends from heaven. Or it may be a statue of Buddha while walking in meditation. It was a custom for the Buddha to rise early in morning to sit in meditation, and then do walking meditation among the forest trees. The main image is detached from its scenic and illustrative context. Some of these images often in bronze are dated fifteenth century.

This type of images are extraordinary examples of innovation visualizing all the marks of a great man. The Teacher advances forward gracefully to announce the doctrine. The body has graceful undulation, hanging arms rhythmically follow curves of the body, hips are curving slightly outward and there is a smooth flowing rhythm of the body and the garments. Each detail is delicately outlined, his head is shaped like a lotus bud and the neck merges harmoniously into shoulders. The theme already occurs in Indian Buddhist works of art. The above-mentioned features of such images can be traced back to the Gandhara school.

DESCENDING FROM THE TRAYASTRIMSHA HEAVEN

Trayastrimsha represented the second of the six Buddhist heavens on the top of Mount Meru. The Buddha went there to meet his mother and preached the philosophy found in the Buddhist text *Abhidharma*. There in the Sudhamma meeting hall he sat on Indra's throne under the *parijata* tree, a characteristic of this particular heaven. The tree bears flowers that shine like the morning Sun. Petals lie scattered on the divine seats. The Buddha is sitting inside a building. A tree is to its right. Behind is the Chulamani Chaitya, where lies the lock of Buddha's hair that he had cut off at the time of renunciation, and the tooth that was placed in the same stupa by Shakra or Indra. In front is a jewel ladder that was made to bring down the Buddha to Sankissa. A shrine was built at the point where his right foot first touched the earth.

COLOSSAL IMAGES

In Thervada countries like Thailand, the sculpted Buddha images were often huge in size. A number of colossal images are lying in the ruined monasteries of Ayutthia or brought to the museums in dilapidated and sad condition. But in the temples in Bangkok there are a number of images overwhelmingly large in size. At the temple of Wat Po, the brickcore image is 150 feet in length. It is covered with plaster and gold leaf. The soles of the Buddha's feet are intricately carved, depicting auspicious signs inlaid with mother of pearl. He is lying on the right hand side holding his face supported by right palm. Buddhas in Bamiyan in Afghanistan were the best known colossi in the Buddhist world. The first colossal image of Shakyamuni in Japan was sculpted soon after its entry there. It is popularly known as Asuka Daibutsu. The Chinese cave temples also house many colossal images.

SIX PERFECTIONS OF THE BUDDHA

Buddha's throne bears six animal figures symbolically representing his attainment of Six Perfections, called Paramitas – the Garuda or divine eagle at the top is the first Paramita of charity (*dana*). The two young Nagas stand for mortal excellence (*shila paramita*). The two dolphins/*makaras* are symbols of forbearance (*kshanti-paramita*). The two dwarfs/*vamanas* represent endurance (*virya-paramita*). The two elephants stand for meditation (*dhyana-paramita*). The two lions below the lotus are the highest perfection (*prajna-paramita*).

SHAKYAMUNI ACCOMPANIED BY THE LORDS OF HEAVEN AND EARTH

Buddha is accompanied by Brahma on the right and Indra on the left, the lords of Earth, the world of living beings and heavens, on the summit of Mount Sumeru. Their association is common both in texts and in iconography. Both of them were present at the time of the birth of Shakyamuni. They heard his teachings and then swore to defend the Buddhist faith. They stand in pairs in halls of worship. They requested the Buddha to set the Wheel of Dharma in motion. It is Brahma who first uses the word 'Tathagata' in addressing the Buddha. It is to Brahma that the Buddha speaks his first words after enlightenment. Brahma and Indra have a gentleness of facial expression reminiscent of the countenance of Bodhisattvas.

BUDDHA AND HIS DISCIPLES

Buddha is often flanked by two of his disciples – Shariputra and Maudgalyayana. They stand as ideal disciples holding the mendicant's staff and bowl. Buddha had once spoken to Shariputra – wise art thou, comprehensive and manifold thy wisdom, joyous and swift, sharp and fastidious. ... The preeminence of Maudgalyayana lies in his miraculous powers.

SHAKYAMUNI SURROUNDED BY SIXTEEN ARHATS

Shakyamuni selected sixteen Arhats from the group of his disciples and asked them to stay in the world to protect the teachings till the time of the descent of Maitreya. Each was assigned a quarter of the world to be dispersed over the globe. They are the apostles of the Buddha who have succeeded in travelling on the Eightfold Path. They are free from all the worldly attachments and the wheel of transmigrations. They have crossed various stages of saintship after a long course of asceticism. Normally they are depicted as wise and venerable. Some of their names are – Ajita, Kanakavatsa, Vanavasi, and Vajriputra.

DIVINE RADIANCE OF THE BUDDHA

In some thangka paintings Buddha is visualized as a wheel representing his radiance. These are rays of spiritual light

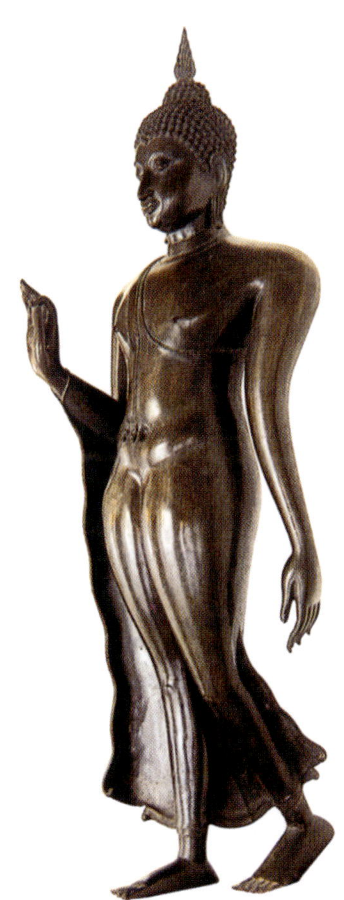

Sukhothai period in Thailand produced masterpieces representing Buddha advancing forward to announce the doctrine portraying complete visualization of signs of a great or a divine man.

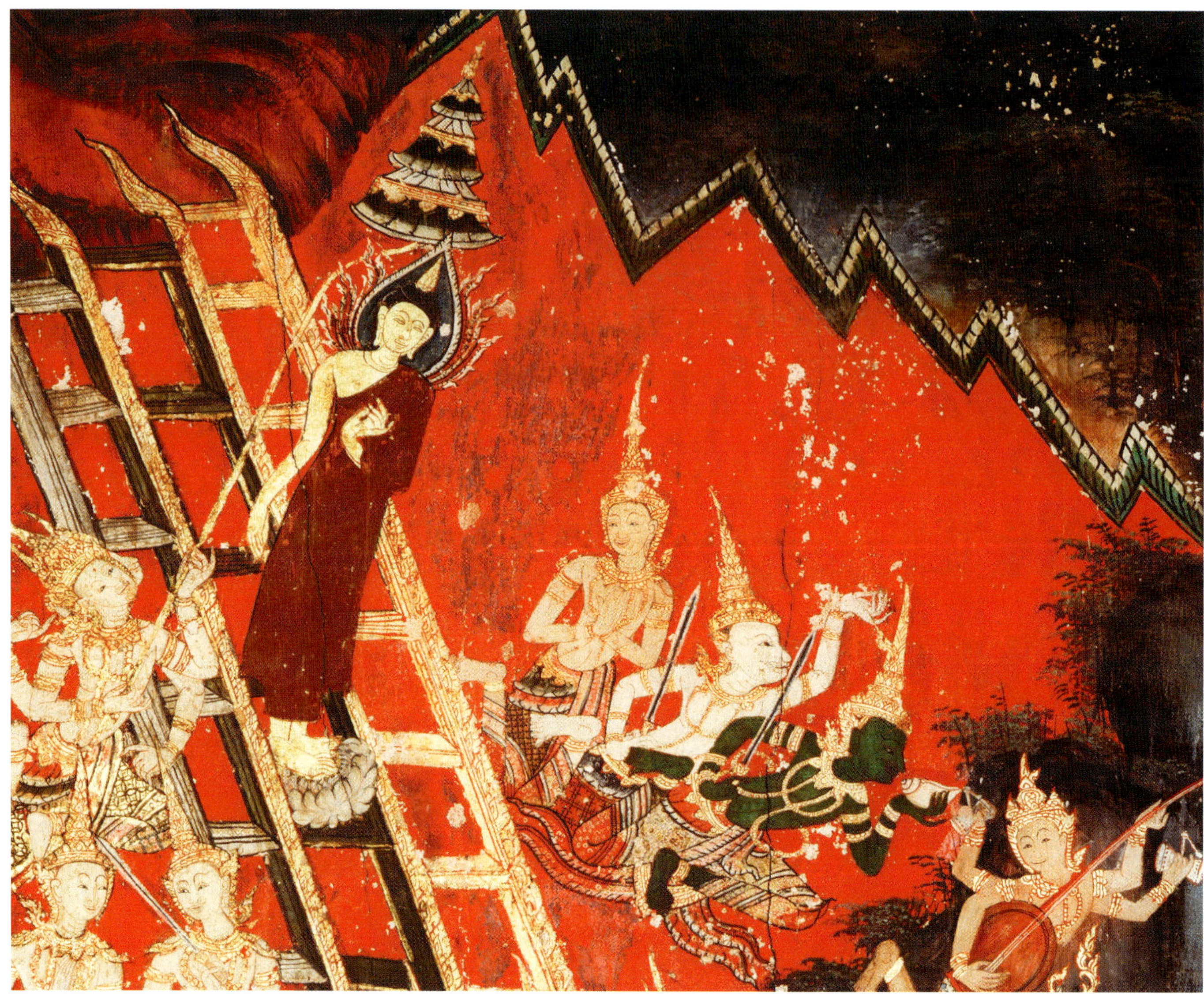

that flood forth from the heart of the Buddha. This is the divine light that lives in the depths of the wise. This is the purest light, the divine spark, which has to be attained.

BUDDHA PROTECTED BY NAGA

Origin of a Buddha image in contemplation, sitting cross legged on a coiled snake and protected by a naga spreading its hoods over Buddha's head goes back to the story of the demon Mara who created a terrible storm and flood to distract Buddha from meditation. The naga had crept out of a hole under the Buddha's tree to lift him above the flood and to give him shelter from rain. Such images were first created in Cambodia combining the familiar Khmer belief of the naga as cosmic source of existence and life with the image of the victorious Buddha as pattern of the king. The Buddha on naga presents an alter ego of the king around whom the universe revolved. Such images also symbolize Buddha's victory over sorrow and death.

MIRACLE OF SHRAVASTI

The Buddha images with flames issuing from his shoulders and a stream of water from his feet while he preached in mid air when he thought of converting the believers,

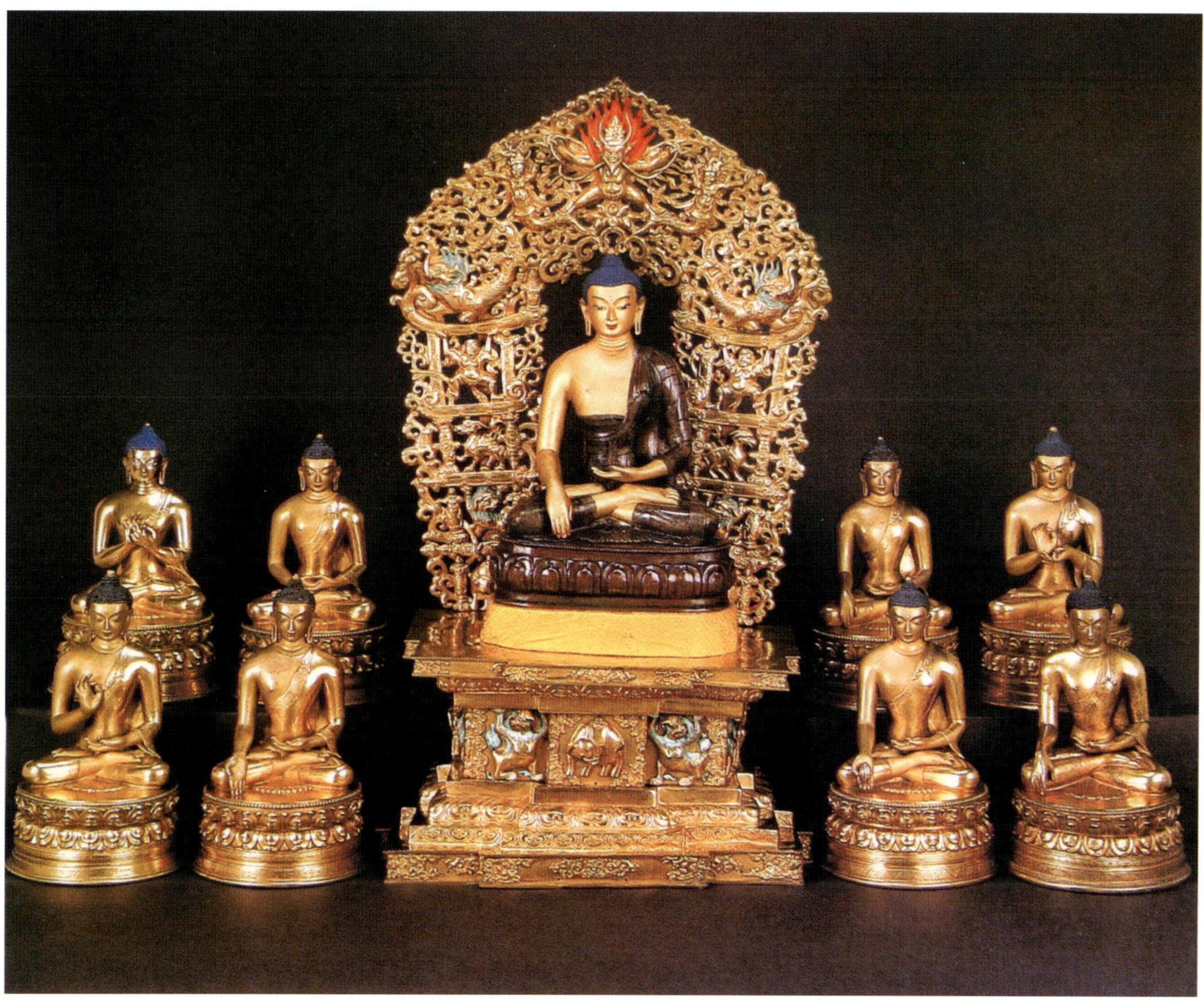

represents the miracle of Shravasti. The Buddha sat on a lotus provided by two naga kings – Nanda and Upananda and caused unending replicas of himself to appear stretching upto heaven. It is recorded that a special pavilion for the performance of the miracle was built by King Prasenajit. This subject became a favourite theme in the Buddhist world.

Fire and water represent two out of four elements acknowledged by the Buddhists maintaining that atoms are not eternal because they possess motion. They are integrated and harmonized by space, the fifth element. Water represents liquidity and fire, heat. Some schools of philosophy argue that atoms are set into motion by merits and demerits and Ishvara, the

ABOVE: *Buddha is sitting with eight Buddhas of medicine, as the supreme physician whose medicines contain prescriptions for liberation from suffering. Practice of medicine has been consistently an important part of monk's life. Healing was also a metaphor for the process of spiritual awakening.*

FACING PAGE: *Buddha's descent from the Trayastrinsha heaven painted on the walls of Buddhaisawan chapel at Bangkok National Museum, Thailand. A ladder made of jewels and nagas is meant to bring the Buddha down to Sankissa. On his left is a golden ladder for Indra and on his right is a silver ladder for Brahma.*

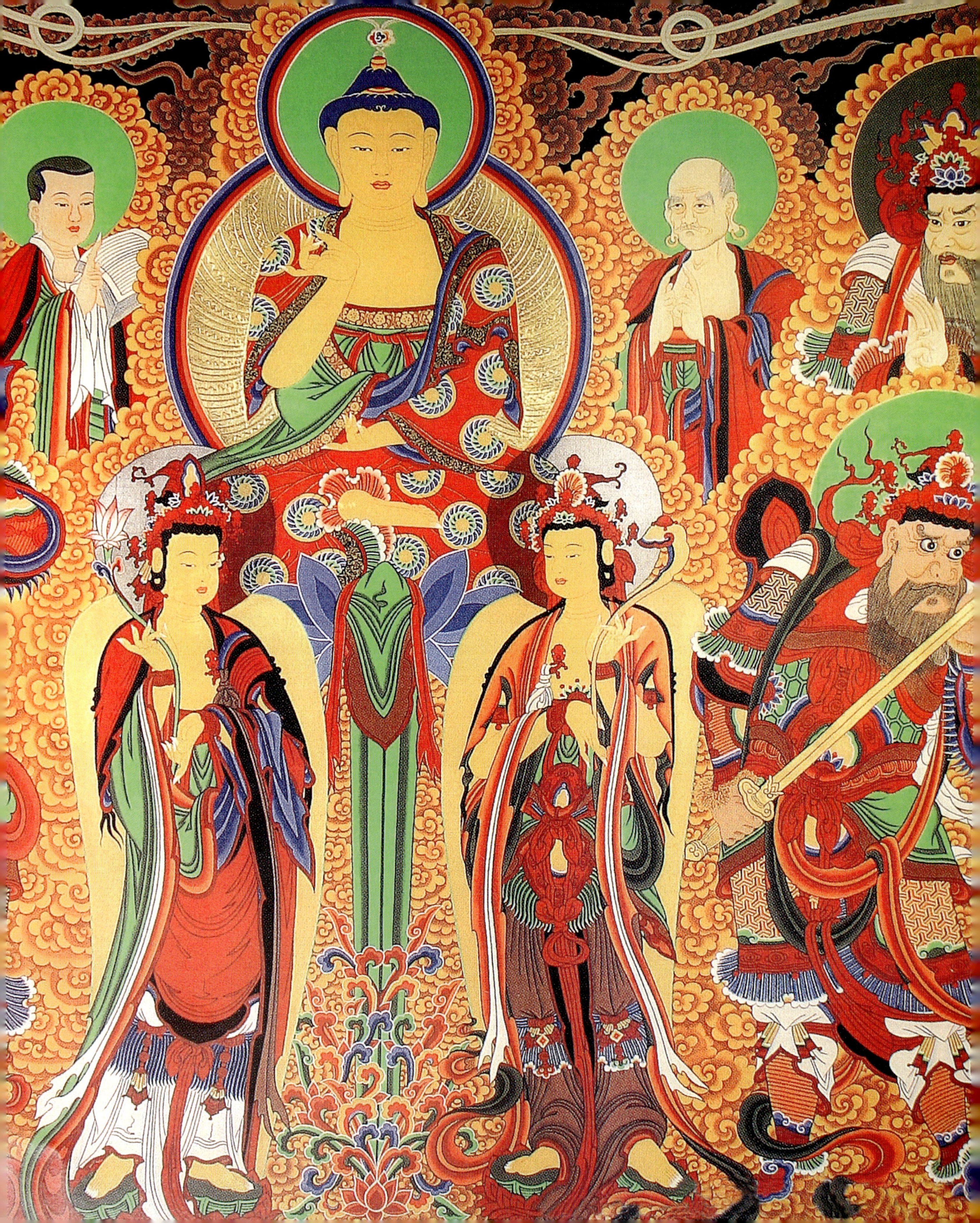

supreme power directs the actions of the atoms. Thus such images may represent Buddha as controlling the flowing and the heating elements in the meditative process.

MAITREYA: THE BUDDHA OF FUTURE

Maitreya is associated with the Sun god, Mitra. It is around him that the light cults came into being. They are represented by Amitabha, Vairocana, and Maitreya. He is also one of the Buddhas of the three times. Dipankara is the Buddha of the past, Shakyamuni of the present, and Maitreya of the future. Maitreya is said to be waiting for the time when he will descend to the earth. He is the hope of civilization expressing the invisible future by means of the visible. Maitreya confers happiness. The time lapse between *nirvana* of Shakyamuni and appearance of Maitreya is four thousand divine years. He is the lord of ten planes of meditation. A Japanese master of Buddhism says, 'The sunlight of the Buddha Shakyamuni has been hidden in the distant cloud, and we have not yet seen the glimpse of the moon light of the merciful Future Buddha Maitreya.'

Huge statues of Maitreya sitting serenely were housed in the Tibetan temples as a symbol of future hope. He is worshipped in the very central cathedral of Lhasa. It is believed that the age of discord, *kaliyuga*, as it draws to an end, will drown mankind in a welter of hatred and destruction. When mankind has sunk to the lowest level of evil, when hunger, pestilence and wars have filled the world with blood and death, Maitreya will descend from the heaven.

The belief in 'Maitreya' comes from Iranian belief in Mithra. The Buddhists living in the Northwest were inspired by the Pashtu speaking people for their mythology of light cults. According to another interpretation, 'Maitreya' comes from *'maitri'*, meaning compassion. Out of compassion for all sentient beings the Buddha abstains from eating meat. Because he is an incarnation of compassion, skin of a black antelope hangs from his left shoulder. Black antelope is believed to be a very kind hearted animal.

Buddhist literature mentions him in three different roles – as a member of Shakyamuni's audience, as a Bodhisattva, and as a Buddha-to-be, who is to return to a purified and happy world, attain enlightenment and lead his countless devotees to salvation. The world to which he was to come is pictured as golden age mentioned both in Hinayana and Mahayana texts. The world then will be ruled without force, by a universal monarch. His capital will be splendid which will need no sun, no moon, as Buddha will give light to it.

Born into this idyllic world, Maitreya will have all the distinguishing marks, the majestic beauty and the radiance of a Buddha. He will attain enlightenment, preach like Shakyamuni but with a much more conspicuous success. Mara will cooperate meekly from the start, instead of doing his best to tempt or discourage. His life span will be immensely long and thus the supreme blessedness of associating with him will be prolonged almost into timelessness.

Believers will go to Tushita where Maitreya is surrounded by a host of great Bodhisattvas. Wonders and pleasures of his heaven are listed in loving detail in sutras. They also state that all of Maitreya's followers in heaven will descend with him to earth in his last incarnation and will share in the ultimate bliss of his Buddhahood.

There are a variety of forms of Maitreya sitting or standing, with various combinations of emblems and mudras. His cult gained popularity in the early centuries of the Christian era. Devotees hoped to be reborn in his paradise to be redeemed by his teachings. He often sits on a high throne or a lotus seat.

Maitreya began to appear as a bodhisattva in the northwestern region of ancient India. He may be shown wearing the dress of a Bodhisattva at the end of the line of Seven Buddhas or Four Buddhas as a diminutive, or as a throned figure at the center of a sculptured pedestal for a Buddha.

Maitreya often sits in a posture with both the legs pendant as if he is ready to descend to establish the lost Truth. His sitting posture in a European fashion is derived from royalty and is known as *bhadrasana* in Sanskrit. It is also popularly known as an asana of Maitreya that sometimes is

FACING PAGE: *Buddha as Amitabha preaches in the heaven called Sukhavati, sitting on a lotus seat emerging out of a pond, joined by two bodhisattvas, Padmapani and Vajrapani, holding a lotus and a vajra, standing in front.*

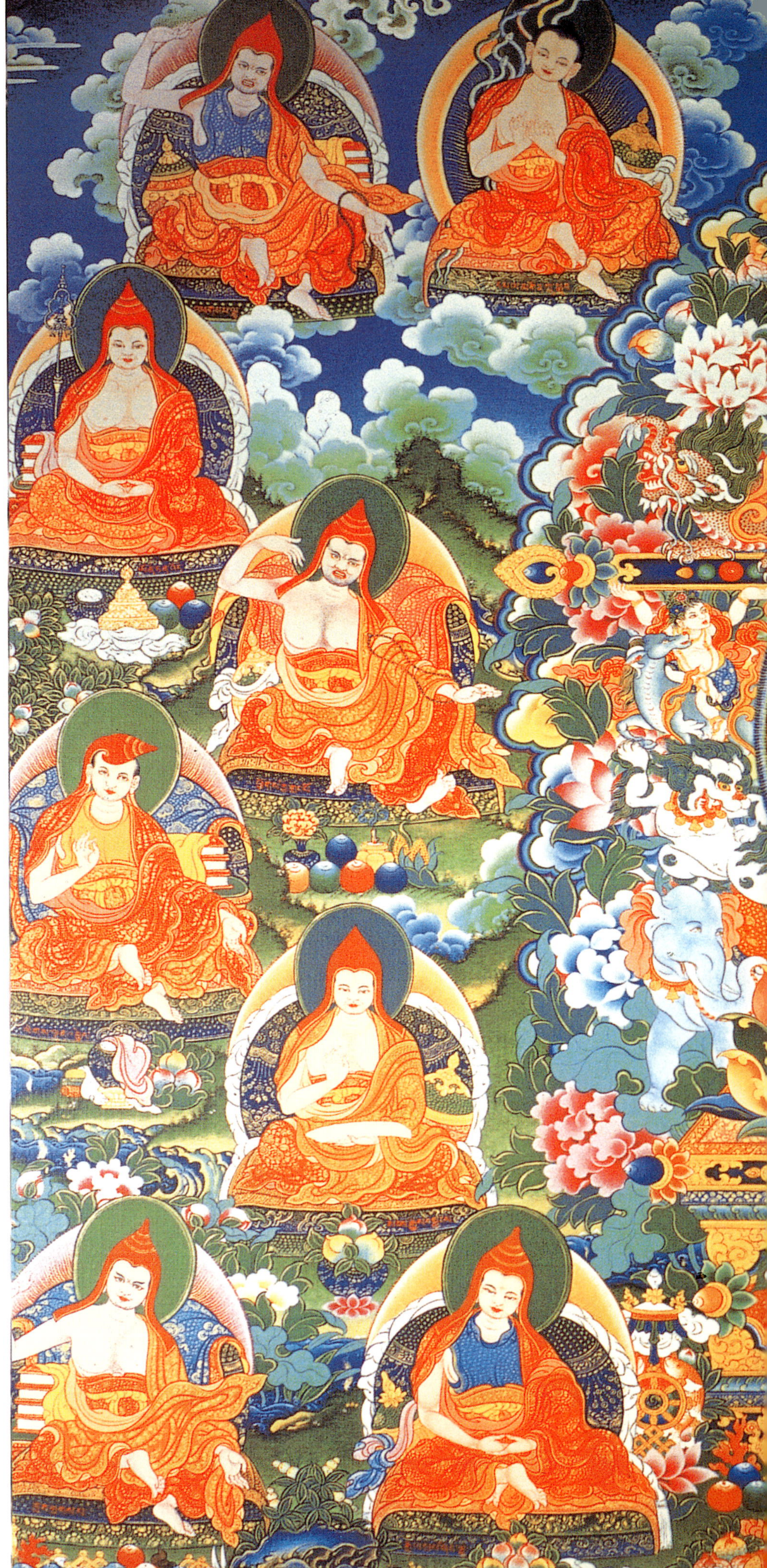

Buddha is surrounded by teachers known as eminents and ornaments. The Six Jewels of Buddhism are – Aryadeva and his teacher Nagarjuna (sitting on top left), Asanga and his younger brother Vasubandhu (sitting on top right), Dinnaga and Dharmakirti (sitting below Gunaprabha and Shakyaprabha) on the left and right. Dinnaga was one of the earliest Buddhist logicians, who studied under Vasubandhu also. Dharmakirti was a master logician who had listened to the teachings of Dinnaga from his disciple Isvarasena. Gunaprabha was one of the four chief disciples of Vasubandhu and Shkyaprabha was a disciple of Shantarakshita in the Vinaya lineage. Atisha, another Buddhist teacher is sitting below the Buddha. He went to Tibet in the eleventh century to preach.

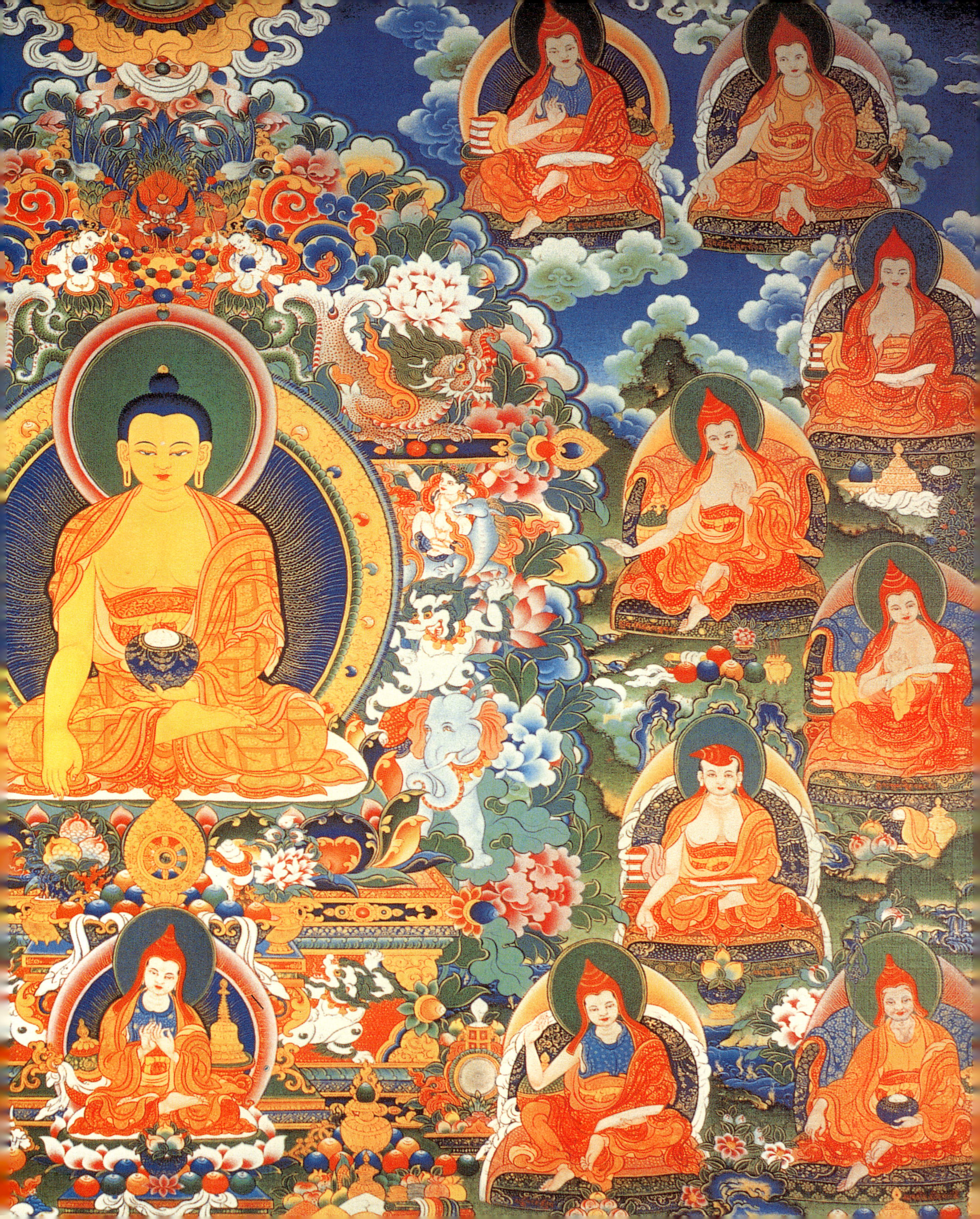

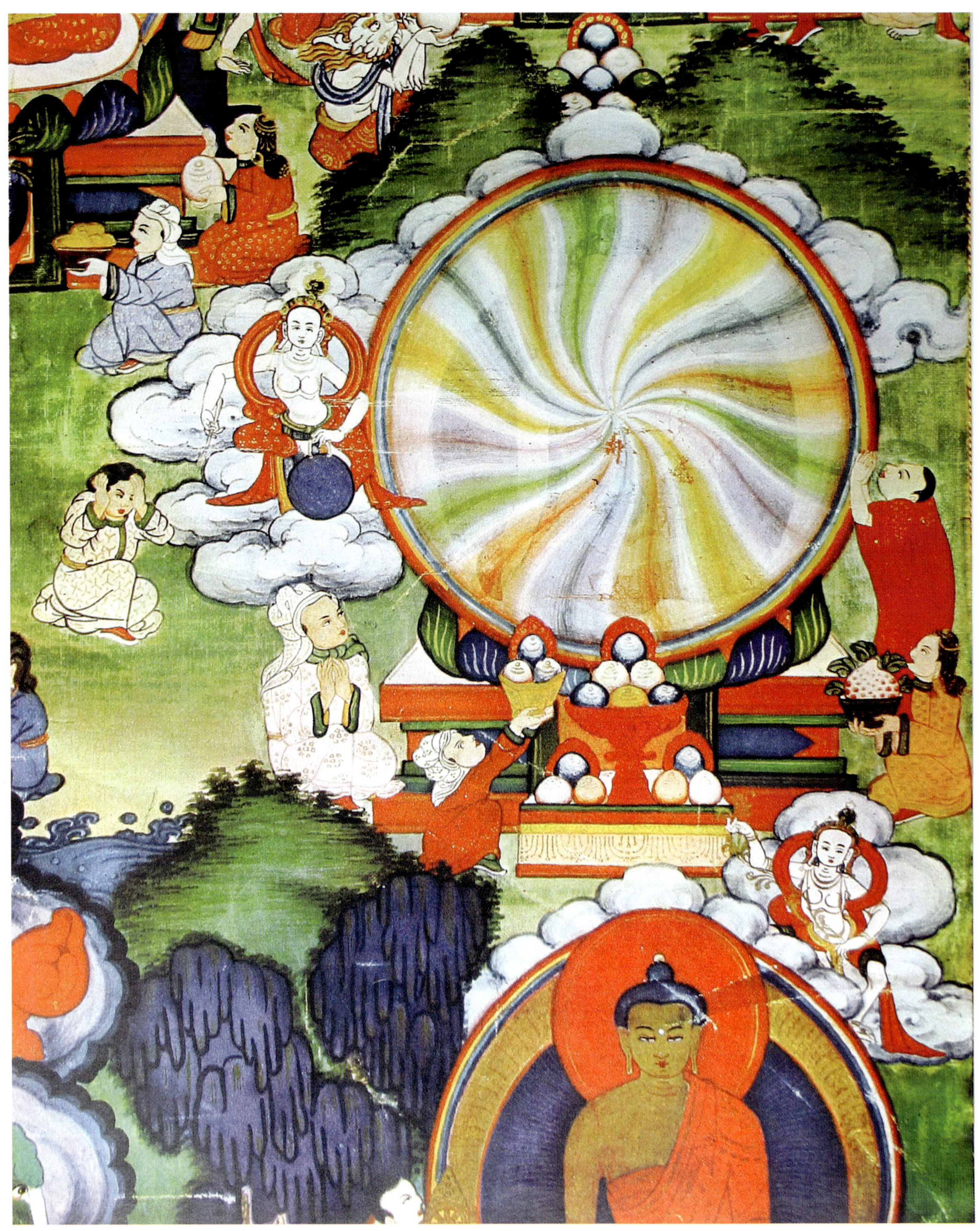

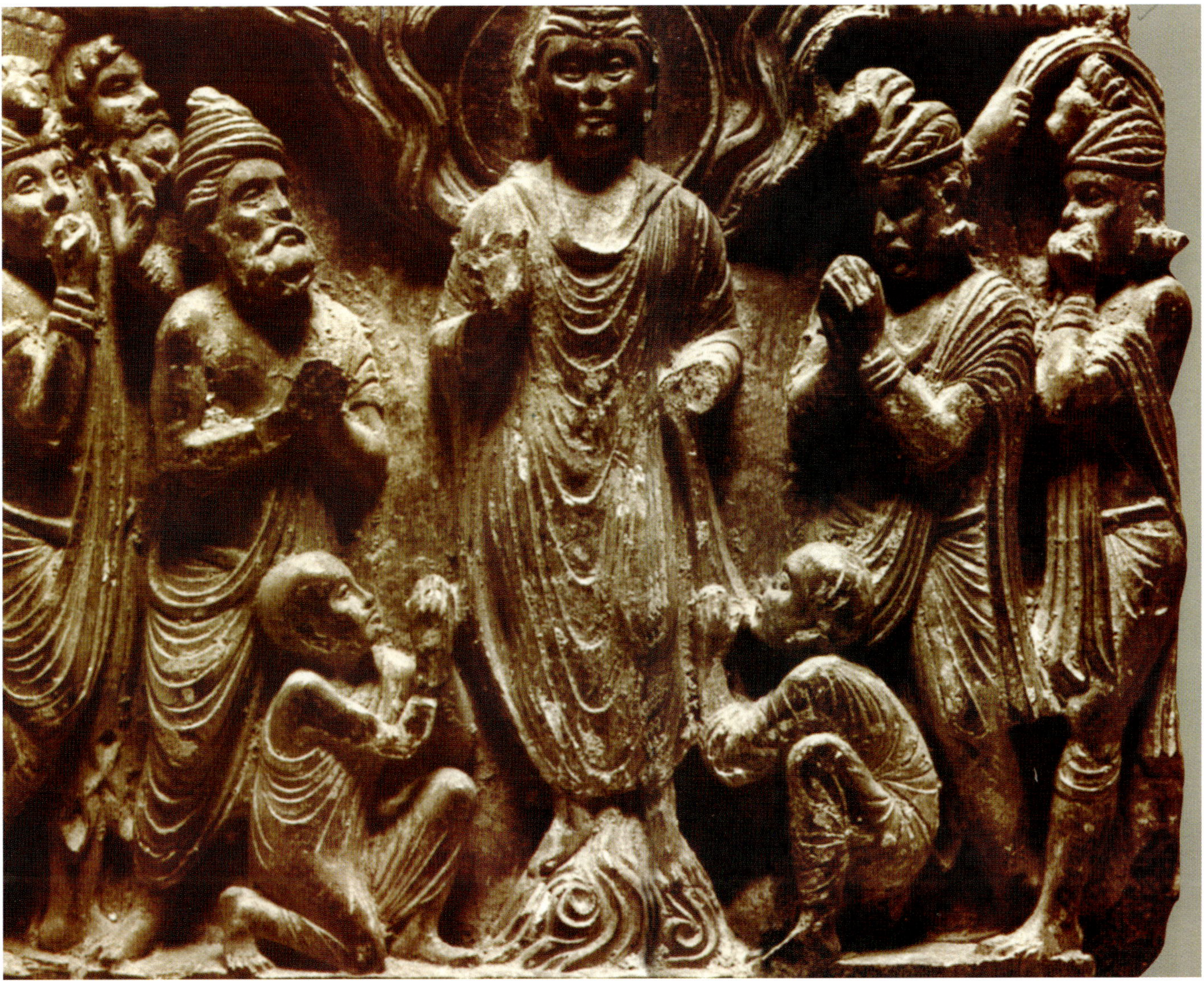

also identified as *Maitreyasana*. Normally in his two armed forms he performs the mudra of teaching or with both of his hands or the mudra of fearlessness with the right while the left may be in the posture of discussion, *vitarka*, benediction or meditation or hold a wheel, vase, stupa, alms bowl, vajra, conch, or a twig of *nagakesara*, or it may rest on the head of a lion, on his knee, or form a fist.

The vase with a narrow neck represents the idea of pouring nectar, the symbol of wisdom of the Buddha, upon those who study the doctrine to take away all their delusions and hindrances in order to gain enlightenment.

In all forms and traditions his body is of golden colour. He looks peaceful and resplendent. His matted hair adornd with a miniature caitya forms his crown. As a Buddha he does not wear any ornaments. The *ushnisha*,

ABOVE: *In order to convert the nonbelievers, the Buddha sat preaching in mid air and caused unending replicas of himself to appear stretching up to heaven. Flames from his shoulders and a stream of water issued from his feet.*

FACING PAGE: *Divine radiance or spiritual power of the Buddha is represented by rays of spiritual light, flooding forth from the heart of the Buddha, who is mysteriously visible from behind the screen of rays. Divine essence or light lives in the depth of man.*

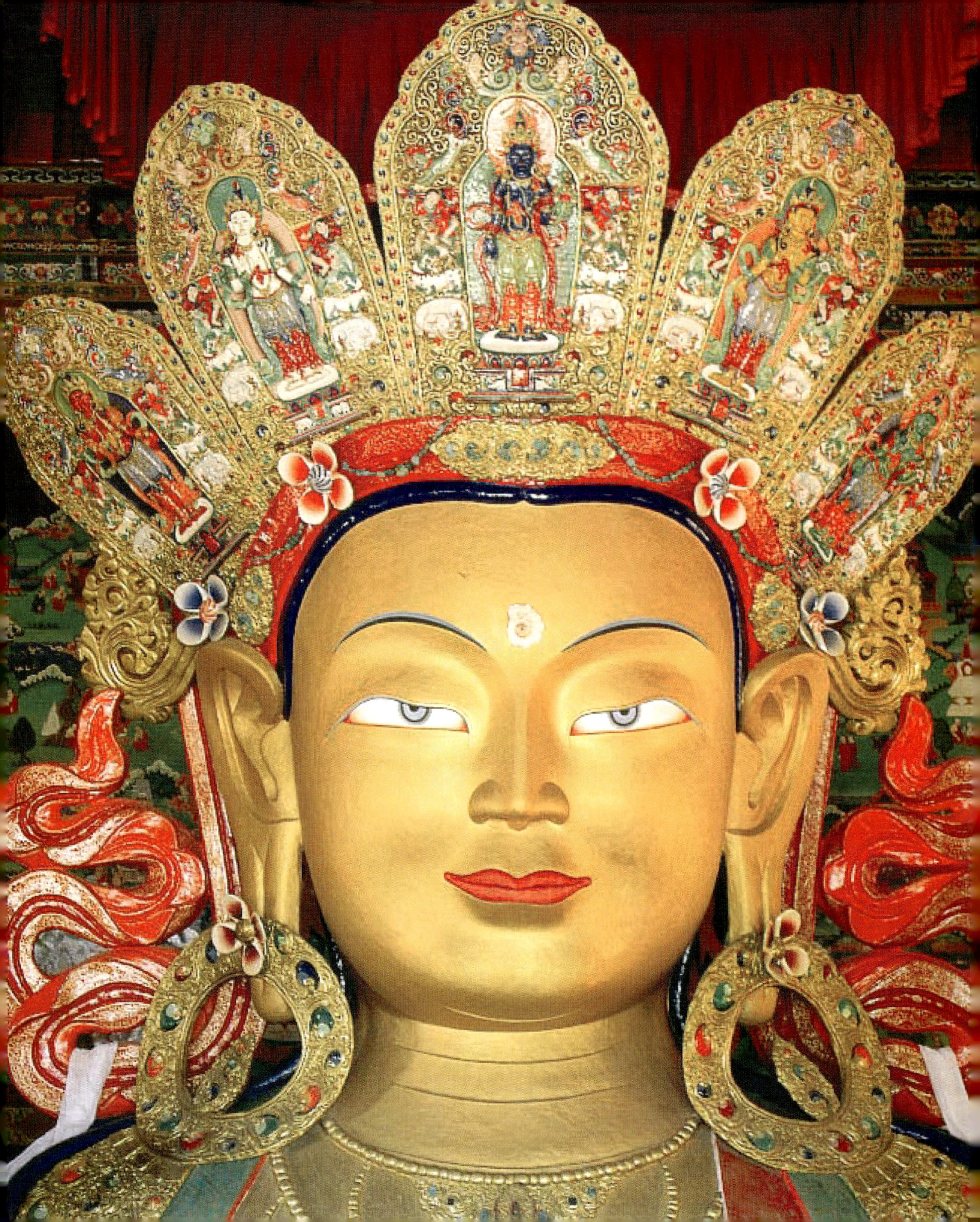

long earlobes and monastic robes indicate his being a Buddha.

Paintings of Maitreya from Kyzyl, Karashahar and other sites in Central Asia; stone, bronze, brass and copper images from Kashmir, Bihar, Nepal, Tibet, Mongolia and Indonesia; drawings and paintings on manuscripts and scrolls are a part of the rich legacy of the Buddhist world. A Buddha of future is apparently a Bodhisattva of present. As a Bodhisattva he wears ornaments and a crown, holds the ewer, besides a three forked stick. The vase holds the ambrosia to be sprinkled during initiation ritual. In images found from Gandhara, as a Bodhisattva, Maitreya holds a vase in his left hand and does the mudra of fearlessness with the right, both in standing and sitting postures.

He is often drawn in Japan and Tibet as a Bodhisattva sitting or standing on a lotus. Sometimes his attribute, a vase is placed on the lotus held by him. Tibetan thangkas show him sitting in Tushita with legs in pendant position. Several Maitreya images have been sculpted and carved in Chinese cave temples. In one of them – Lung-men, there is a pair of lions beneath the seat of a youthful, smiling image of Maitreya, and a pair of acolytes sitting on both the sides as mirror images. The attending figures are the teachers, Asanga and Vasubandhu. Chinese produced a number of gilded metal statues sometimes decorated with inlaying precious stones. Korea produced a colossal statue of Maitreya 21.45 meters high at Kwangchok-sa monastery in the tenth century. The benign smile, half closed eyes in meditation, and pursed lips endow him with an introspective beauty and spiritual peace.

Painting Maitreya on scrolls and murals on the inside walls of temples, descending from his abode to receive the soul of the deceased became a fashion in Japan, following popularity of devotion to Amitabha. He sits or stands on a lotus placed on clouds accompanied by his retinue. A number of such paintings are preserved in museums and monasteries.

Maitreya images in Tibet and Mongolia are often gigantic in size. In China, Buddhas sitting in this posture are famous as chaired Buddhas. There are caves in the Gansu province of China dedicated to Maitreya with myriad icons. Such images are also found in the caves in the western part of India. Many of them lie on trade routes frequented by merchants coming from the Northwest. A gigantic statue of Maitreya has been sculpted in Korea, which is 33 metres above the ground and is cast in 160 tons of bronze. The Koreans believe that when they build an image of Maitreya in their hearts too, all lives on earth

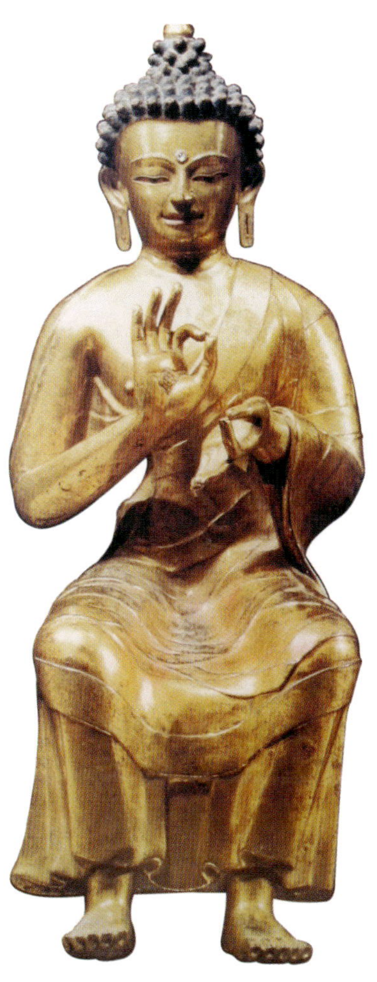

ABOVE: *Image of Maitreya, sitting in bhadrasana, with both legs pendant and hands in dharmacakrapravartana mudra. The posture signifies that he is about to get up to come down to this world from the Tushita heaven to renew the dharma to humanity. This form is also known as Vyakarana Maitreya.*

FACING PAGE: *Maitreya fulfilled many needs, both spiritual and political. He was the model for kings and emperors who saw themselves as enlightened cakravarti rulers. Tibetan and Mongolian monasteries usually housed Maitreya images which were especially worshipped during annual Maitreya festivals instituted by Tsongkhapa. The Future Buddha is also portrayed as a young bodhisattva.*

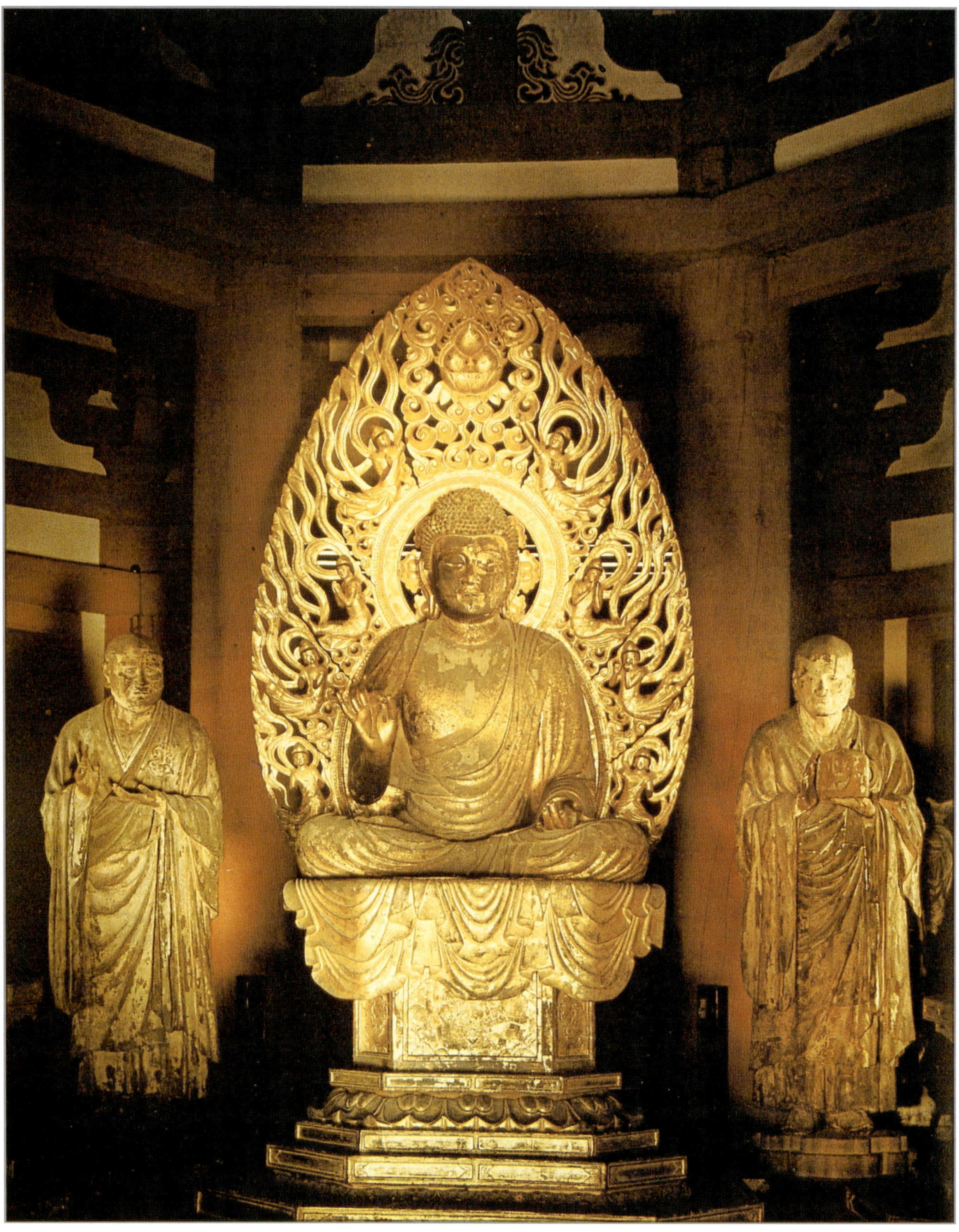

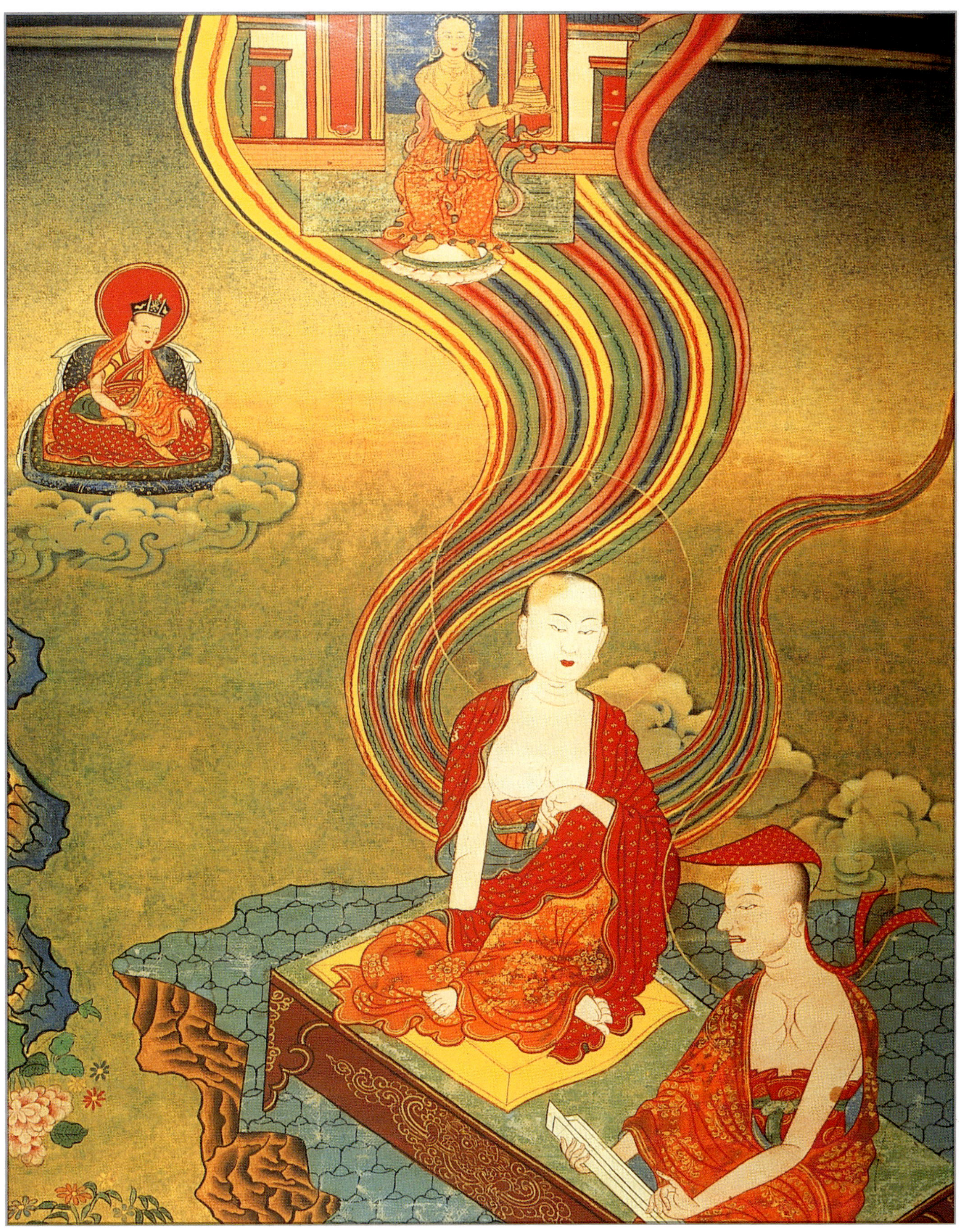

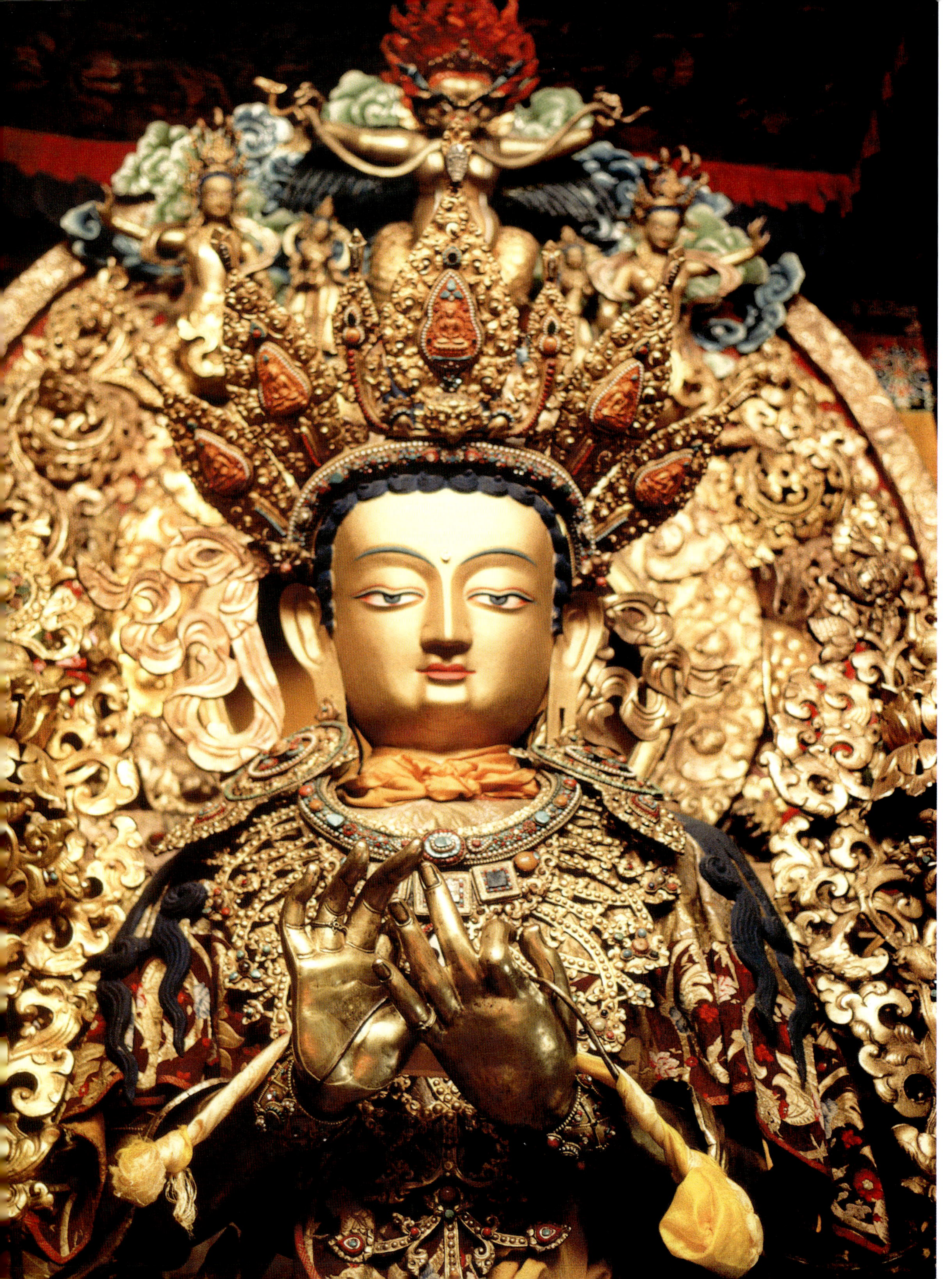

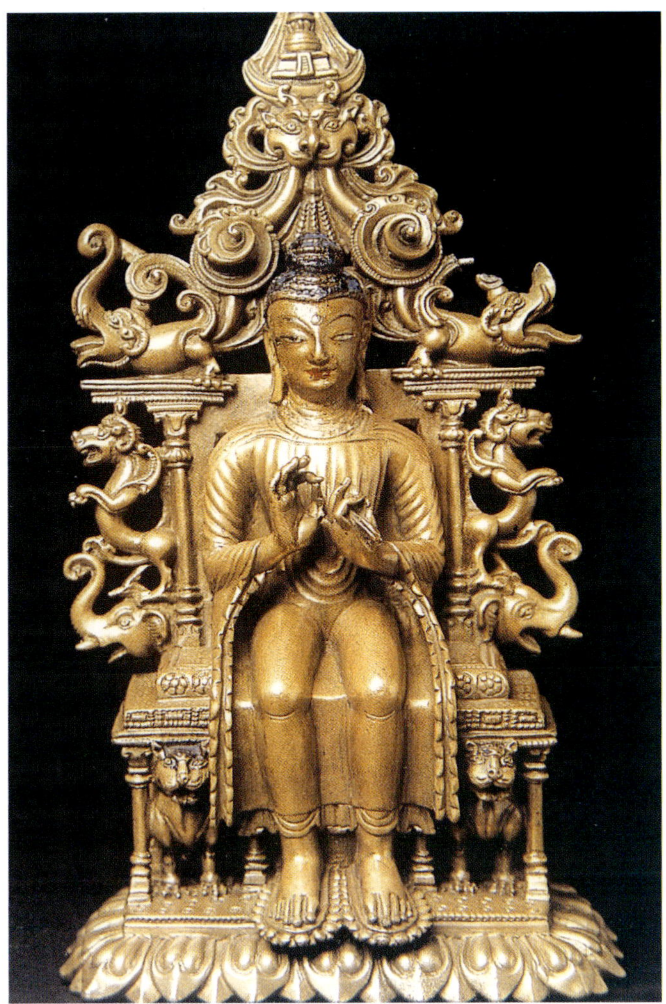

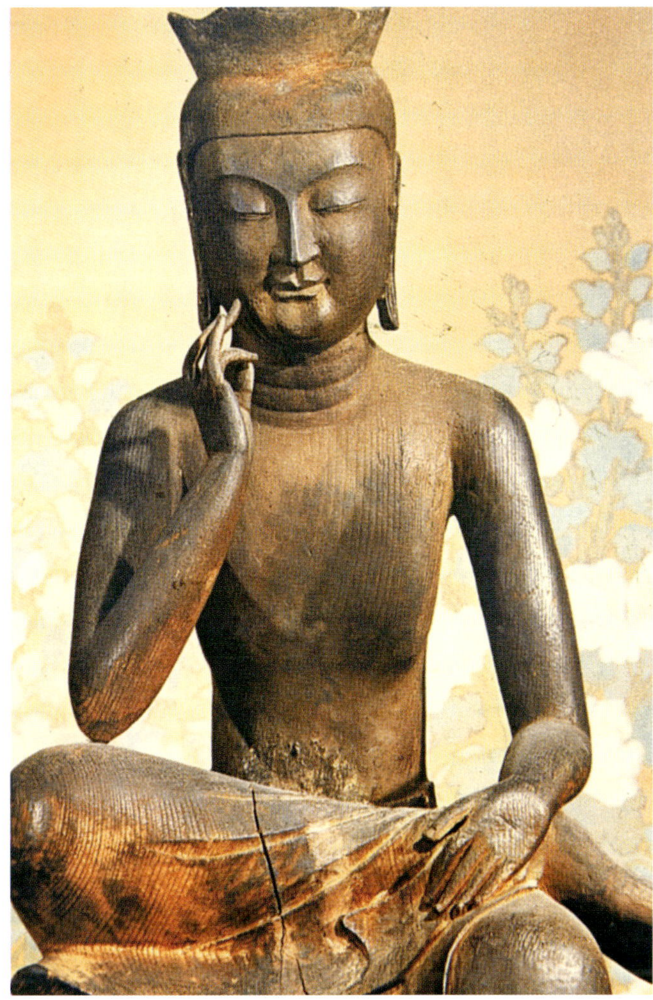

will turn into lotus flowers and the world around them would become a pond of joy.

Maitreya attains a pensive form in China, Japan and Korea. He raises his right foot to the left knee, wears a monk's cap, brings his right hand to the chin touching the cheek with fingers, and sits in a pensive mood with the left hand resting on the ankle. The posture is reversed in some images in China and Korea. The shape of his seat looks unusual, like a wickerwork stool, which is hidden under his drapery. The way he sits is comfortable, natural and conducive to thinking. According to a recent research this type of image is of Maitreyacharya, a teacher Maitreya.

The devotees of Maitreya perform Dharma action not only for themselves to avoid the wrong path and

PRECEDING PAGE, LEFT: *Maitreya flanked by Asanga and Vasubandhu is a yogi in Absolute Truth attained by inner illumination.*

PRECEDING PAGE, RIGHT: *Maitreya descends from his heaven Tushita and comes on a cloud holding a stupa.*
The ray of Maitreya which comes down splits into five different colours, touches Asanga and then ends its course in a white flame.

FACING PAGE: *Maitreya is performing the mudra of turning the Wheel of Law. As a divine saviour he resides in the Tushita heaven, waiting to come down to the earth to establish the dhrama.*

ABOVE, LEFT: *Maitreya in gilded broze in Kashmiri style.*

ABOVE, RIGHT: *Maitreyacarya is popularly known as Miroku or Maitreya in pensive mood. The meditating image is of infinite grace, sweetness and softness.*

false knowledge but also to help others follow the path of Maitreya.

Two scholars flank Maitreya: Asanga and Vasubandhu. The ray of Maitreya that comes down from the top splits into five different colours, touches Asanga and ends its course in a white flame. So Asanga is white, which is an expression of his illumined consciousness. Asanga was a professor at Nalanda and spent much time in Ayodhya, a centre of learning. His younger brother was Vasubandhu, a scholar of philosophy. Their distinctive personalities are brought out in thangka paintings. Asanga is calm and serene while Vasubandhu is energized thought.

The coming of Maitreya signals the new age. In Tibet, Maitreya festival has been the focus of the New Year's day since it was initiated by Tsonkhapa in 1409. It was introduced in Mongolia by Zanabazar in 1657. A 54 feet high Maitreya image was enshrined in a temple in the middle of Ulaanbaatar in the nineteenth century by the fifth Bogdo Gegen. Best Mongolian masters cast the statue from bronze in Dolnur which was installed and consecrated in the temple in 1826. Today thousands of Mongols and Tibetans flock to hail Maitreya's return as a symbol of new age.

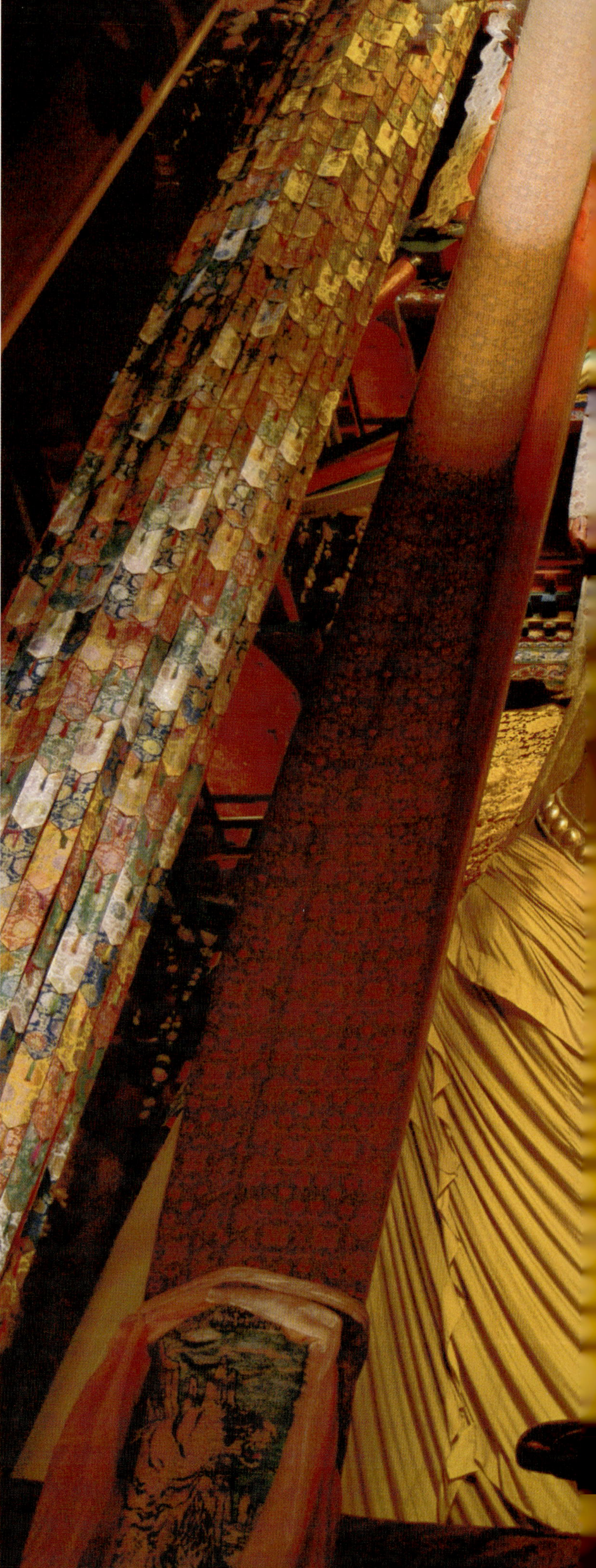

The image of Maitreya from Tashilumpo monastery is the largest of its kind. Such colossal images were often carved out of rocks made of clay.

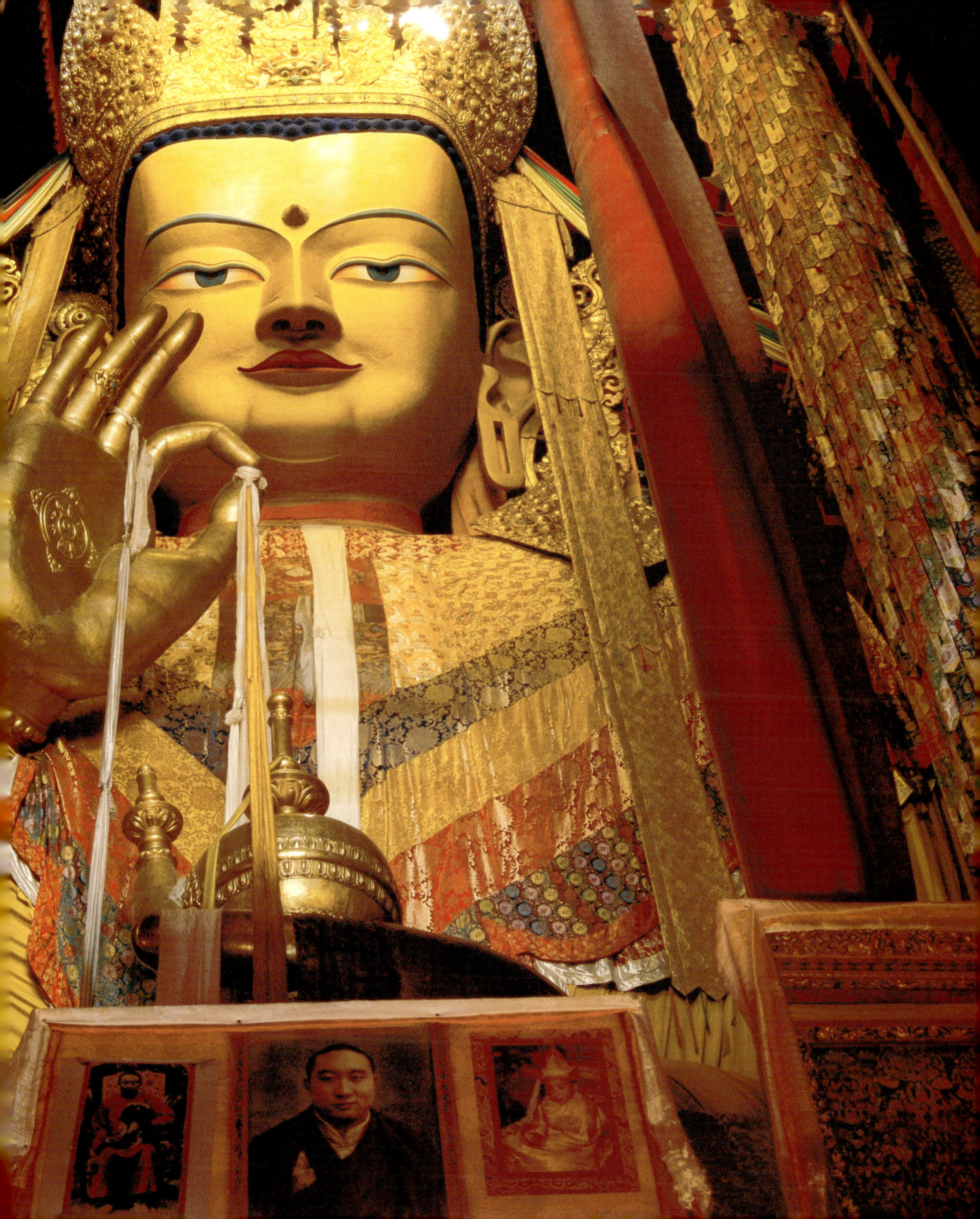

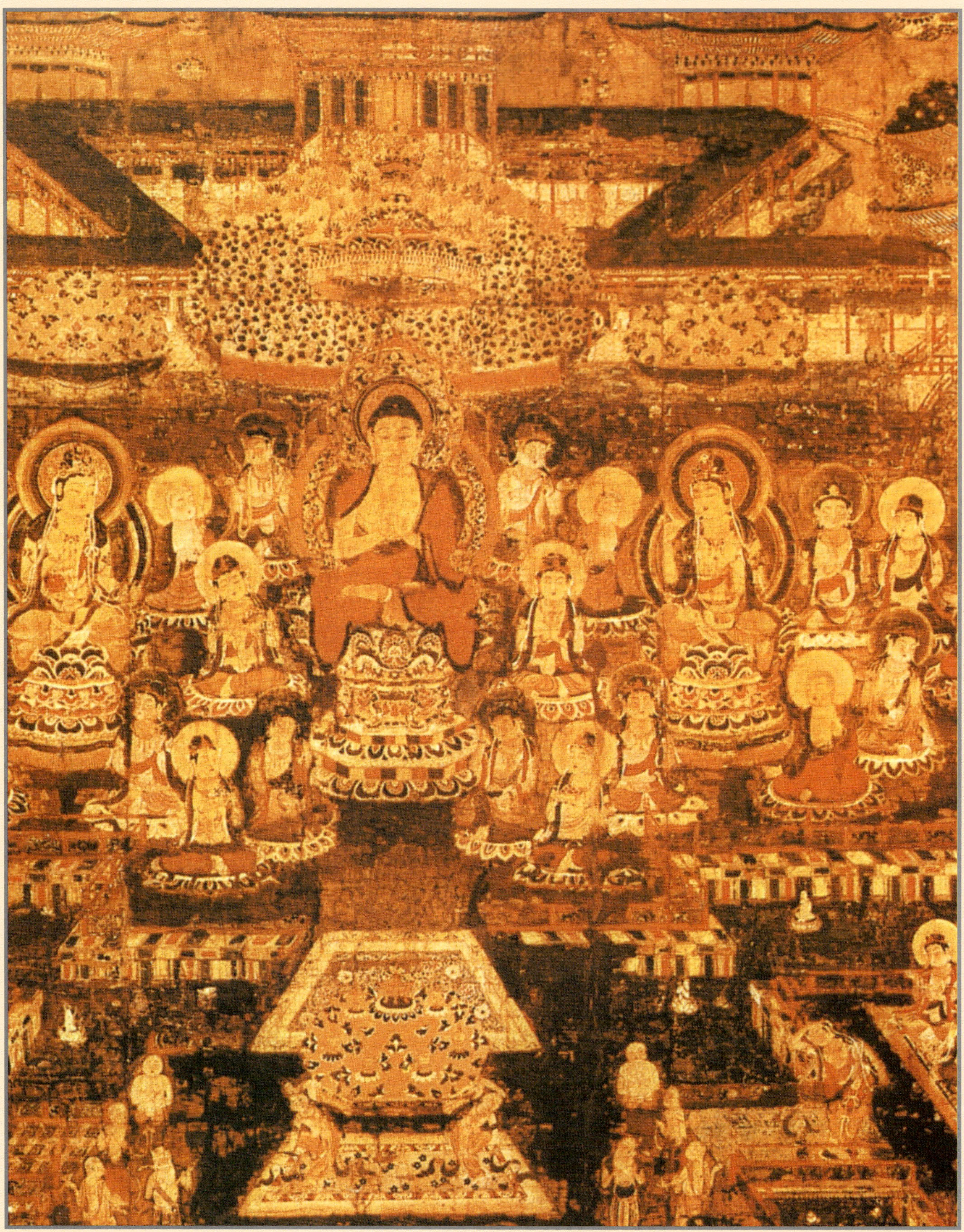

Trikaya Manifestation

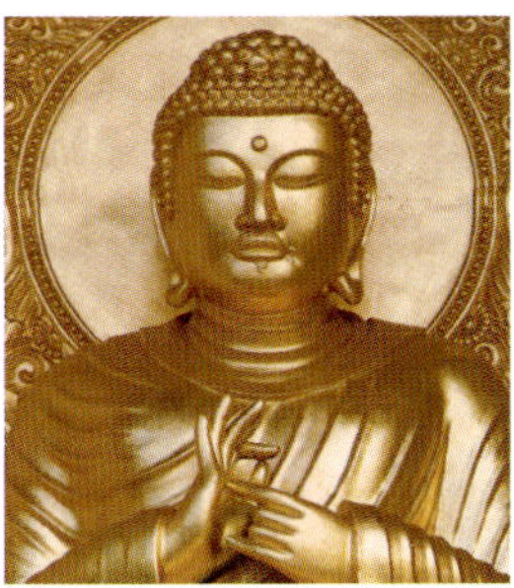

According to the doctrine in Mahayana Buddhism, Buddha manifests himself in three modes or dimensions: *dharmakaya*, *sambhogakaya* and *nirmanakaya*. There are references to the 'physical body' *(rupakaya)*, or to the second body, known as the 'mind-made body' *(manomayakaya)* in early Mahayana Buddhism. The precise nature of the Buddha had been ambiguous: on the one hand he was born and lived as a human being and on the other, he transcended human nature through his enlightenment. Having realized the Dharma meant that he had identified with it. The Buddha himself had stated – He who sees the Buddha sees the Dharma, and he who sees the Dharma sees the Buddha. The Buddha as a great yogi possessed supernatural powers by means of which he could travel through the heavens and manifest himself in the form of a magical body to preach the doctrine to the gods.

It is the true nature of the Buddha, which is identical with transcendental reality, the essence of the universe. The *dharmakaya* is the unity of the Buddha with everything existing. At the same time it represents the 'law' (*dharma*), the teaching expounded by the Buddha.

The *dharmakaya* was initially identified with the teachings expounded by the historical Buddha Shakyamuni. It is timeless, permanent, devoid of characteristics, free from all duality; it is the spiritual body of the buddhas, their true nature, which all buddhas have in common. Various names are applied to the *dharmakaya* depending on whether it is being taken as the true nature of being or as the true nature of the buddhas. In many schools the *dharmakaya* is regarded as impersonal, in others as personal. The *dharmakaya* is realized through *prajna*.

It is believed that all the Buddhas are in their essential nature identical with the ultimate truth or absolute reality known as the Truth Body, *dharma-kaya*. This is their first

ABOVE: *Buddha sitting in the posture of setting the Wheel of Dharma in motion, representing his first sermon delivered at Sarnath, from a pagoda built in the Battersea Park, London.*

FACING PAGE: *Buddhas in their sambhogakaya manifestations populated their respective paradises such as Sukhavati, Abhrati, Tushita etc. Buddha Amitabha sits in the Western Paradise, Sukhavati surrounded by Bodhisattvas. In the lower section souls are painted, reborn in his paradise.*

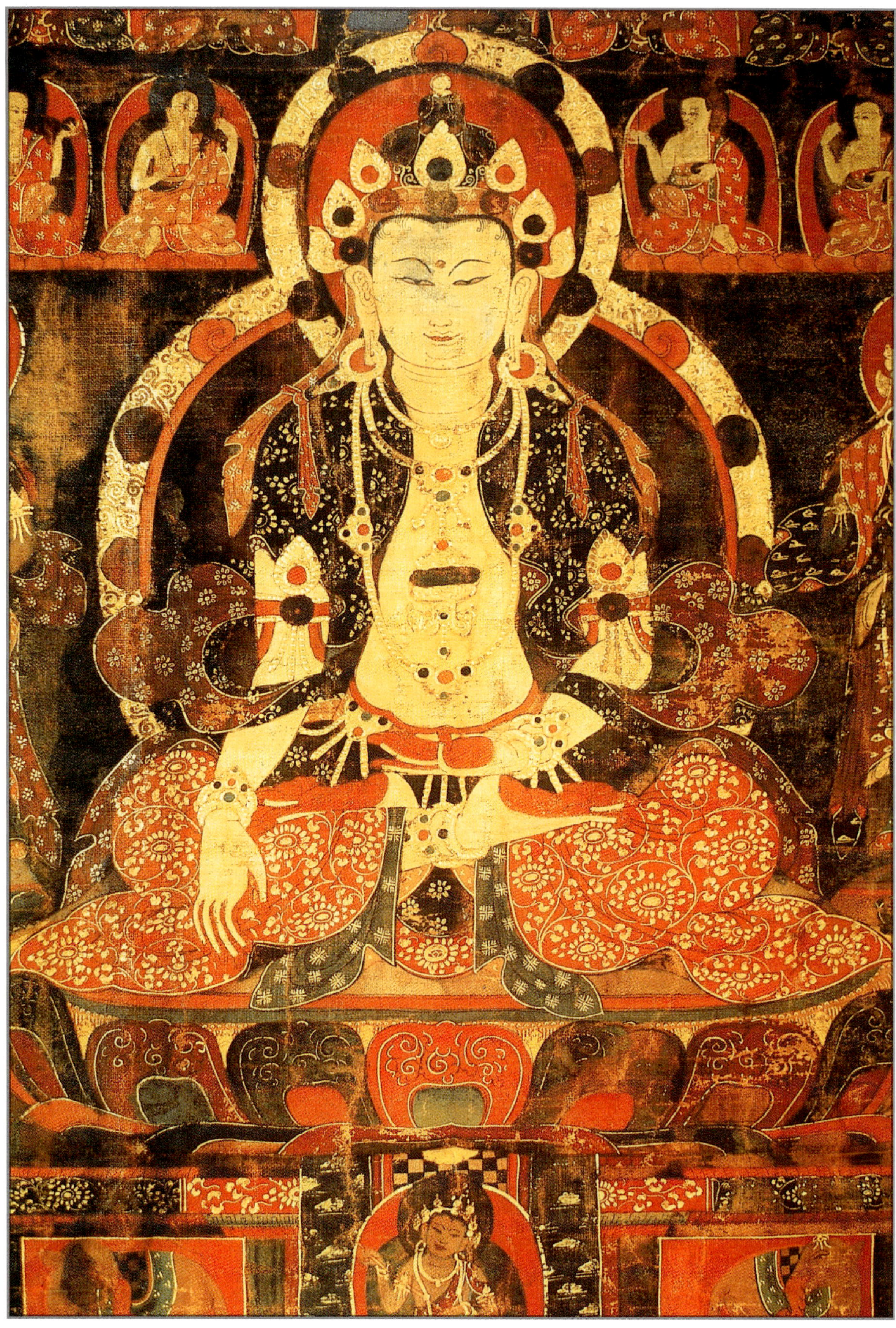

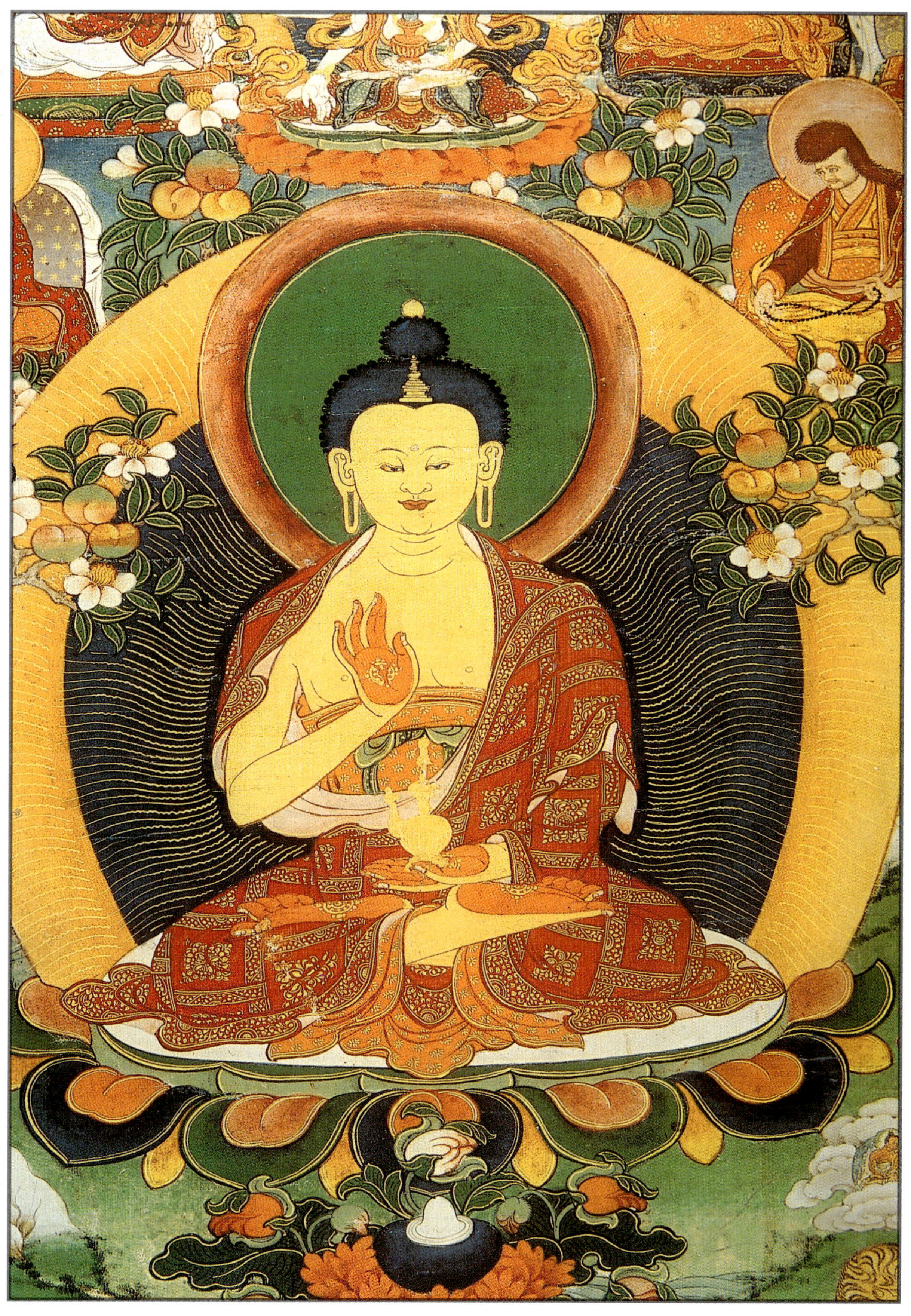

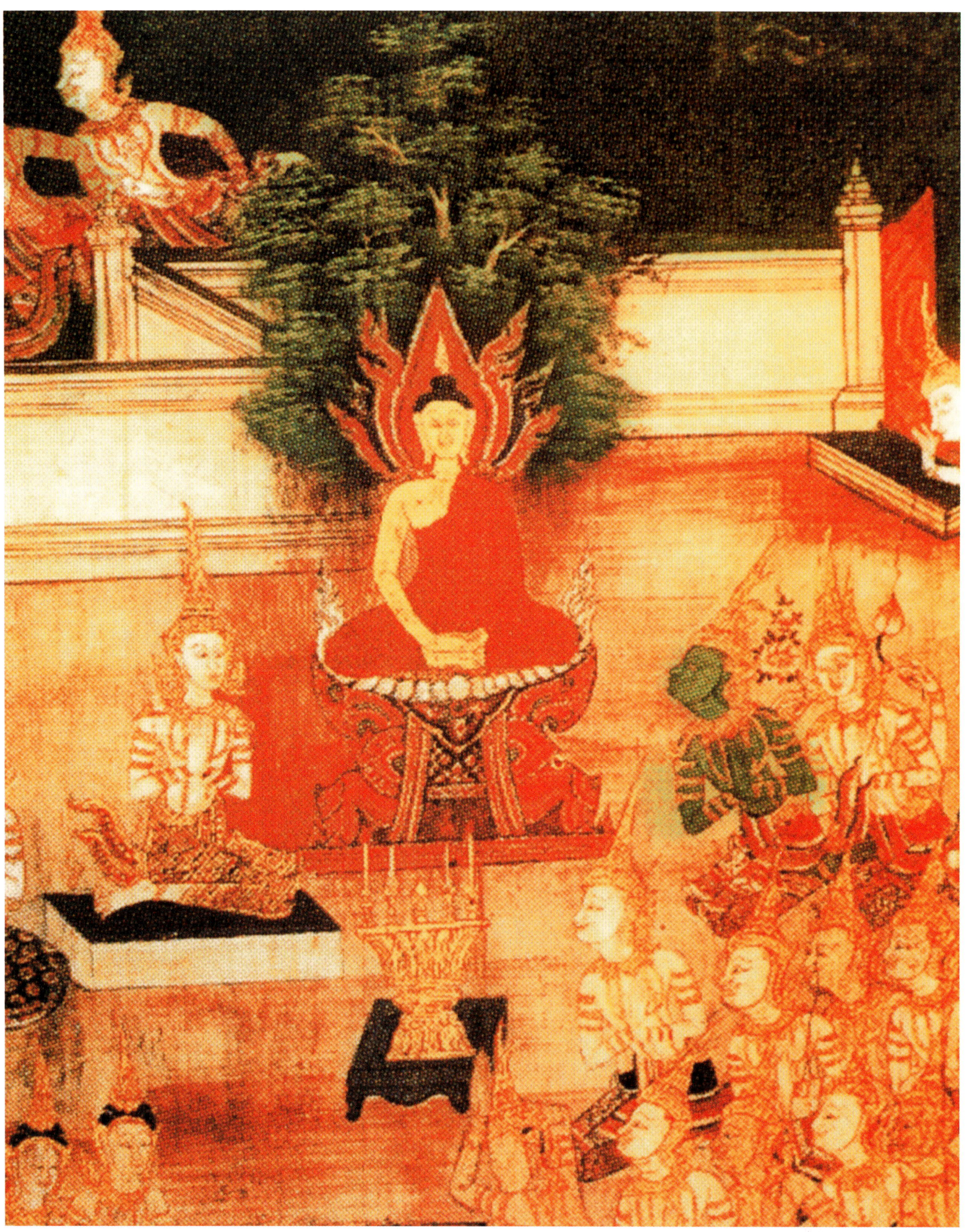

'body'. At the same time, Buddhas have the power to manifest themselves in a sublime celestial form in splendid paradises where they teach the doctrine surrounded by hosts of Bodhisattvas and supernatural beings. This is their second body, known as the Enjoyment Body, *sambhogakaya*. This is the body of the buddhas, who in a 'buddha-paradise' enjoys the truth that they embody.

The *sambhogakaya* is the result of previous good actions and is realized, as a result of a bodhisattva's accumulated merits in enlightenment. It exhibits the thirty-two major marks and the eighty minor marks of a Buddha, and can be perceived only by bodhisattvas who have attained the last stage of a bodhisattva's development. This 'body of delight' represents the Buddha as an object of devotion. The descriptions of the buddhas introduced in the Mahayana sutras refer to this aspect. The buddhas in their *sambhogakaya* manifestations populate the buddha-fields (Sukhavati, Abhirati, Tushita, etc.); to be reborn in these buddha-fields is the hope of many Buddhists.

Motivated by boundless compassion, Buddhas project themselves into the world of suffering disguised in a manner through the use of 'skilful means' so as not to frighten or alarm, but to provide which is most necessary and useful. This is their third body, the Emanation Body, *nirmana-kaya*. It is the body of transformation, the earthly body in which Buddhas appear to men to fulfil the Buddhas' resolve to guide all beings to liberation.

The *nirmanakaya* is embodied in the earthly Buddhas and bodhisattvas projected into the world through the meditation of the *sambhogakaya* buddhas as a result of their compassion. The task of the *nirmanakaya* manifestations is to expound the teaching. They are guides on the way to liberation from suffering, but cannot bring beings to this liberation directly. Like all human beings, they are subject to the misery of illness, old age, and death, but possess the divine eye and divine hearing. The individuality of *nirmanakaya* Buddhas dissolves after their deaths.

In the *Vajrayana,* the trikaya concept expresses different experiential levels of enlightenment. The *dharmakaya* stands for the fundamental truth of emptiness, the all-pervading supreme reality, enlightenment itself. The *sambhogakaya* and the *nirmanakaya*, the 'form bodies', are seen as means for conveying the experience of the absolute. In Tibetan Buddhism, the body, speech, and mind of the master are equated with the three bodies and symbolized by the mantra *om ah hum*.

The developed doctrine has played a central role in Mahayana Buddhist thought but did not have much influence in Theravada Buddhist countries, where the Buddha continues to be regarded for the most part as simply a remarkable human being who, through his attainment of *nirvana*, has forever gone beyond the possibility of involvement in human affairs.

In Zen Buddhism the three bodies of a buddha are three levels of reality, which stand in reciprocal relationship to each other and constitute a whole. The *dharmakaya* is the cosmic consciousness, the unified existence that lies beyond all concepts. This substrate, characterized by completion and perfection, out of which all animate and inanimate forms as well as the moral order arise, is embodied in Vairocana. Symbolized by Amitabha, the *sambhogakaya* is the experience of the ecstasy of enlightenment, of the *dharma* of the Buddha and the patriarchs, and of the spiritual practices transmitted by them. The *nirmanakaya* is the radiant, transformed buddha-body personified by Shakyamuni. The reciprocal relationship between these is illustrated in Zen by the following analogy: the *dharmakaya* can be compared to medical knowledge; the *sambhogakaya* to the education of the doctor through which he or she gains this knowledge; and the *nirmanakaya* to the application of this knowledge in treating patients, who through it are changed from sick to healthy persons.

PRECEDING PAGE, LEFT: *Shakyamuni is depicted as universal monarch and is adorned with the eight jeweled ornaments that symbolize royalty: a jeweled crown, a pair of earrings adorned with silk ribbons, a pearl choker, a jeweled pendant, a precious necklace, armlets and bracelets, anklets and a studded belt.*

PRECEDING PAGE, RIGHT: *Lord Buddha visited the Trayastrimsha heaven to preach his mother, Mahamaya and the deities residing there. Buddhaisavan chapel. Bangkok National Museum.*

FACING PAGE: *Shakyamuni Buddha, sitting in the posture of touching the earth, summons the firmament of the earth as witness to his supreme and ultimate enlightenment. His nimbus in this picture is green and the gloria blue and purple with golden rays emerging from it.*

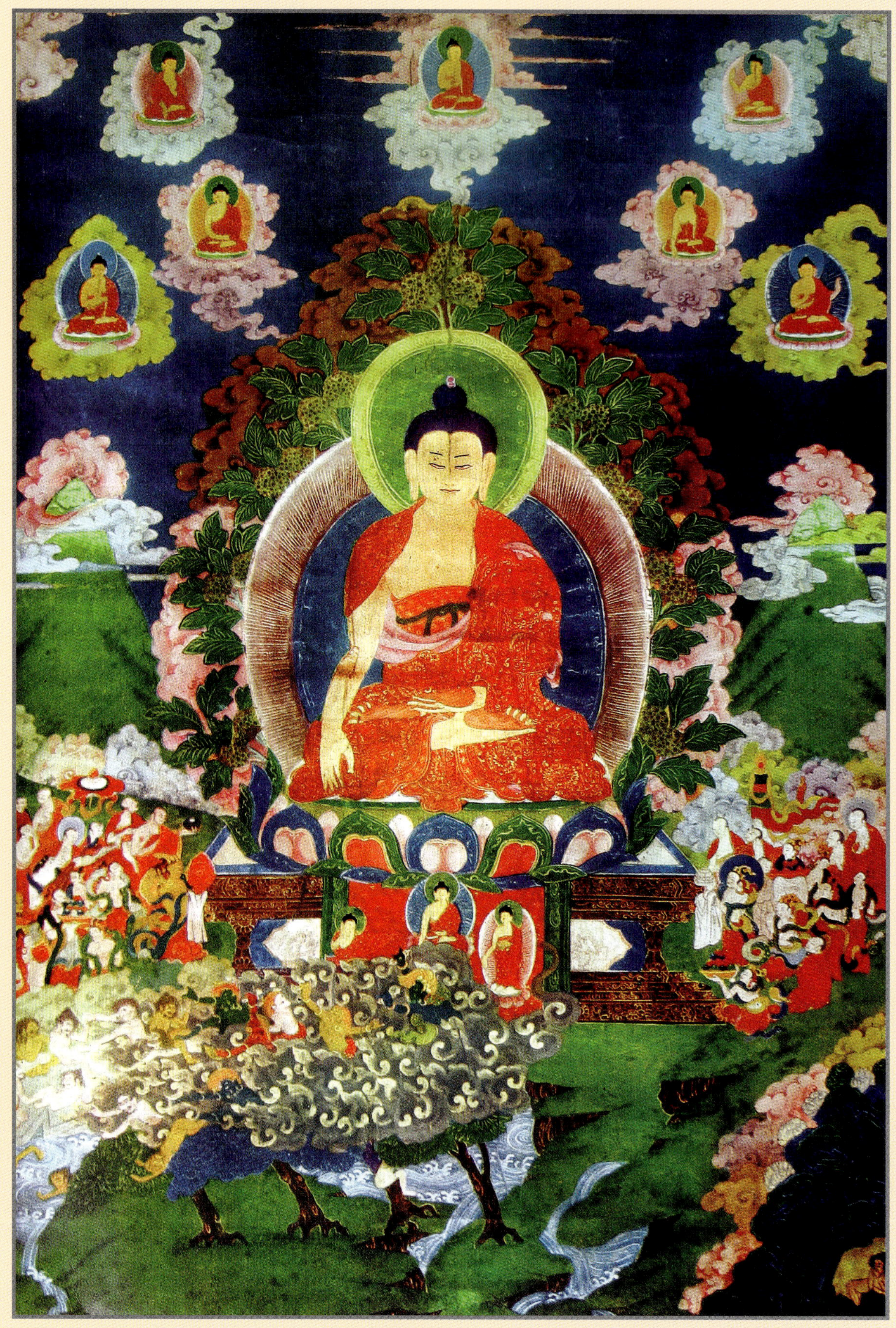

Seven Historical Buddhas

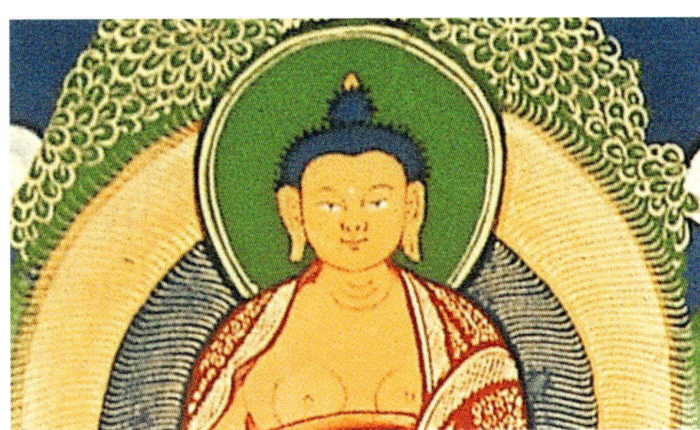

The Mahapadana sutra accepts that Shakyamuni Buddha was preceded by six other incarnations, and presents names of their parents, places of birth, and trees of enlightenment, etc. The Buddhavamsha goes beyond enumerating the Seven Buddhas as well as their predecessors. Evidences to their worship can be traced in Chulavagga. They are identical both in the Theravada and Mahayana traditions. As a group they enjoyed greater prestige in China than in contemporary India.

Vipashyin, the first was thought to have had his career ninety-one aeons ago. Shikhin and Vishvabhu divided between them the thirty-first aeon. These three belong to the previous glorious kalpa. Krakucchanda, Kanakamuni, Kashyapa and Shakyamuni are the first four of the Thousand Buddhas of Bhadrakalpa. There was a heretical Buddhist sect that claimed its descent from Shakyamuni's cousin Devedatta. One of the Ashokan pillars records his devotion to the cult of Kanakamuni. Its inscription tells that in the fourteenth year of his reign he rebuilt the past Buddha's stupa in an enlarged form, and in the twentieth year came in person to visit the place and pay homage. Hsuan-tsang mentions stupas of Four Buddhas of Bhadrakalpa near the capital of Konkan.

The earliest sign of their existence in aniconic forms can be traced in the seven trees of enlightenment carved on the railings at Bharhut and gateways at Sanchi dating from the first century BC to AD. The trees are carved singly or in a row alternating with stupas. The Kushana reliefs at Gandhara and Mathura depict them in rows of seven Buddha figures usually terminated by an image of Maitreya dressed like a Bodhisattva, pointing to the eighth, who will descend as a saviour in future.

The Chinese pilgrim Hsuan-tsang has mentioned images of Seven Buddhas at the royal monastery of King Shiladitya. According to him the places of birth of the Seven Buddhas and monuments erected in their honour

ABOVE: *Vipashyin, the first among the Seven Historical Buddhas is sitting in 'touching the earth' posture.*

FACING PAGE: *Buddha Shakyamuni is sitting at the centre of the thangka painting. Seven Buddhas are painted in the upper part of the scroll. Below the lion throne are scenes of torture in hell where unenlightened souls migrate.*

were located in the neighbourhood of Shravasti and Kapilavastu. Seven Buddhas alongwith Maitreya are represented at Ajanta cave number twenty-six, dated AD 481. They are painted on the doorway of its cave number seventeen, each with an inscription. They are also seen in cave number four and seven of Ajanta, two and three of Kanheri, and twelve of Ellora. Sutras add further details of the Seven Buddhas by supplying names of their casts and gotras and the places of birth.

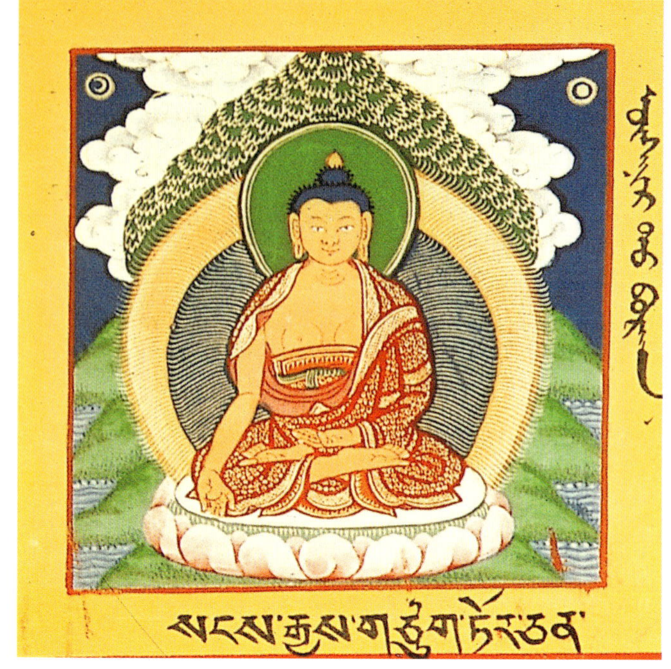

2

Names of the Buddhas, their respective directions and the mudras given in Tibetan 500 icons:

1. Shakyamuni	Explaining the dharma	Centre
2. Vipashyin	Bhumisparsha/dhyana	East
3. Shikhin	Varada/dhyana	NE
4. Vishvabhu	Abhaya/dhyana	SE
5. Krakucchanda	Samadhi	West
6. Kanakamuni	Explaining dharma/dhyana	SW
7. Kashyapa	Varada/holds robe	NW
8. Mahakrodha	Noose/sword	South

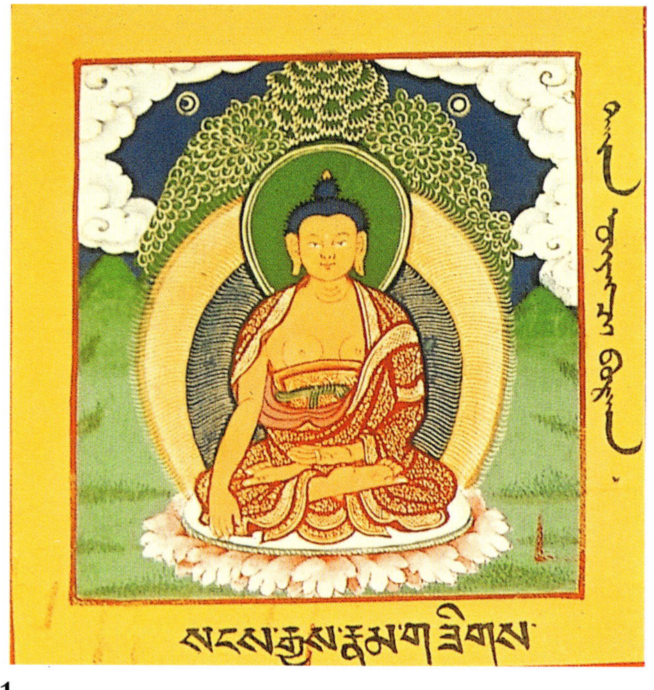

1

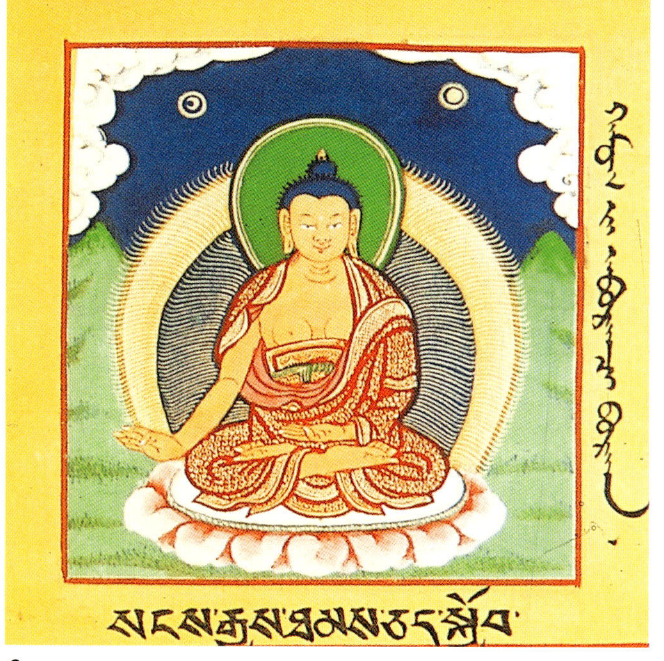

3

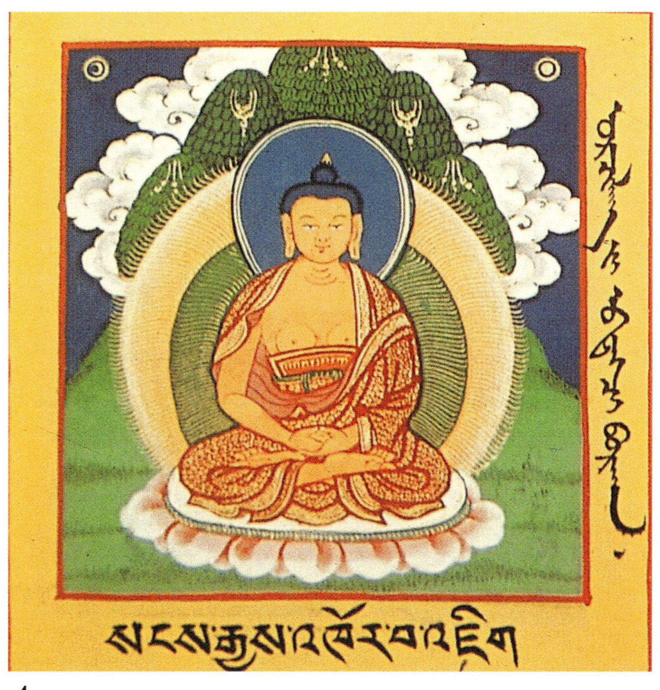

4

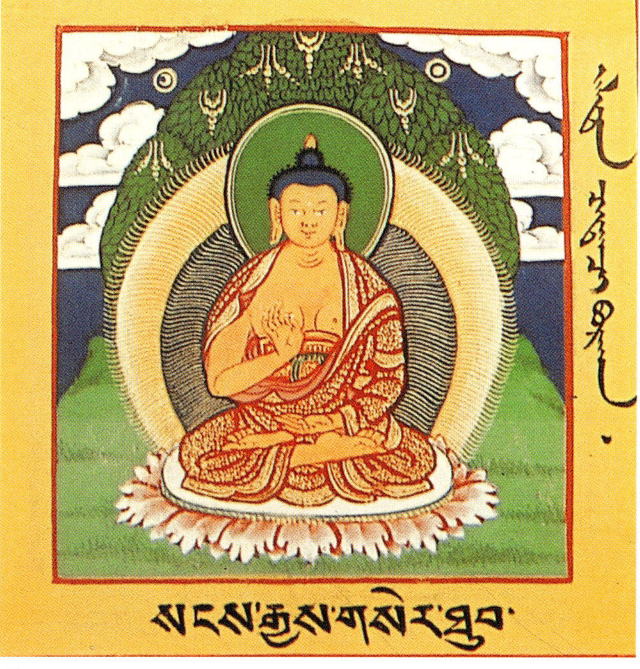

5

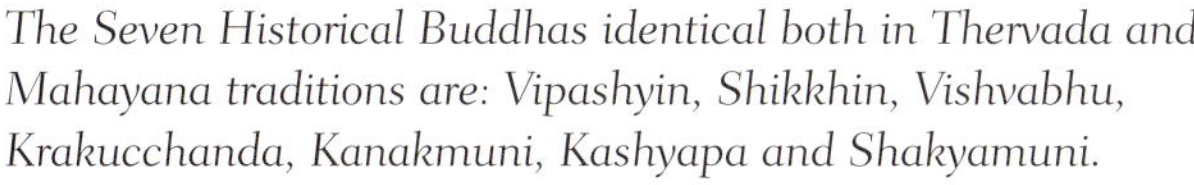
The Seven Historical Buddhas identical both in Thervada and Mahayana traditions are: Vipashyin, Shikkhin, Vishvabhu, Krakucchanda, Kanakmuni, Kashyapa and Shakyamuni.

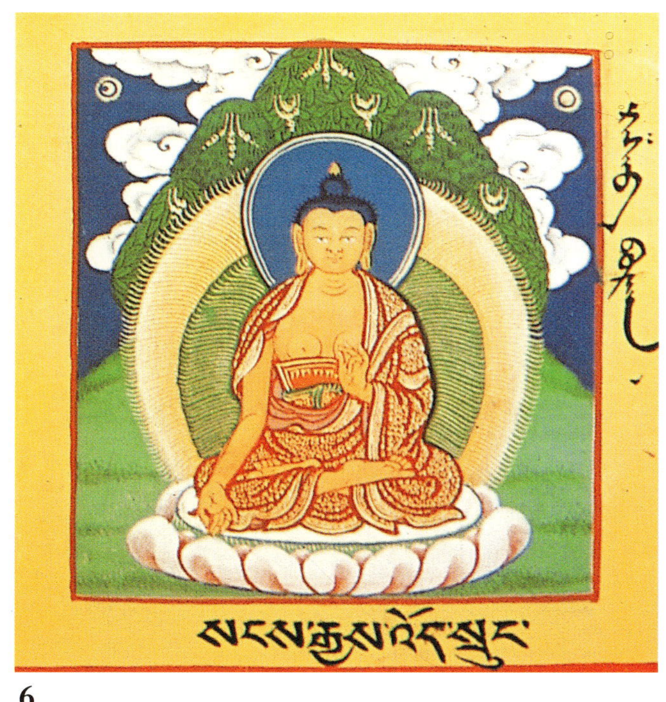

6

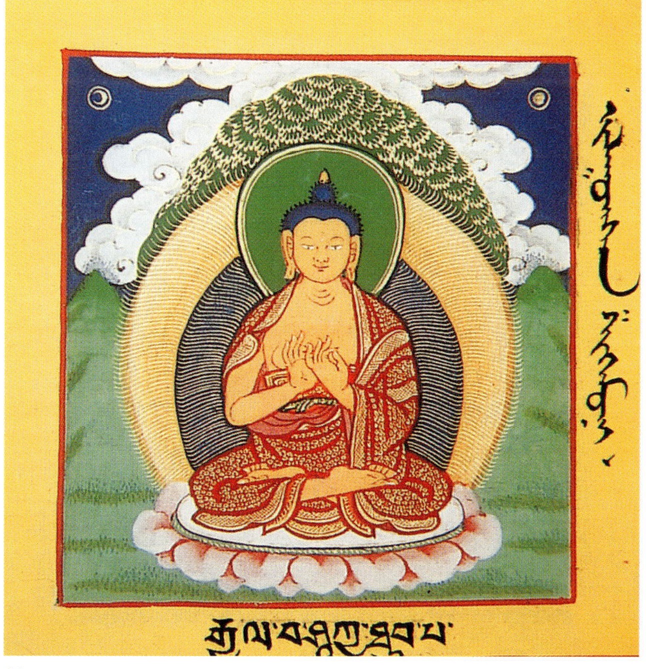

7

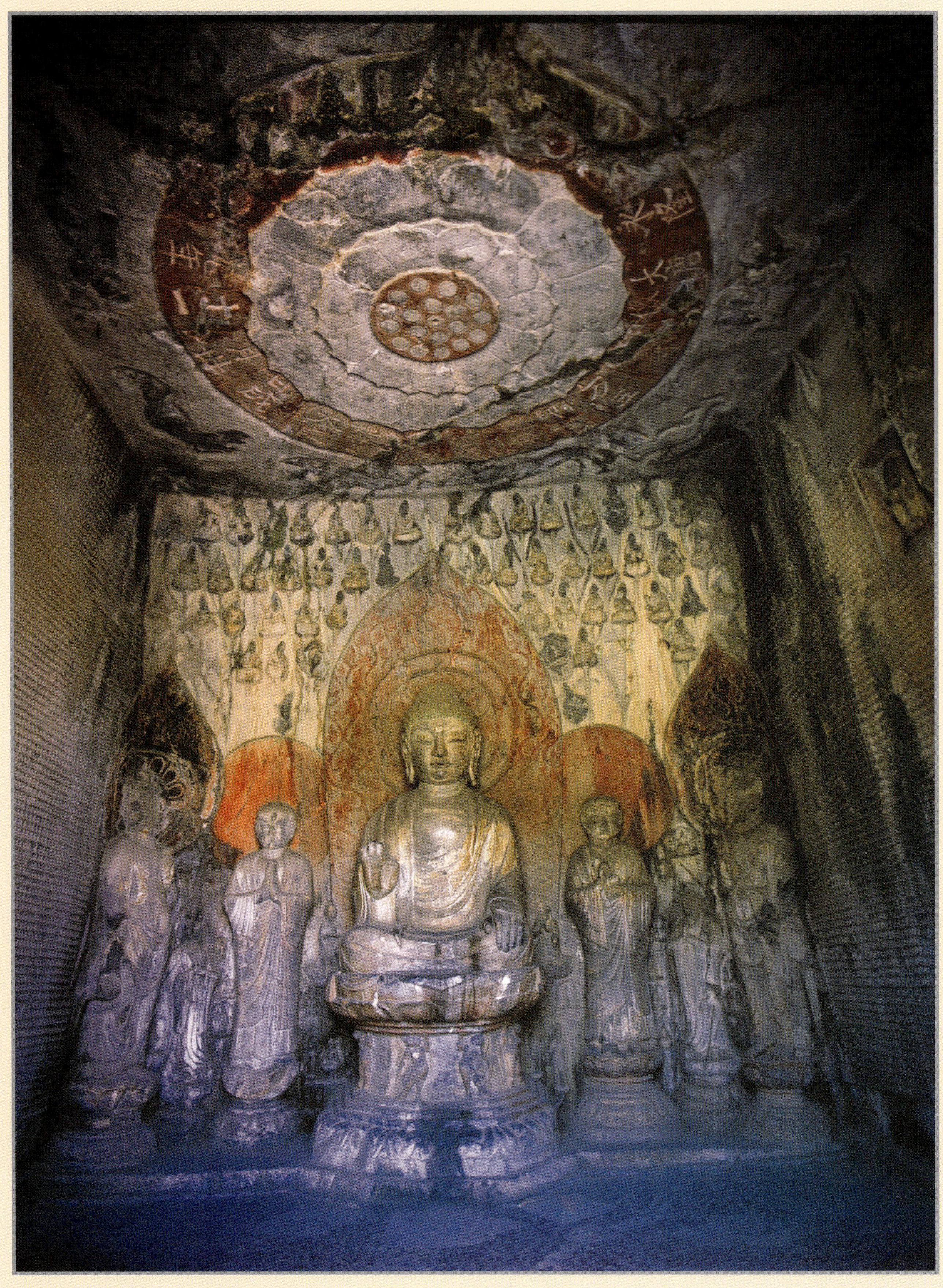

Thousand Buddhas

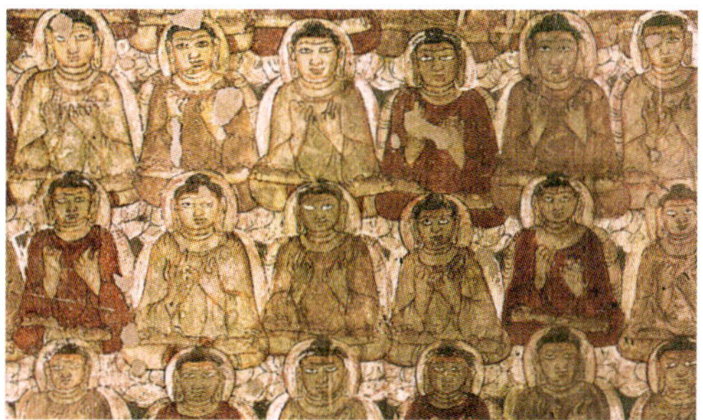

Buddhism is eternal. The founder, the Sage has benefited the world beyond count through thousands of lives. The recollection of pre-incarnations gave an authentic background to his historical life. The idea of multiplying the names of the Buddha lies behind Mahayana development. Thousand became an integral element in the concept of state and in the symbolization of power as a visible element of the palladium. It represented a thousand-fold power of a kingdom. Thousand Buddhas bless the present aeon. The number played a preeminent role in stabilization of the state. The Sanskrit word for thousand is '*sahasra*', derived from '*sahas*' meaning might.

Recitation of the names of the Thousand Buddhas was eulogized in the *Bhadrakalpika-sutra* as – any worthy man or woman who hears the names of the World-honoured Buddhas of the past, present and future *kalpas,* who believes in them joyfully and reads and recites them without injurious intent; who may be able to copy them out by hand so that they may be explained to others, or who may be able to have painted Buddha icons fashioned, or may be able to worship them with incense, flowers and music ...

Indic tradition produced a number of texts supplying thousand names of various deities. Names of the thousand Buddhas of Bhadrakalpa pertain to the same category of literature. Among these thousand names several relate to illumination, to Buddha as light of the world. It was believed that the present age of the world, the Bhadrakalpa together with its immediate predecessor and successor have been assigned a total of three thousand Buddhas, to be evenly divided between them. The names were compiled in a penta-lingual text in Sanskrit, Tibetan, Manchu, Mongolian and Chinese.

ABOVE: *The mural illustrates the Miracle of Sravasti when the Buddha multiplied himself a thousand times. This event consequently served as the basis for iconographic elaboration in thangkas symbolizing the notion of Thousand Buddhas. Ajanta Cave 2, sixth century.*

FACING PAGE: *Thousand Buddhas are often painted or carved filling up the space behind the main image of a Buddha. The entire alcove enshrining the colossal Buddha Maitreya at Bamiyan was decorated with rows of Buddhas representing Thousand Buddhas. In the Yun-kang caves in China also Maitreya is surrounded by them.*

The sutra of Bhadrakalpa was translated into Chinese in late third century. Three consecutive sections give names of the Thousand Buddhas, details about their birthplaces, families, parents, disciples, ages, number in their audiences, duration of the Dharma that each establishes and so on. Another sutra that speaks about the Thousand Buddhas is *Brahmajala-sutra*. It says – I am called Rocana and live in the ocean of lotus world ... I incarnate myself into one thousand Buddhas. Thus Thousand Buddhas were an integral aspect of Rocana in early third century. There are several other sutras translated into Tibetan and Chinese that gave a foundation to the perenniality of Buddhism and a theological importance to the Thousand Buddhas.

Thousand names or epithets of divine beings are seen as a common phenomenon in the Indic religious tradition. In Buddhist art the number thousand for Buddha represent their being innumerable or thousand. Buddha has a thousand epithets which underwent an apotheosis as the Thousand Buddhas and they became a thousand pictures or a thousand icons more or less of identical form who are often painted in rows of equal size on walls or scrolls. One of the best examples is the Thousand Buddhas painted on the wall is in the Dun-huang caves in China. When they are painted on scrolls, for example, Tibetan thangkas, they are often divided into four, with each thangka containing 250 icons. Woodblock prints of Thousand Buddhas were created as votive offerings. Some of such prints are also discovered from inside the images of Buddhas.

The idea of Thousand Buddhas resulted in creation of three thousand Buddhas of past, present and future and even ten thousand Buddhas. Theoretically, there could be as many Buddhas as there are grains of sand in the Ganges. Thousand Buddhas bless the present aeon of *Bhadra-kalpa*.

Sir Aurel Stein recovered a 70 feet long scroll from Khotan containing names of Thousand Buddhas. There is a story given in *Gandavyuha-sutra* in which Queen Maya says that she is the mother of the Buddha, as also the past Buddhas Krakucchanda, Kanakamuni, and Kashayapa. So she will also be the mother of all the Buddhas of the present aeon. When the time comes for Maitreya to manifest, and descent from Tushita heaven, she will be his mother. Just as she will be the mother of Maitreya, so she will be the mother of other Buddhas of the *Bhadrakalpa*. She enumerates the names of the Buddhas of Bhadrakalpa, beginning with Simha and ending with Abhyucchadeva. She repeats that she will be the mother of countless Buddhas, among whom Maitreya is prominent.

Thousand Buddhas are depicted in both the Tibetan and Sino-Japanese traditions in the outer enceinte of the *Vajradhatu-mahamandala*. They are repeated without any distinction. The same form is stenciled over a thousand times.

The sutra on Thousand Buddhas gained popularity in the renowned centers of Buddhism in China. 'Caves of Thousand Buddhas' were carved to the southeast of the main oasis of Dun-huang. According to the legend they owe their existence to a monk who had seen a cloud in his dream with Thousand Buddhas above the valley. A stone stele of 698 from the T'ang dynasty states that the first chapel named 'Cave of Unequalled Height' was constructed by an Indian pilgrim in AD 366. The fifth century witnessed popularity of Thousand Buddhas in China reaching to its zenith. During this period Thousand Buddhas were painted in caves, arranged symmetrically with the main image of a giant statue of a Buddha. For example, the largest cave at Yun-kang is filled with Thousand Buddhas with Rocana at the centre. In another cave a colossal image measuring 44 feet, is a seated Buddha, which bears miniature Buddhas on its nimbus. Similarly, they can be seen on the nimbus behind the main image of Rocana at the Toshodaiji monastery in Japan. Thousand Buddhas are represented over the entire outside surface from top to bottom. They may be painted in the uppermost zones of the wall as well as surface of the octagonal pillars.

Inner surface of the walls of a portable shrine called Tamamushi-no-zushi, kept at the Horyuji monastery, situated near Nara is the earliest example portraying Thousand Buddhas in Japan. It is an embodiment of the Lotus-sutra. On the basis of its philosophy a plaque with

FACING PAGE: *Buddha had a thousand epithets which underwent an apotheosis as the Thousand Buddhas and they became a thousand pictures or thousand icons, more or less of identical form. Sets of ten scrolls comprising one hundred Buddhas each were painted illustrating Buddhas in a geometric pattern of squares.*

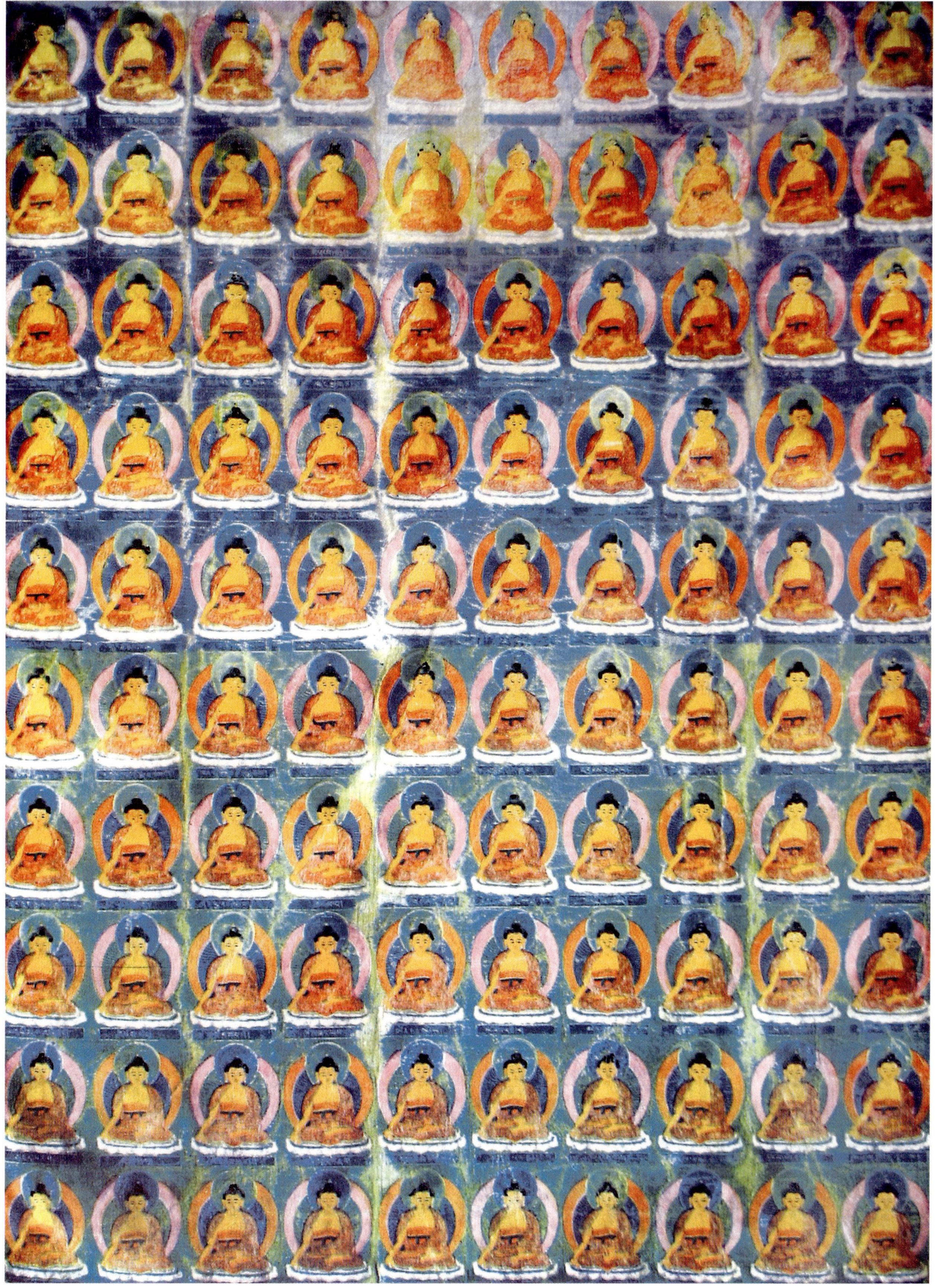

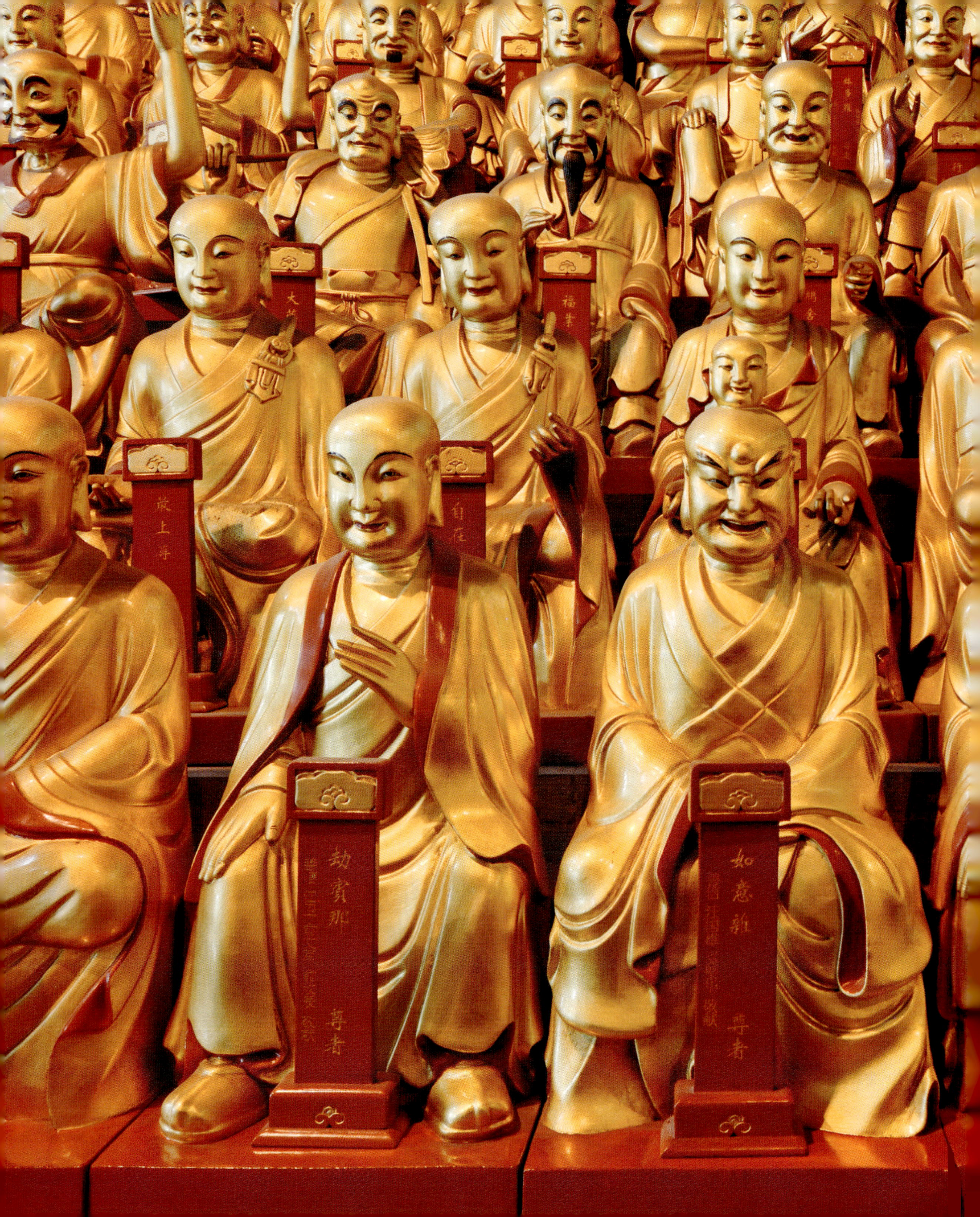
劫賓那尊者
如意難尊者

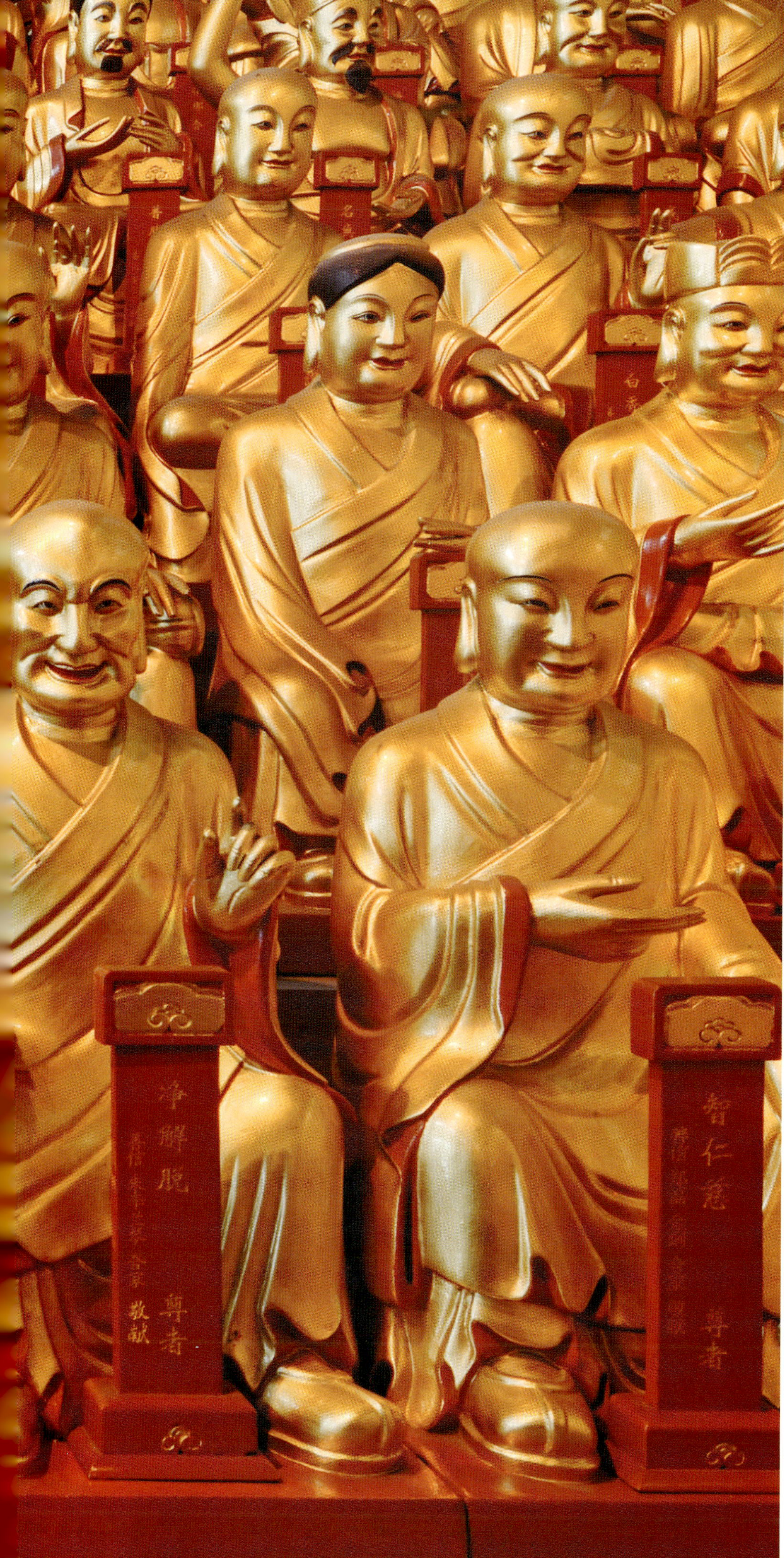

Monasticism is central in Buddhism. Monks are self discplined wanderers seeking delivarence from bonds of existence and misery. (There is no caste bar.) Entry to sangha is open to the richest and the poorest, to the highest and the lowest. Everybody is bound by the vow of poverty, relinquishing personal possessions of worldly goods, pursuing the highest ends, undistracted.

Thousand Buddhas was moulded for the Hase-dera temple in Japan. The sutra gives a marvellous exposition of timelessness of the teachings and infiniteness of the Buddha. An apparition of a stupa on the plaque contains Buddhas in the upper background.

At Borobudur in Indonesia in Java, Thousand Buddhas sanctify in iconic form. Ninety-two Buddhas sit in each of the four directions, sixty-four in the fourth gallery and seventy-two in the semi-enclosed stupas. All the images of the six groups perform different mudras – *bhumisparhsa, varada, dhyana, abhaya, vitarka* and *dharmacakra*. The total number comes to five hundred and four multiplied by two, that is one thousand and eight, as a pilgrim bows to them during his upward journey and while descending.

Horyuji monastery owns a print of the Thousand Buddhas. Another print was discovered from inside a statue of Maitreya in the Kofukuji monastery. Still another print of three thousand Buddhas was found from another Maitreya statue at the Shomyoji monastery. Such prints eventuate from the practice of printing by wood blocks on sheets of paper, folding and inserting them into statues.

From Tibet there are xylographs, representing the Thousand Buddhas, wood printed at the Potala palace of the Dalai Lama. A festival of the Buddha names was celebrated by the Japanese emperors from AD 830 to 1467 to purify the court and the country from sins committed in the course of the year. A number of such examples of the worship of the Thousand Buddhas can be given from the history of Buddhism in Asia.

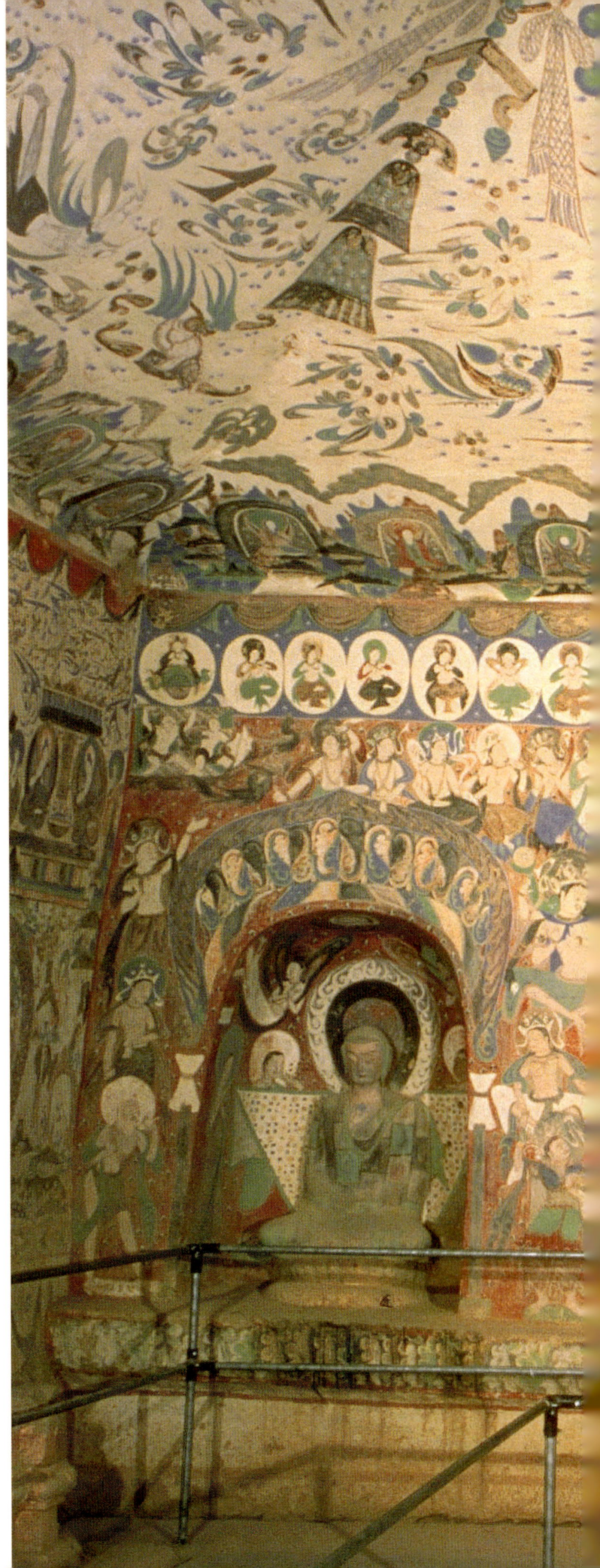

The world renowned grottos at Dunhuang in China are identified as the 'Caves of Thousand Buddhas'. A special sutra, the Bhadra-kalpika-sutra is devoted to them. It was translated into Chinese by a native of Dun-huang Dharmaraksha, who had lived from AD 265 to 313.

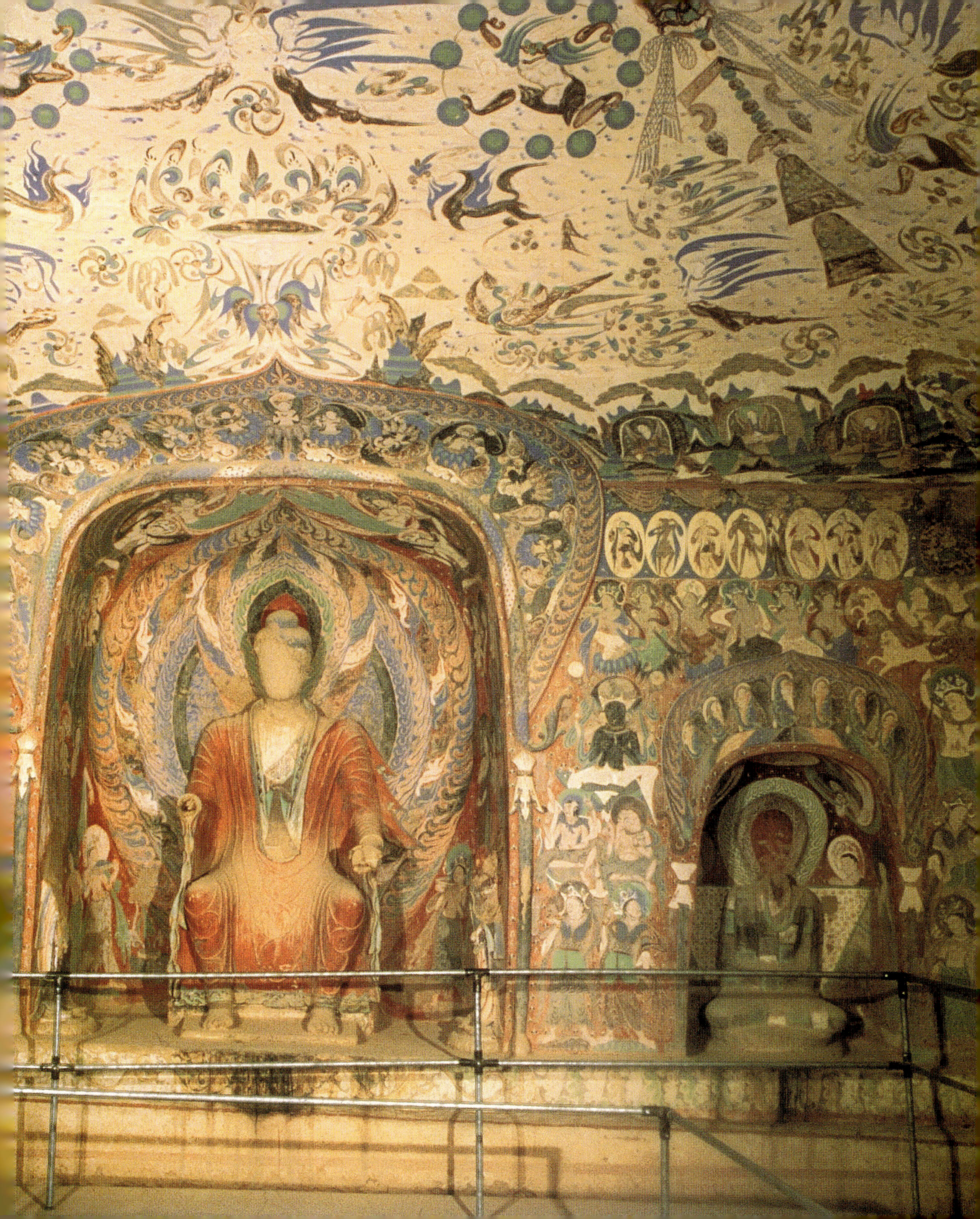

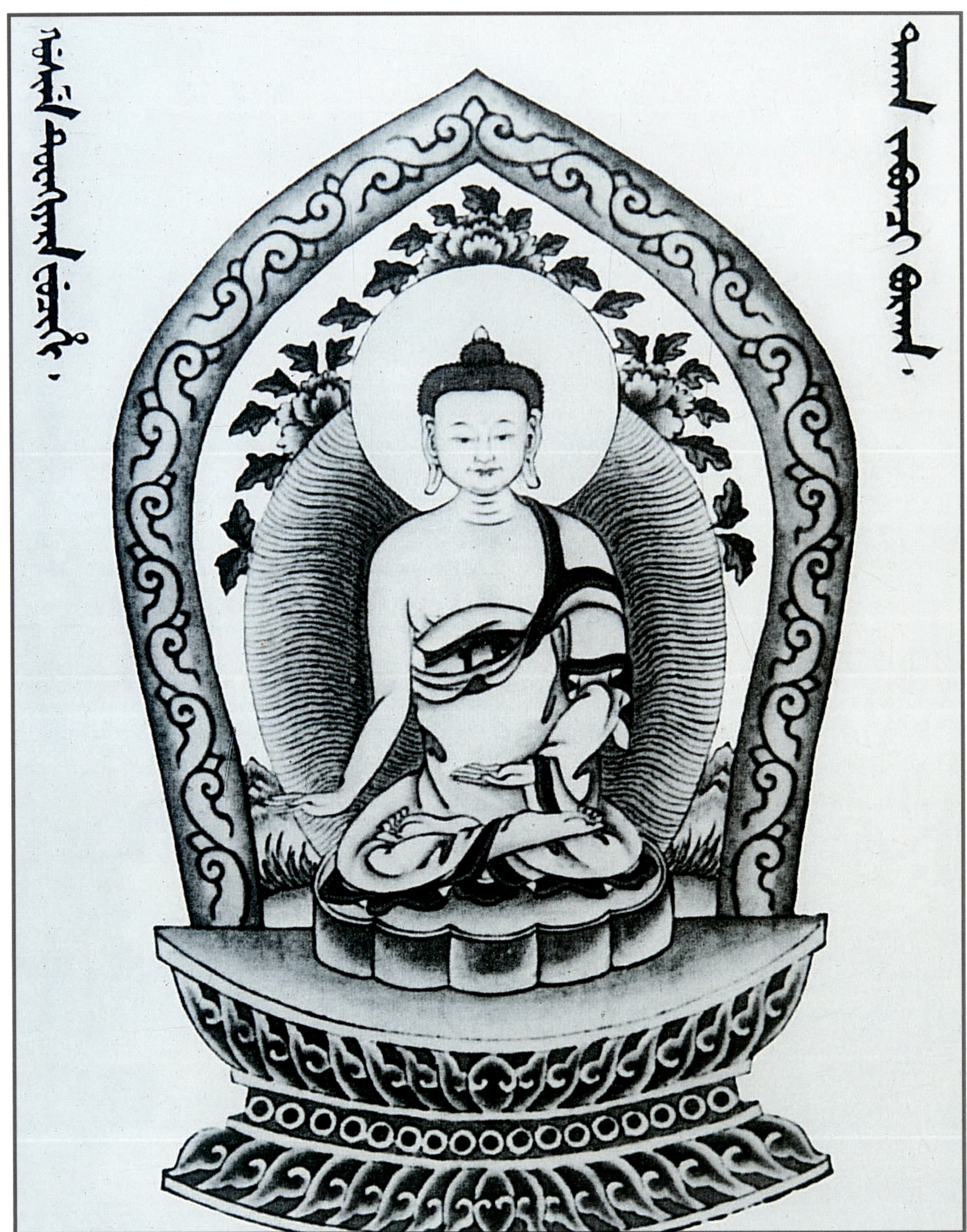

Buddhas of Ten Directions

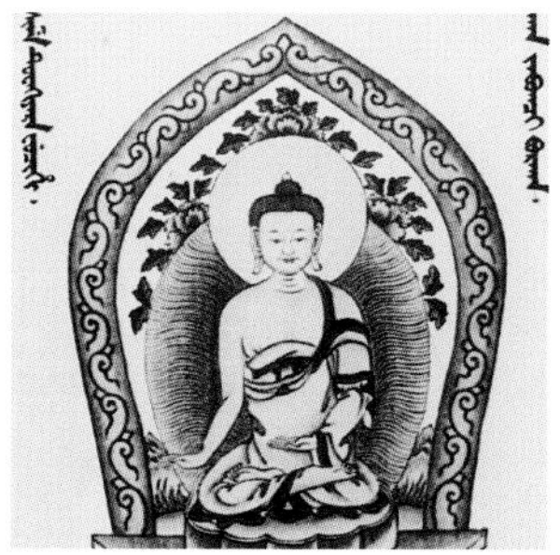

The concept of Buddhas of Ten Directions remained important for centuries at every level of thinking in Mahayana Buddhism. Whereas in Hinayana texts, Shakyamuni denies the possibility of plurality of Buddhas, there can never be two Buddhas in the world at the same time, and to meet a Buddha is a rare experience. But in Mahayana theology ten directions, including eight points of compass and the sphere above and below, are pervaded by an incalculable number of Buddhas. Acceptance and rejection of the Ten Buddhas is found in the Chinese texts. A question is put – why no one has ever met one of these Buddhas. The answer comes very simply – the Buddhas of the ten quarters and their Bodhisattvas, even relatively nearby Buddha Maitreya, do not visit the earth because mankind is so sinful, so blinded by ignorance that their coming and going would pass unnoticed. In this phase of Buddhist teaching, it is told that though a Buddha is theoretically omnipotent, he cannot or will not aid those who lack even the minimum readiness to receive him.

A Buddha in reality has two types of bodies – one is the physical body given by his parents, and the other is the spiritual body, *dharmakaya,* which fills the ten quarters of space, immeasurable and infinite … . He is able to convert the beings of the world throughout the ten quarters by assuming every kind of body, name and condition of birth. It is also believed that Shakyamuni possesses an immeasurable supernatural power that enables him miraculously to create Buddhas in the ten quarters, so as to preach the Law and emit light and convert all beings.

There is no fixed list of the names of the Ten Buddhas. Their names are given in the *Prajana-paramita* texts, followed by two Bodhisattvas, accompanying each of them and the names of the worlds in which they reside. In India they are painted in the upper registers of the south and north walls of the assembly hall at Tabo monastery, belonging to the tenth century AD.

ABOVE: *One of the Buddhas of Ten Directions.*

FACING PAGE: *First among the Buddhas of Ten Directions painted in the 300 icons and represented as statuettes in the Pao-hsiang Lou pantheon.*

Names of Ten Buddhas and the accompanying Bodhisattvas:

Bodhisattva	Buddha	Bodhisattva
E Samantarashmi	Ratnakara	Bodhisattva
SE Padmahasta	Padmottamashri	Bodhisattva
S (Vigata) Ashoka	Ashokashri	Bodhisattva
SW Bodhisattva	Surya-mandala-prabhasottama-sri	Bodhisattva
Nadir Bodhisattva	Padmashri	Padmottara
W Arya Avalokiteshvara	Ratnarcish	[Caritramati]
NW Bodhisattva	[Ekacchatra]	[Ratnottama]
N Bodhisattva	Jayendra	Jayadatta
NE Bodhisattva	Samadhi-hastyuttara-shri	Vijaya-vikramin
Zenith Manjushri	Nandashri	Nandadatta

The above list cannot be considered final. There are a number of series of names of Ten Buddhas given in Tibetan, Chinese and Japanese traditions, and in various sutras and their translations into Chinese and Tibetan. In Japan the Ten Buddhas along with other Buddhas and Bodhisattvas are worshipped in Zen monasteries at daily meals. They are – Vairocana, Rocana, Shakyamuni, Maitreya, Amitayus, all the Buddhas of the ten directions, and of the three times, Manjushri, Samantabhadra, Avalokiteshvara, and Mahasthamaprapta. It is widely believed that one gains merits by invoking the names of the Ten Buddhas, by hearing them and by repeating the names. On the south and north walls of the assembly hall at Tabo monastry are painted the Buddhas of the Ten Directions with their attendant Bodhisattvas, turning towards them.

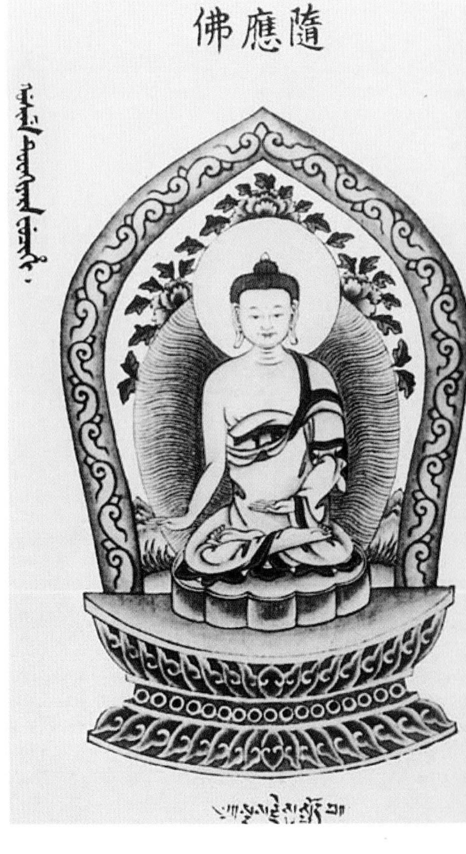

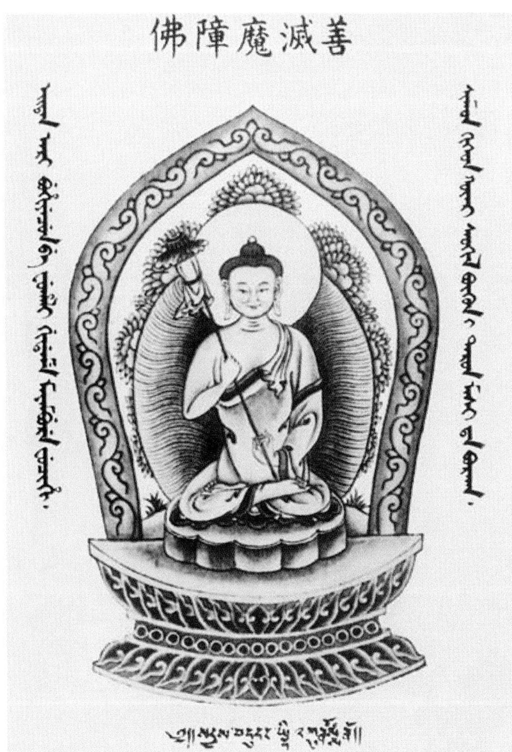

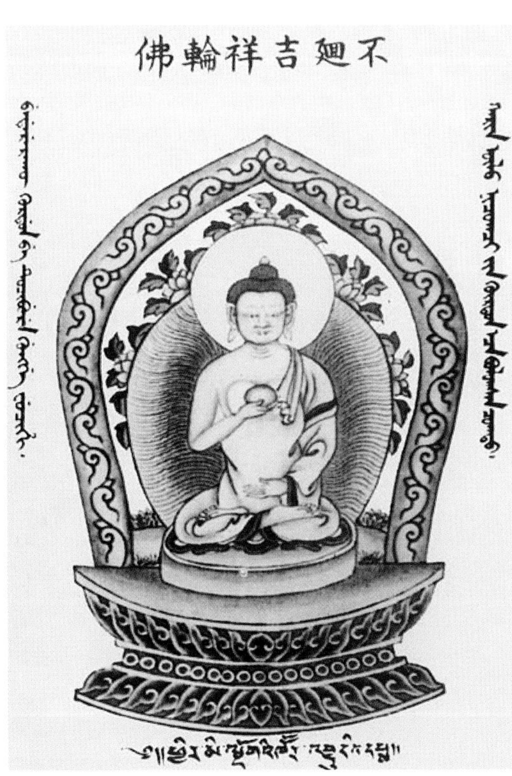

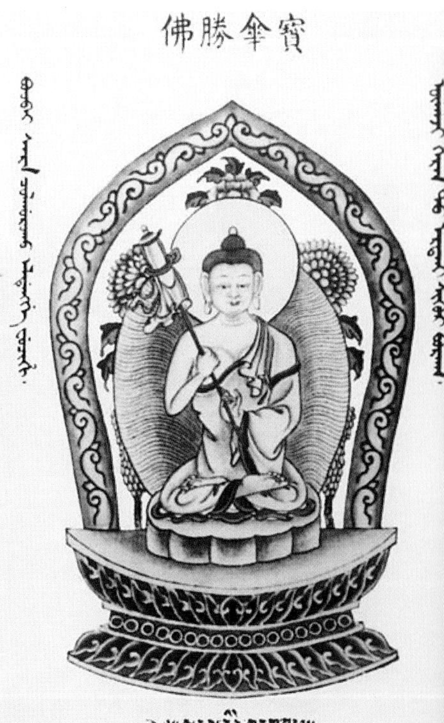

顯聖王佛

善滅諍訟佛

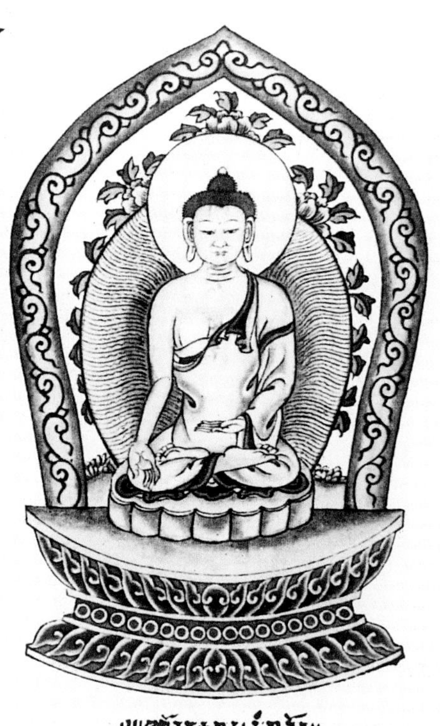

寶身光輝佛

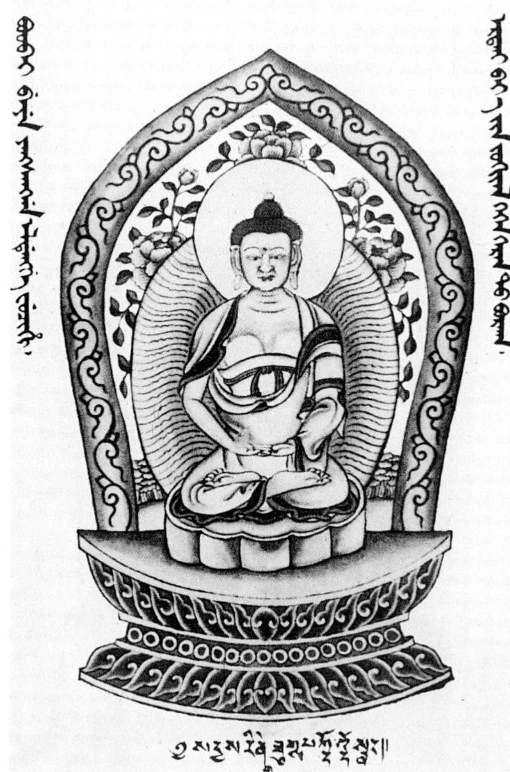

隨引菩提佛

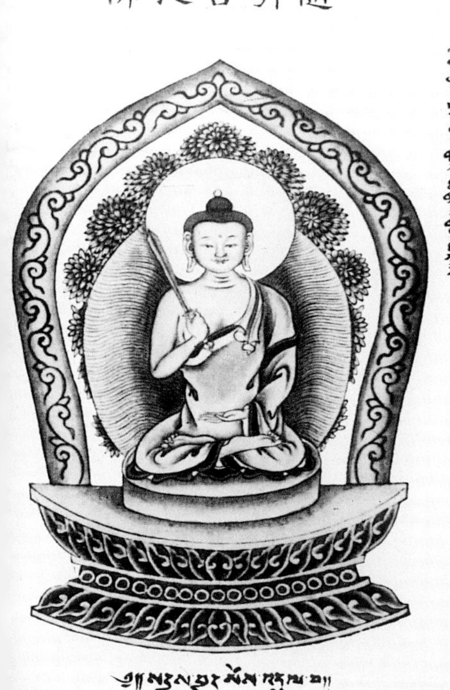

無畏滅冥佛

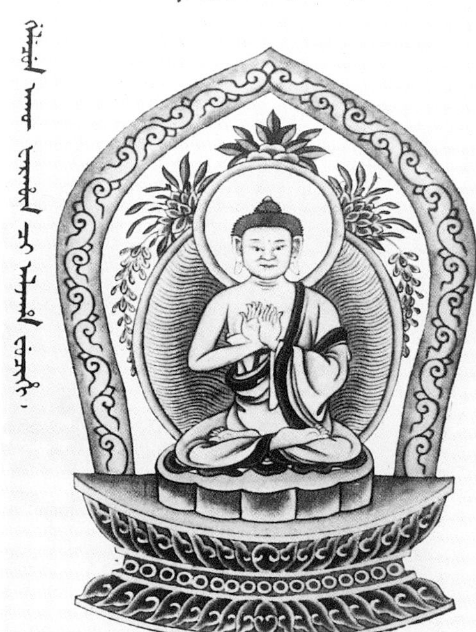

初慈决疑佛

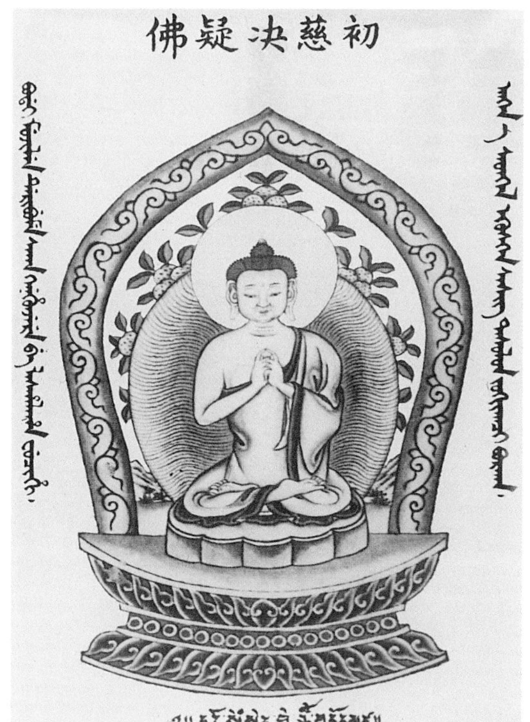

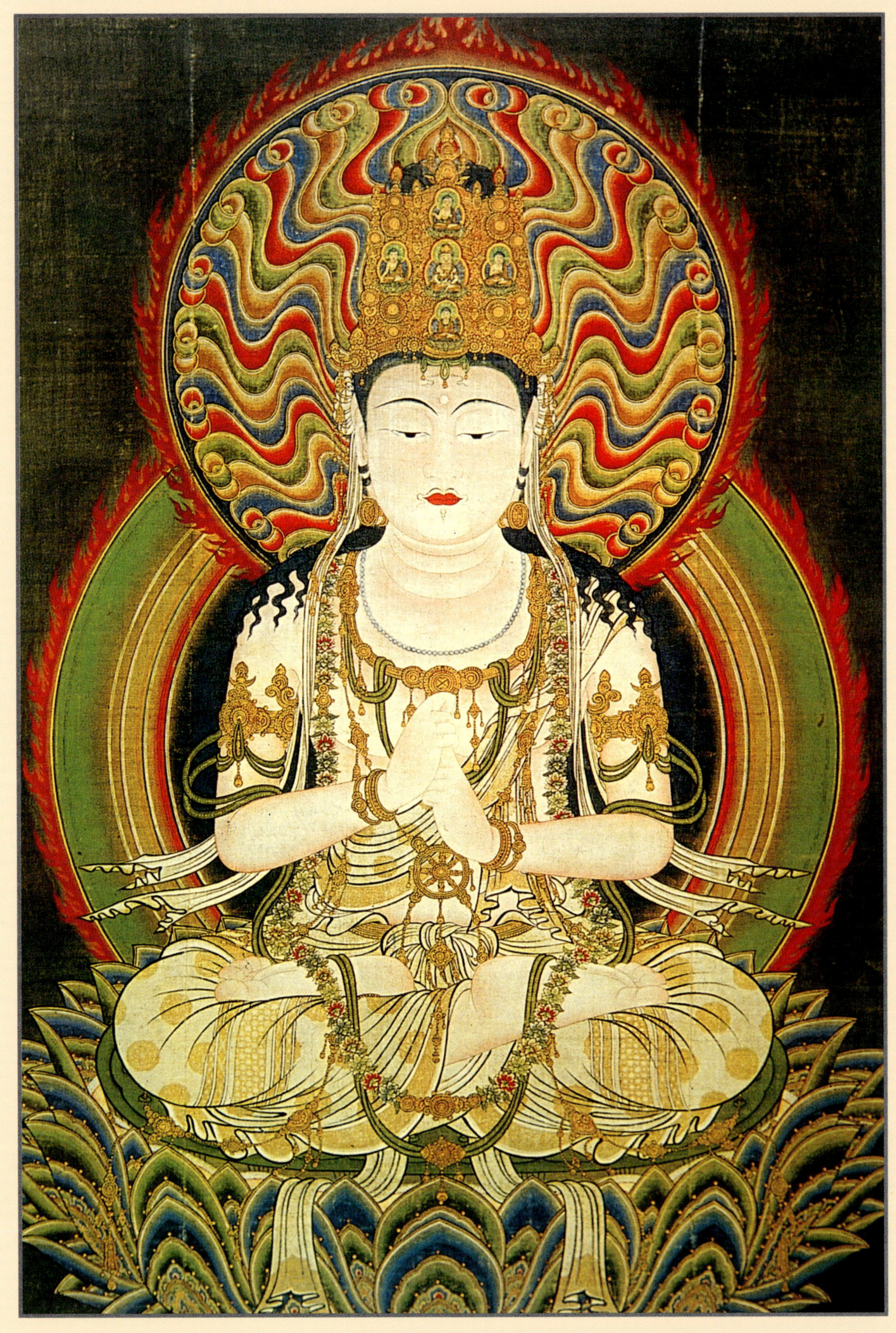

Buddhas of the Light Cults

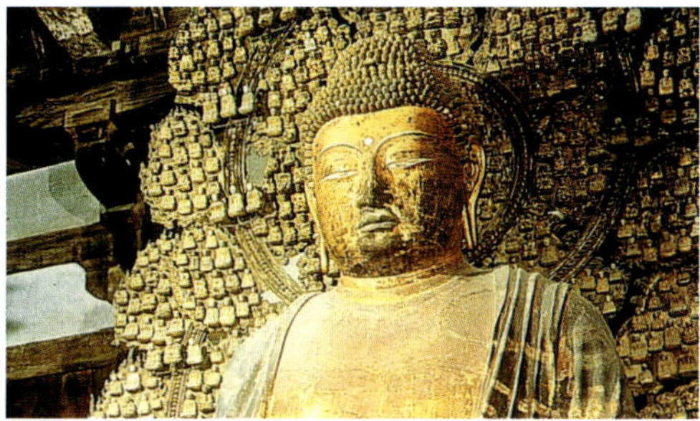

Manifestations of the Buddha as Vairocana, Amitabha and Maitreya belong to light symbolism, which predominates in Mahayana Buddhism. From where it was infused into Buddhism, is not certain, but its most consistent and strongest manifestations occurred in the northwest, in the region penetrated by Iranian influences. The Pashtu speaking people covered a much wider area than present day Iran, and besides language they had shared values. Their macro level of light cults inspired remythologization from eternal Buddhist premises. Buddhism underwent a qualitative change under these influences. The idea of a divine saviour in future is alien to the early teachings of Buddhism. It has unmistakable parallels in Iranian belief. The light cults developed on two distinct lines: first being Amitabha, translated as Infinite Light or Transcendent Sun; and Vairocana, the Light (of knowledge) representing luminous symbolism while the second, Maitreya, on the other line is Sun himself, as the word comes from Sanskrit 'Mithra' meaning sun. Standing Buddha figure was first presented with an aureole of light about his whole body, like the sun god, on the coin of Kanishka. It is plausible that Maitreya Ajita has an Iranian origin in Mithra Invinctus.

VAIROCANA

Buddha Dipankara was apotheosized as Amitabha and later as Vairocana. Amitabha is the first among the Tathagatas mentioned in the *Gandavyuha sutra* while Vairocana is the last. Transition from Shakyamuni to Vairocana was inherent in the lineage of the Enlightened One. Vairocana, the term comes from the root '*ruc*' in Sanskrit meaning light, luster and brightness, so Vairocana is light apotheosized. He is the metaphysical sun; the light of the sun of wisdom, the

ABOVE: *Vairocana is translated as the Great Sun, known as Dainichi in Japanese. He dissipates lies and errors, vile and evil, the malevolent and the malicious, just as the Sun dispels darkness. As the Sun shines for all times, in the same manner, Mahavairocana, the Great Sun as the supreme Buddha eliminates untruths and errors by the light of his wisdom. He performs the posture of supreme enlightenment, called bodhyagri mudra.*

FACING PAGE: *Rocana is sitting with Thousand Buddhas carved on the halo behind him. According to the Brahmajala-sutra they are his incarnations. He lives in the ocean of lotus worlds.*

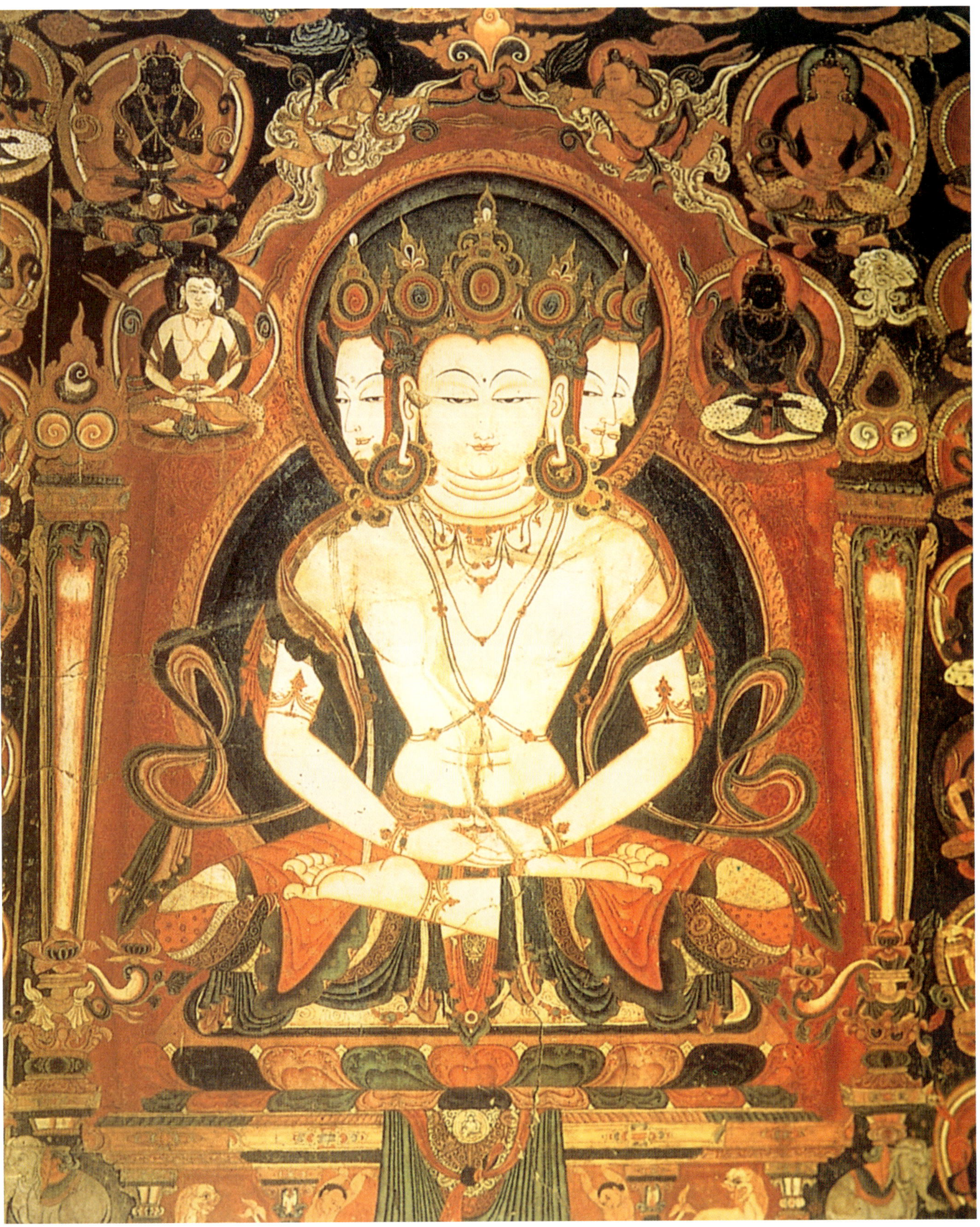

universal light that transcends all limitations. Every human being has an inherent potential or seed that can be nourished in the womb of compassion to attain enlightenment.

Vairocana has attained several forms such as – Rocana, Abhisambodhi Vairocana, Vairocana of Vajradhatu-mandala, Maha Vairocana of *sarvadurgati-parishodhana* in dharma-cakra mudra, and Sarvavid Vairocana. There is a distinct line of development from Amitabha to Rocana of Avatamsaka, then Vairocana of Garbhadhatu, culminating in Vairocana of Vajradhatu. The first three perform the same mudra of meditation, which culminates in enlightenment, that is *bodhi*, the transcendental wisdom. Vairocana is said to be a jewel in Mahavastu. He is refered to as a spokesman and it also comes as a name of a *cakravartin*, a former incarnation of Maitreya.

Due to similarity in names – Vairocana and Rocana are often not clearly distinguished. But the Japanese make a clear distinction between them. Rocana is called Roshana as Roshana Daibutsu in Nara, and Vairocana is known as Birushana and Dainichi Nyorai. In the Zen monasteries Rocana and Vairocana are eulogized as two different Buddhas. Popularity of Buddha as Rocana owes to *Avatamsaka-sutra*, which was closely connected with the area around Bamiyan, from where it was transmitted to China, Korea and Japan. It reached China in the second century AD with translation of the epithets of the Buddha. The first colossal image of Rocana was carved at the Yun-kang caves of China measuring 30 feet in height. The tradition of sculpting Rocana images was carried on in China through the seventh century. In AD 632, the Chinese pilgrim Hsuan-tsang reached Bamiyan and witnessed the splendour of the two colossal images, their precious ornaments, draperies and the overall richness. Hsuan-tsang had identified the smaller statue as Shakyamuni. But according to the recent researches the smaller statue was that of Rocana while the other was of Maitreya. As a tradition, Rocana is backed or surrounded by a Thousand Buddhas. A few fragments of frescoes lower down on the sides of the niche indicating that once the entire alcove was decorated with rows of seated Buddhas. The image needs comparison with Rocana enshrined in the monastery of Toshodaiji where he sits on a huge lotus pedestal. It is a lacquer statue and the halo behind made of wood bears a number of clusters of tiny Buddhas, all looking similar in size.

Thousand Buddhas were said to be incarnations of Rocana in early third century in *Brahmajala-sutra* – I am called Rocana and live in the ocean of lotus world ... I incarnate myself into one Thousand Buddhas.

Vairocana is portrayed in paintings and sculptures as two armed, four, six or eight armed. He is white in colour and suppresses obtuseness and ignorance. His abode is located in the east and attains different forms in different traditions, e.g. according to the *Avatamsaka sutras* he is the principal Buddha and is visualized in *sambhogakaya*. Vairocana is immeasurable luminosity that emanates into Five Tathagatas, which reminds us of the five elements of cosmology.

Vairocana representing the state of universal dominion is known as *Ekakshara Chakravartin*. He is the sovereign of sovereigns. As a sovereign, he has two forms: he holding a wheel in the bowl-bearing mudra or performing jnana-mushti (fist of knowledge) or bodhyagri mudra (gesture of supreme knowledge). In a number of illustrated Japanese pantheons, he is portrayed with seven jewels of a universal monarch: the wheel, wish-granting jewel, horse, elephant, queen, general, and minister. His abode, Sumeru has terraces of various jewels and his palace is equated with the residence of Indra.

The Japanese Emperor Shomu accepted Vairocana as the symbol of national unity and enshrined his colossal image at the Todaiji monastery in Nara confirming his integral association with the state. He is the image of totality, which lives in the ocean of a lotus world surrounded by one thousand petals.

He is the lord of the twin mandalas, Vajradhatu and Garbhadhatu in the esoteric tradition. In Vajradhatu mandala, he is seated on a lion in the middle of a pavilion atop Mount Sumeru surrounded by seven seas, continents, and sub-continents. In Garbhadhatu mandala, he is represented as the body of principle, *dharmakaya*, as it exists in the totality of phenomenal existence. He symbolizes

FACING PAGE: *Sarvavid Vairocana is white in colour, has four faces and two arms. Adorned with ornaments and crown, he performs the posture of meditation with his hands placed in his lap holding a wheel.*

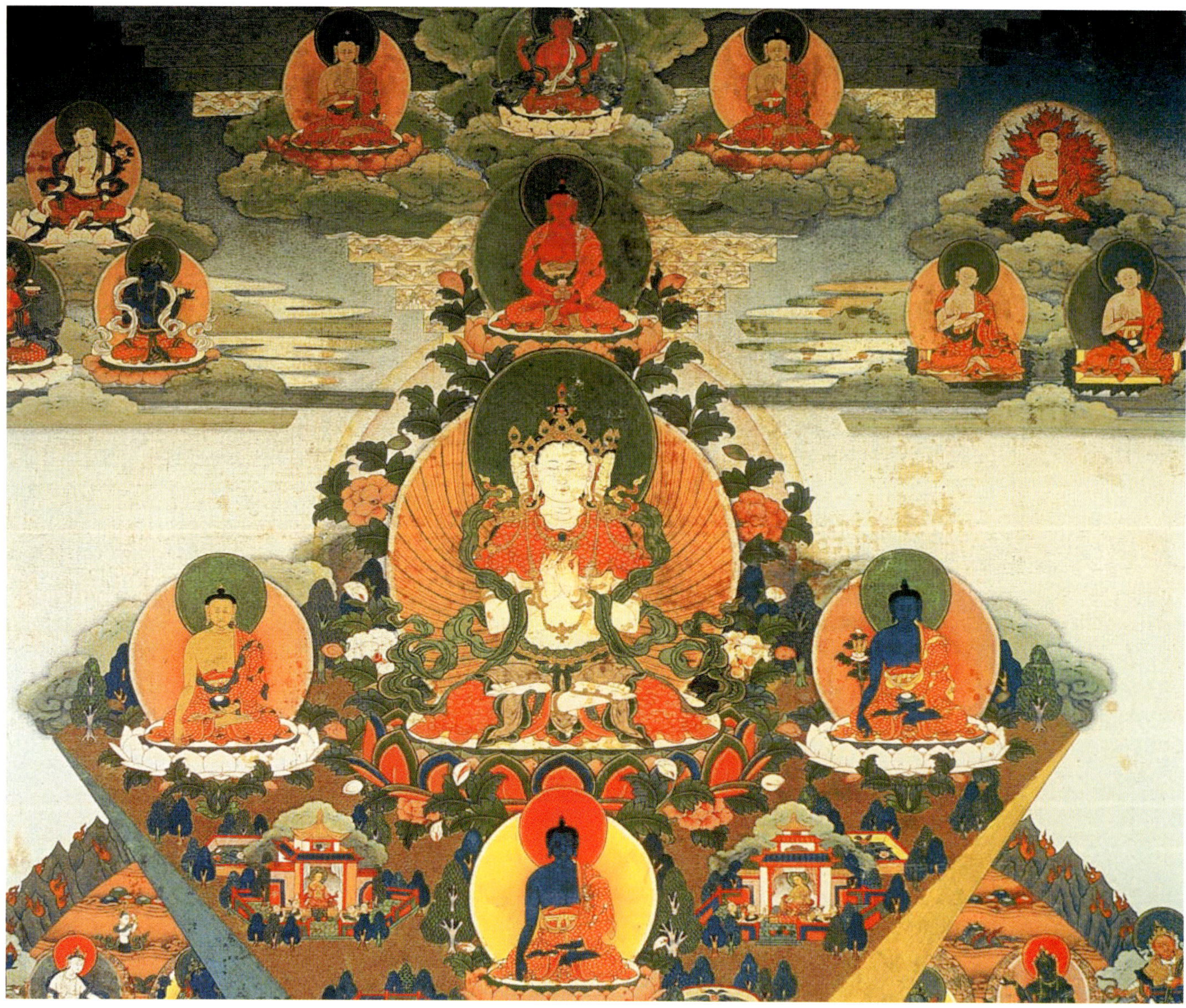

compassion, growth, and potentiality of the world of enlightenment. He sits on a white lotus and is crowned with a jatamukuta, wears a silk lion cloth, is gold coloured and radiant. Representing pure consciousness, he makes the dhyana mudra, the posture of concentration bringing the two hands together with thumbs touching in an upward point. At the centre of Garbhadhatu mandala is an eight-leafed lotus that represents the heart of beings. It is the solar matrix, the mysterious sanctuary where the Sun returns each night to be reborn. Four Dhyani Buddhas and four Bodhisattvas sit on the eight petals.

At the monastery of Tabo in India and the caves of Dunhuang in China he is represented as *Sarvavid Vairocana* with his hands in the posture of meditation holding a

ABOVE: *Four faced Vairocana symbolizes germinal luminosity. He sits in diamond posture, is white, effulgent like the sun, and wears a bejeweled crown. His essence is present in the four directions of space, hence four faces. He wears the five ornaments: crown to indicate mirror-like knowledge, earrings – discriminative knowledge, necklace – equality knowledge, bracelets of arms and feet – dharmadhatu knowledge, and sacred belt – procedure of duty knowledge.*

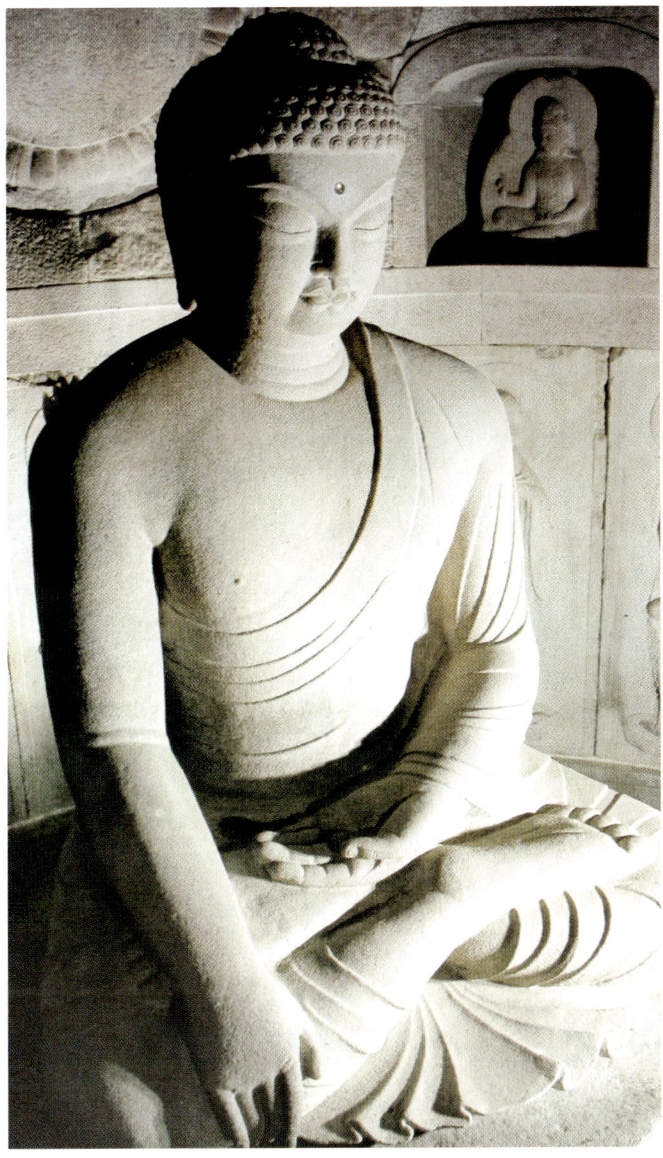

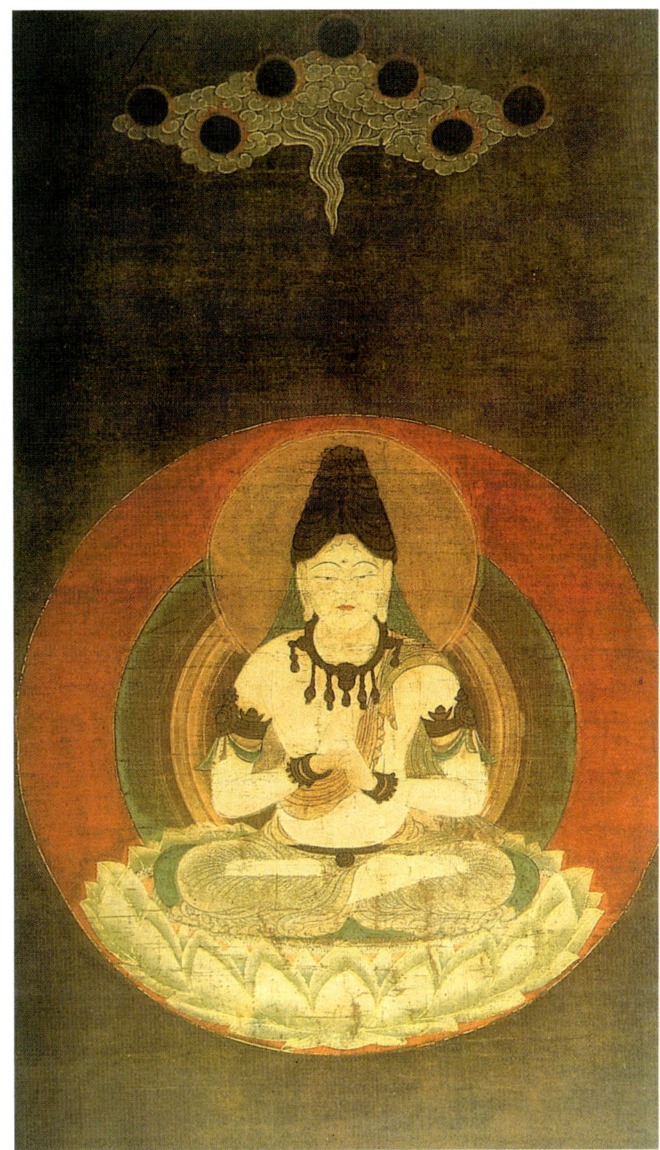

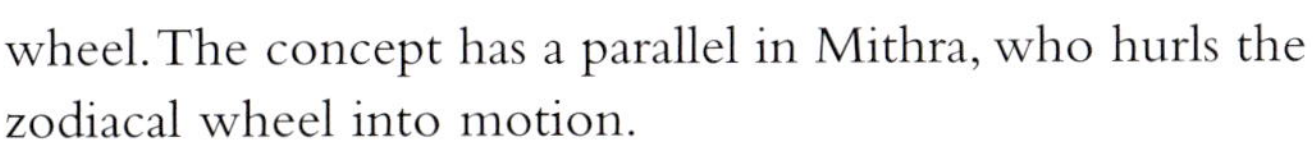

wheel. The concept has a parallel in Mithra, who hurls the zodiacal wheel into motion.

Vairocana in the posture of preaching the dharma is found in Tibetan mandalas, Indian images in sand stone, Nepalese drawings, and manuscript illustrations.

Bodhi of Gautama, the Buddha was transmuted into abhisambodhi of Vairocana, the Tathagata who sits in dhyana mudra like Amitabha. Amitabha and Vairocana are flanked by the same acolytes – Padmapani and Vajrapani. And thirdly there are eight great Bodhisattvas in the train of both of them. In this form Vairocana wears a crown.

According to the Nepalese tradition, Vairocana is the Adi Buddha or the first of the Dhyani Buddhas. When he is placed in the sanctum of a stupa, he is the master of the

ABOVE, LEFT: *The sokkuram grotto in Korea enshrines a colossus sixteen-feet-high image of the Buddha. First rays of the rising Sun touch its forehead jewel. He in turn has cast his sheen on the waters of the eastern seas, exactly on the spot where King Munmu sleeps in eternity.*

ABOVE, RIGHT: *Vairocana, sitting in the posture of supreme enlightenment, representing the light of the sun of wisdom.*

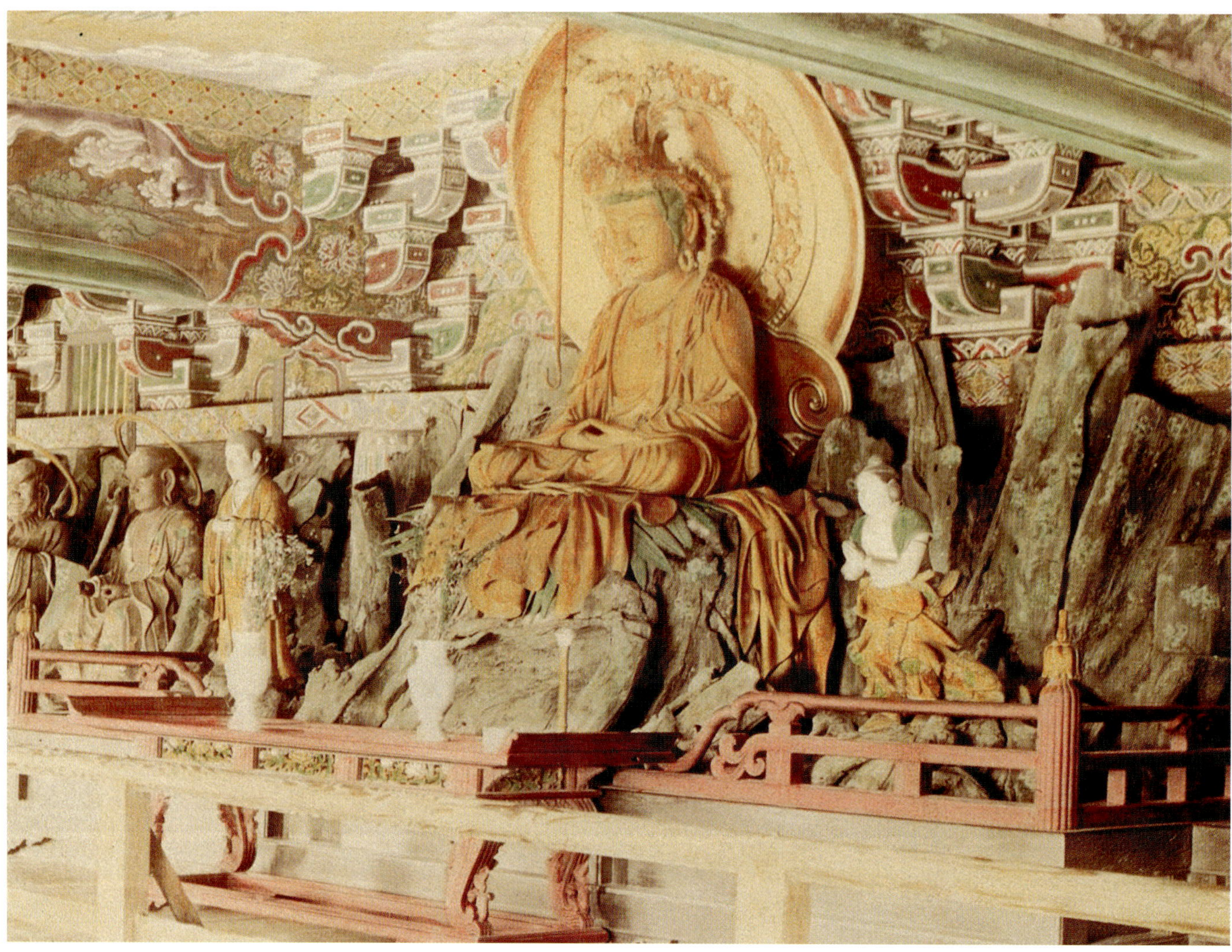

whole temple. He may also be placed between Akshobhya and Ratnasambhava. In Japan he is the highest vehicle for the union of the individual and the universal spirit. He wears a crown and ornaments when he is seated at the centre of a mandala. His colour is white, *akasha* (sky) is said to proceed from him as are the organs of sight and all the colours.

Vairocana is also worshipped as the great sun, *Dainichinyorai*, meaning Great Sun Tathagata painted and clothed in white, seated on a white lotus, wearing an ornate crown and making dhyana mudra. In Tibetan thangkas he is painted as sitting cross-legged making the mudra of enlightenment, bodbyagri mudra. But as a Dhyani Buddha, he wears a monk's robes and his hands are in the dharma-chakra-pravanana-mudra. He assumes the posture in a standing position also with legs wide apart. Sometimes he has four faces while making this gesture with his hands.

Colossal images of Vairocana are also created in Korea and Japan. In Southeast Asian countries, in India and Tibet his statues in bronze and clay are striking in glory and spiritual contemplation. In Tibet he is given royal robes and boots, while in Indonesia a royal parasol is seen as an

ABOVE: *Amitabha is light beyond measure. He is the inexpressible luminous essence, represented in the Western Paradise when his immeasurable light shines upon the devotees, all his grave sins and hinderances of action are nullified.*

additional attribute. There is a long tradition of painting and drawing Vairocana figures in Tibet, China and Japan. The famous Mongol sculptor Zanabazar sculpted an image of Vairocana, which stands out for its contemplative mood and standard of execution.

Popularity of Vairocana gave way to production of a number of forms from the serene to the ferocious, from single faced to three and four faced, from two armed to multi armed, sometimes in yabyum form embracing his consort in Tibetan tantric style. In Tibetan illustrations he even dances embracing his consort holding attributes of war like a goad, a sword, a chain and a cranium. Moreover, he manifests in symbolic forms individually and in mandalas.

AMITABHA: THE BUDDHA AS TRANSCENDENT SUN/IMMESURABLE LIGHT

Amitabha, the Buddha of immeasurable light or the transcendent sun, is one of the Five Dhyani Buddhas: Vairocana, Akshobhya, Amitabha, Amoghasiddhi and Ratnasambhava. His light outshines all the other Buddhas. Explaining his quality Sukhavati-vyuha-sutra says, 'The light of the Buddha shines with immeasurable brilliance in the countries of ten directions and in no place is obstructed. He presides over the western quarter. Sukhavati, the Land of Eternal Bliss is his paradise.' Chinese pilgrims have mentioned in their memoirs of the devotion to Amitabha in India and of shrines dedicated to him. Authors like Nagarjuna and Vasubandhu have also written about him. Devotion to Amitabha is based on Larger Sukhavati-vyuha-, shorter Sukhavati- Amitabha- and Amitayuradhyana-sutras. Parthian Prince An-shih-kao first introduced the tradition into China, from where it was carried to Japan.

Amitabha is idealized from the historical Shakyamuni and has been given many titles and epithets. He gained such an immense popularity in Mahayana countries that sometimes Amitabha seems to have eclipsed even Buddha himself. Completely ignored by Theravada tradition, he was not known to the ancient Buddhist world. Birth of his cult is one of the obscure problems in the history of Mahayana. Attempts have been made to establish a foreign origin such as Zoroastrial heaven of boundless light corresponding to the name of Amitabha. However, Indian tradition might be responsible for the origin of this cult as there are a variety of solar myths attached to it. Some scholars have also tried to seek its origin on the northwestern borderland around the Gandhara region of ancient India where Buddhism was exposed to a strong Iranian influence.

As the most popular divinity in the Pure Land sect, Amitabha pledged to create his own Buddhaland, which would combine all the excellent features of various Buddha lands. Anyone, who invokes the name of Amitabha with a sincere heart can achieve rebirth in his paradise, painted by the Chinese, Japanese, Koreans, Tibetans, and Mongols in a variety of forms. When the immeasurable light of the Buddha shines upon the devotees, all their sins and karmic hindrances are annuled. The Buddha contemplates and preaches the Dharma according to the respective capabilities of the beings. As one of the five Tathagatas, Amitabha is bejewelled. His crown and jewels mark him out as a sambhoga-kaya in all regal splendour. His hands in the samadhi mudra, he wears monastic robes, red in colour and places his hands in the posture of meditation in his lap, sometimes carrying a bowl for alms. Over the centuries he has attained a variety of forms. He is often flanked by two attending Bodhisattvas – Padmapani Avalokiteshvara on the right and Vajrapani Mahasthamaprapta on the left. Peacock, his ride is often painted or carved on the throne.

According to the doctrine associated with his name, he is a superhuman saviour who has created an ideal world into which all those who are reborn, stay until they reach *nirvana* by surrendering to his saving power. In Nepal the highest devotions are rendered to him at the Swayambhunatha temple, as he is the Buddha of the present aeon. Beautiful offerings are bestowed on him in the western quarter of the shrine.

In Japan, Amitabha is known as Amida Nyorai. Nowhere in Sanskrit documents do we find a name reduced to Amita, which could correspond to this epithet. The Larger-sukhavati-vyuha-sutra mentions him as Amitabha except once as Amitayur. The Japanese abbreviation of both Amitabha and Amitayus is 'Amida'. Amitayus is the Buddha of Immeasurable Life and Amitabha, the Buddha of Immeasurable Light. Later the two Sanskrit names were transliterated as Amidayu and

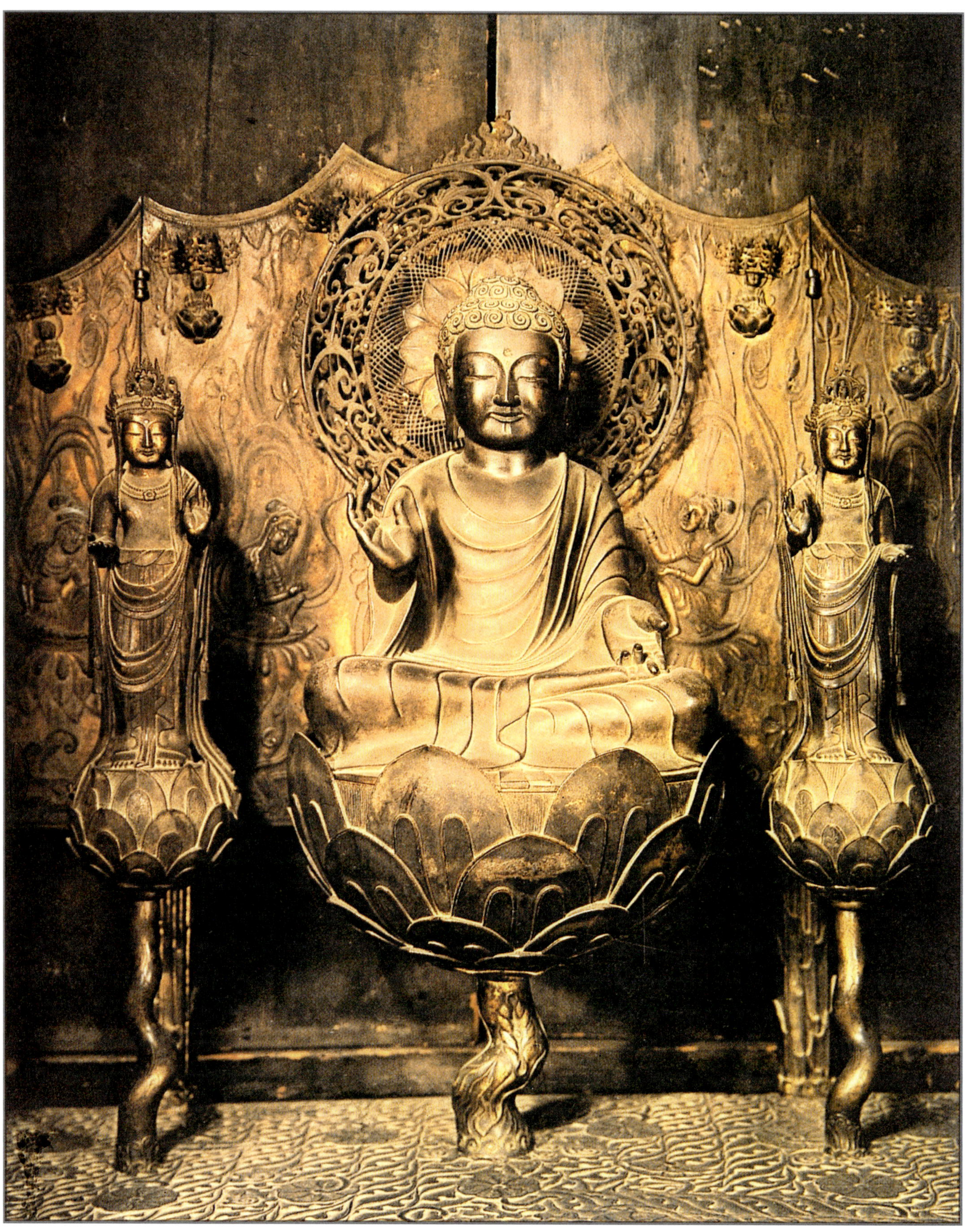

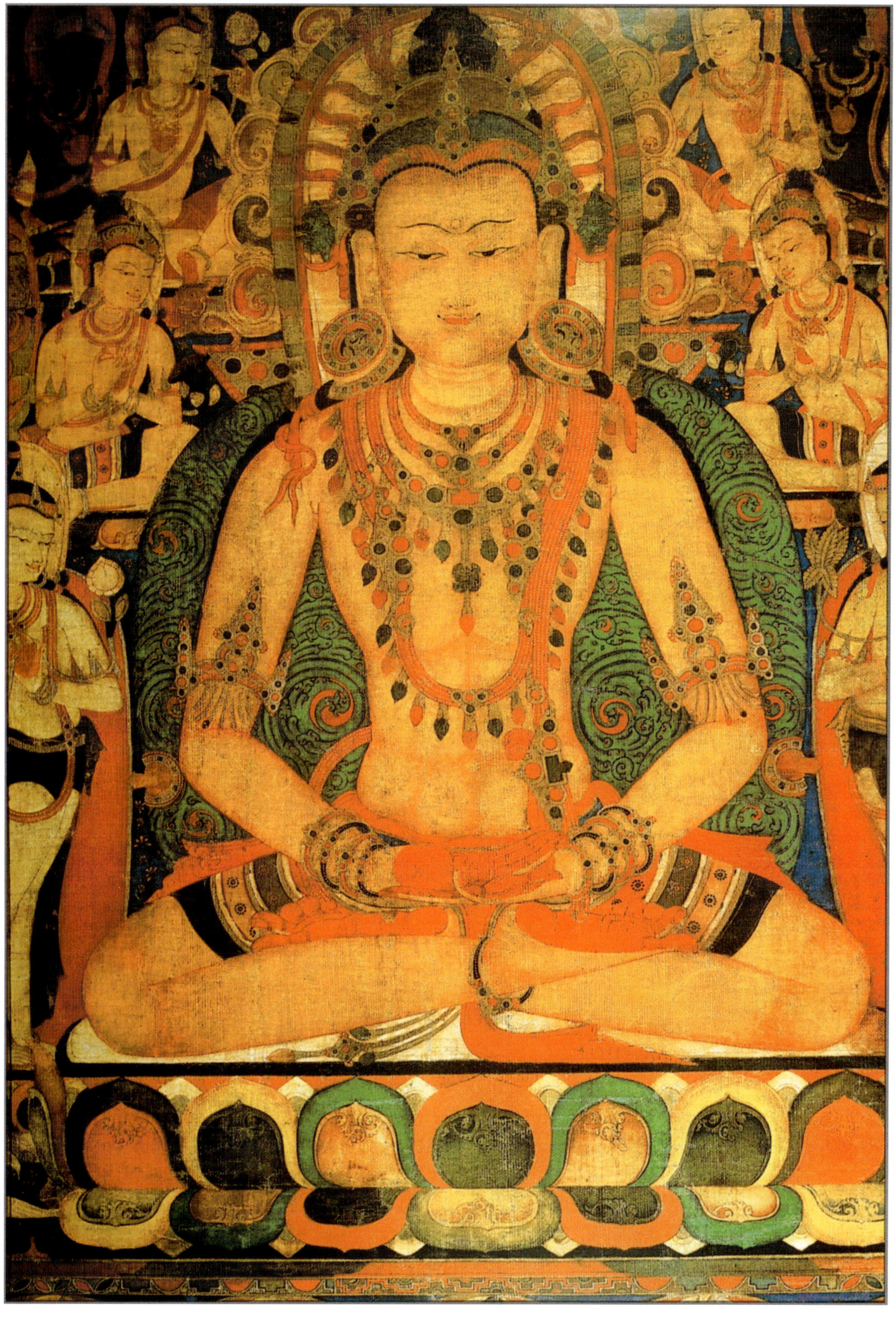

Amidaba. Then 'yu' and 'ba' were omitted resulting in the name 'Amida'.

It was quite common for priests to study sutras and use an image of Amitabha as an object of meditation. Different sutras were recognized as authorities by various sects. Generally speaking, Amitabha was worshipped in two aspects: as an ideal Buddha and as a living personality preaching in the western paradise. Belief in heavenly bliss of his paradise seems to have been budded forth in the early years. Devotion to Amitabha was primarily designed for prosperity in the present life. The paradise of Amitabha is painted on the western walls of temples where the departed souls sit on lotuses.

Visualization of the paradise of Amida is based on *Amitayurdhyana-sutra*, preached by Shakyamuni to Queen Vaidehi in Rajagrha. The idea of representing the Pure Land of Amitabha had originated in China where existed a strong faith in him among people of all classes. Pure Land mandalas were painted in Dunhuang caves a number of times. It became very popular under the Sung Dynasty (960-1279) among the people of both lay and religious societies. In Japan the most prosperous age for this mandala was from seventh to twelfth century. During the Nara period the emperors' families commissioned these representations. Horyuji murals present one such early examples.

Shakyamuni, Amitabha, Bhaishajyaguru and Maitreya come as a group in *Suvarnaprabhasa-sutra*. Amitabha is one of the four Buddhas in the *Mahakaruna-garbha-mandala*. Mahavairocana sits in the centre of the eight petalled lotus in the central mansion. On the eight petals of the lotus sit four Buddhas and four Bodhisattvas. Amitabha occupies the western petal of the central mansion.

Belief in Jodo or Pure Land in Japan can be traced back to the early sixth century AD. The first known reference appears in the writings attributed to Prince Shotoku-taishi, for whom the mandala of the Land of Heavenly Longevity was produced posthumously, after a vow had been made that his soul may rest in the heaven of Amitabha. During the early Nara period, priests of the Kegon, Hosso, and Sanron sects used to study the Pure Land sutras. Monk Chiko of the Sanron sect created a Pure Land Mandala after 640 A.D. Pure Land sect flourished later during the late Heian and Kamakura periods (ninth to thirteenth centuries).

Pure Land belief came to play an increasingly important role. An image of Amitabha was placed for the beginners to meditate attempting to visualize the Pure Land mentally. At an advanced stage the devotee was directed to meditate on the formless Amitabha.

Amitabha wears a monk's robes, has short curls, sits on a lotus, his face has a golden hue, the colour of autumn, which corresponds to west, gold also symbolizes plentitude and indestructibility. He sits in dhyana mudra with his hands resting on his lap with palms up, placed one upon the other. The last two phalanges of his index fingers are verticle and touching back to back. The thumbs come together with the tips touching index fingers. It is the mudra of meditation. The two hands represent two worlds. The left being the world of beings, the Matrix world, and the right the world of the Buddhas, the Diamond world. The right hand supports the left, showing that the world of Buddhas sustains the world of phenomena. The circle formed by the thumbs and the index fingers represent the perfection of Dharma in the two worlds, since the circle is a symbol of perfection. This mudra was attained by Shakyamuni when he was meditating under the Bodhi tree.

Sukhavati-vyuha-sutra expounded the nine grades of rebirth in the Pure Land. Several halls with images of nine forms of Amitabha as saviours of the nine levels of people were constructed.

PRECEDING PAGE, LEFT: *Amitabha flanked by two bodhisattvas – Padmapani Avalokiteshvara on his right and Vajrapani Mahasthamaprapta on his left, is sitting on a lotus seat in his paradise with Seven Buddhas and departed souls carved behind on the screen-like halo.*

PRECEDING PAGE, RIGHT: *Amitabha in his sambhogakaya form wears an elaborate crown and resplendent jewels mark him out in all regal splendour. He wears six ornaments – earrings, necklace, garland, armlets, wrist bands and anklets. He sits on a red lotus surrounded by eight bodhisattvas.*

FACING PAGE: *The paradise of Amitabha is painted according to Amitayurdhyana-sutra. Episodes of the life of Ajatashatru and Vaidehi are painted on the outer left court, thirteen meditations on the right and the lower court deals with three contemplations divided into nine stages that correspond to the nine possible degrees of birth in Sukhavati. The central sanctum is the vision of Queen Vaidehi with Amitabha at the centre.*

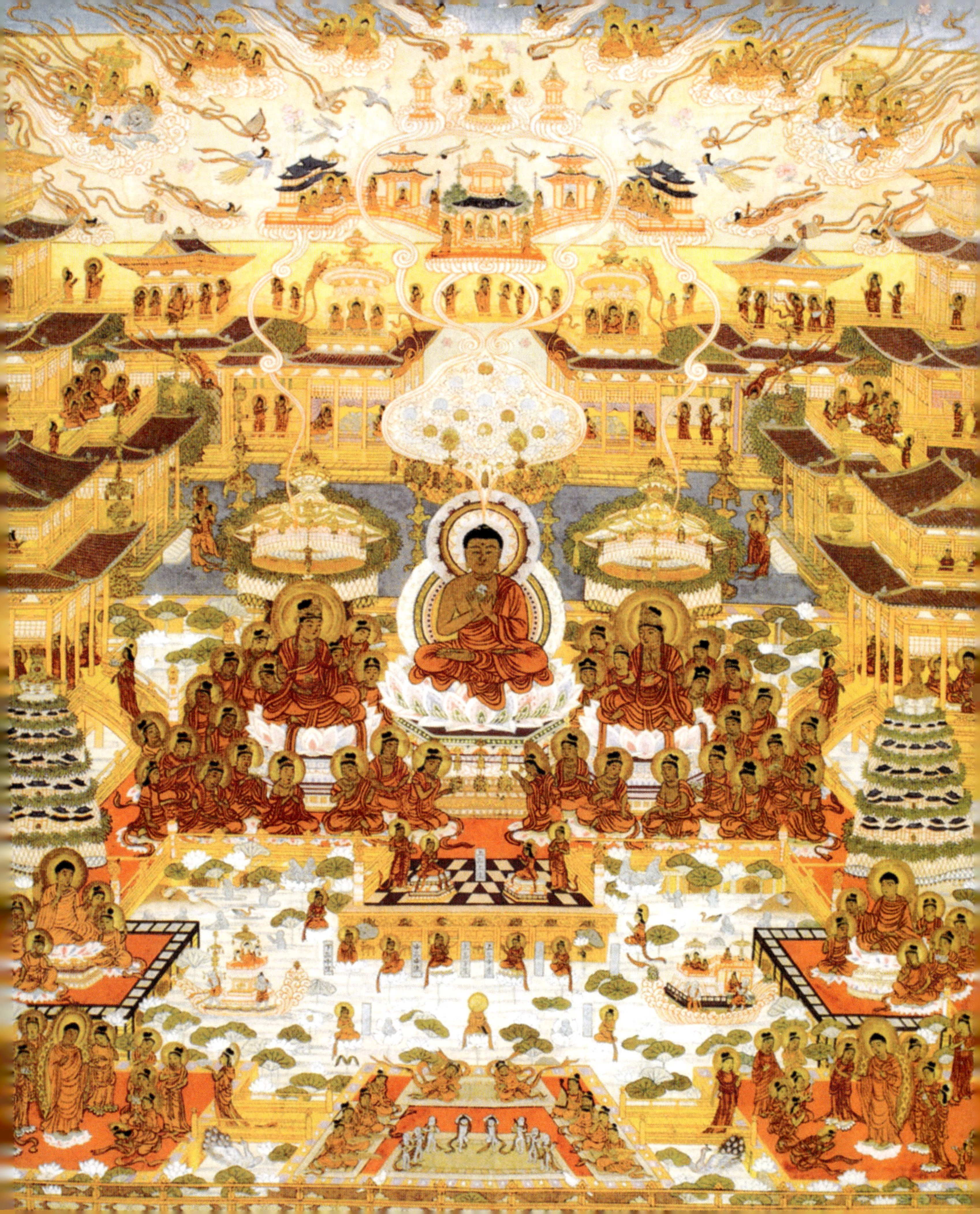

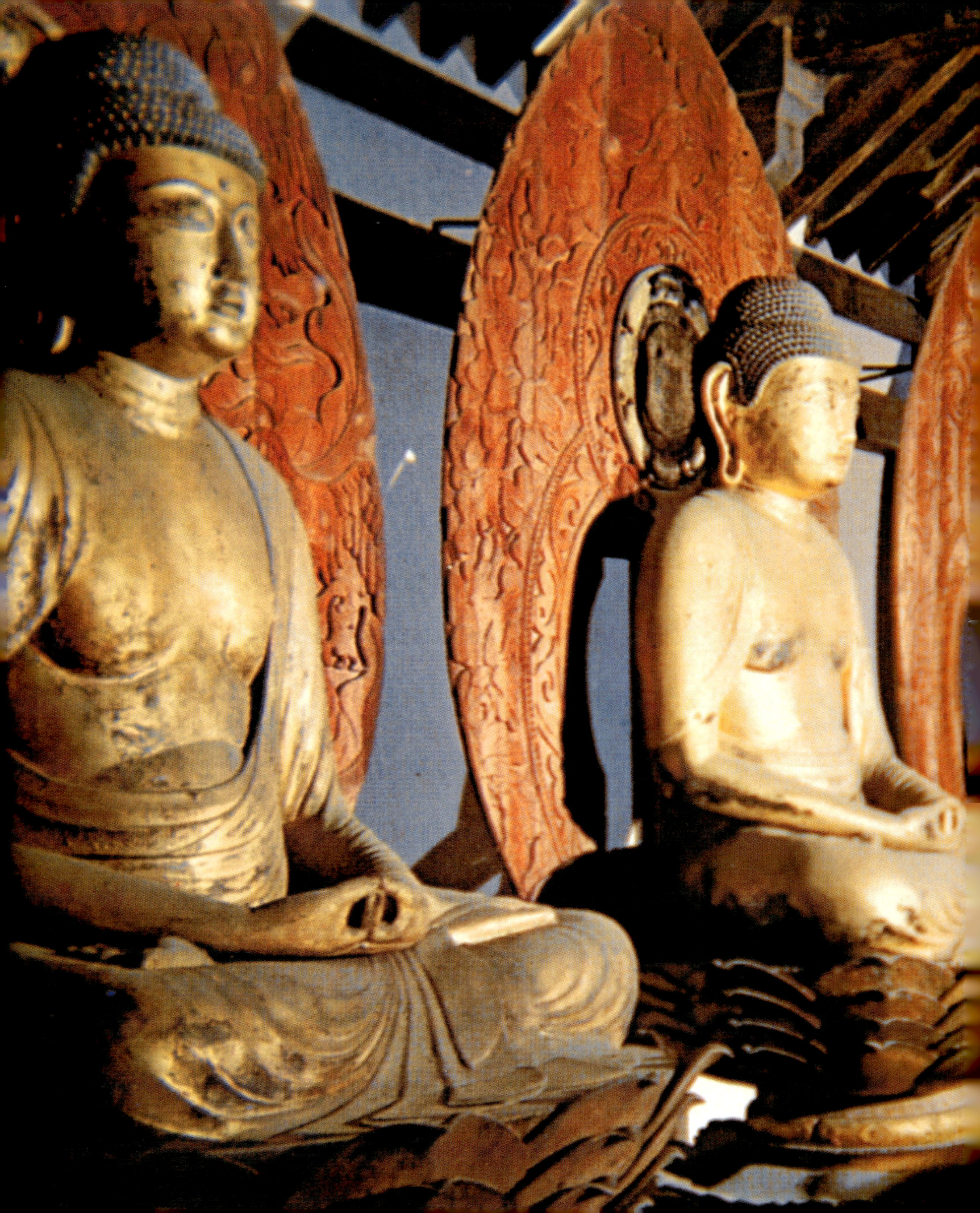

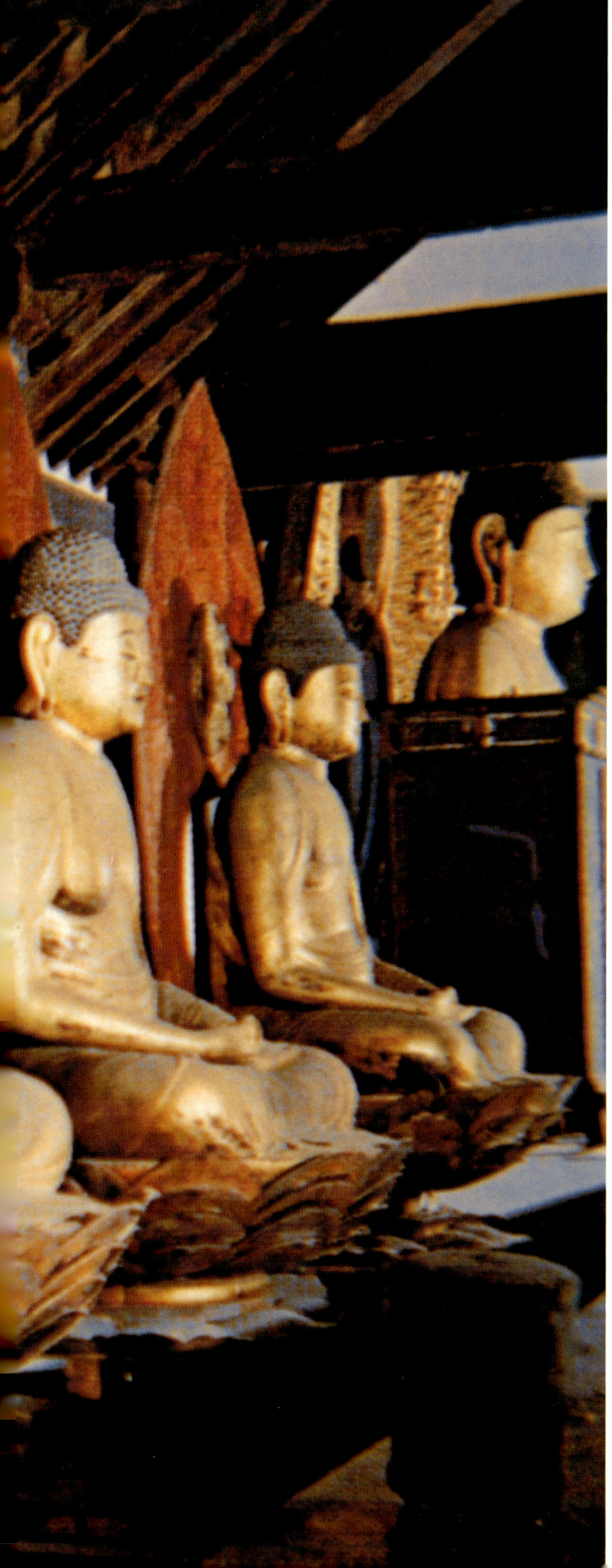

Faith in Pure Land was fostered by active monks in Japan. The statement about Amitabha's descent to receive the soul of the deceased became very influential inspiring painters who visualized the Buddha's descent from the heaven to receive the soul of the dying faithful into his Pure Land. It gave birth to a variety of such paintings. Amitabha is accompanied by twenty-five Bodhisattvas looking joyous and playing on musical instruments, holding banners, bringing materials for worship and Avalokiteshvara brings an empty lotus seat for the soul of the deceased to be flown back.

In the nine-fold sets of images of Amitabha he is envisioned as the saviour of the nine classes, the top degree is attributed to saints, the second to the virtuous beings and the third to sinners. Such a group is dominated by a large central figure, seated in dhyana mudra.

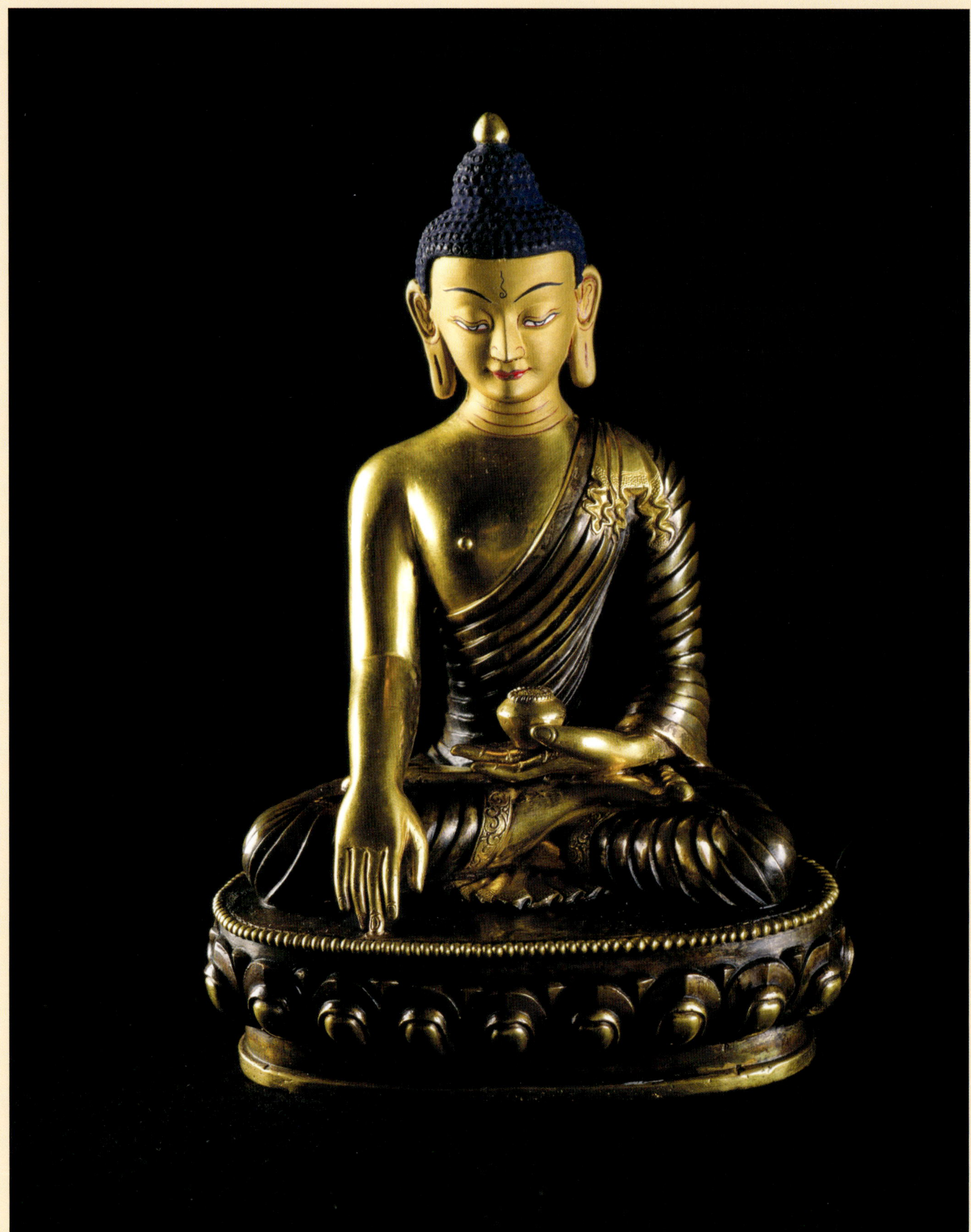

The Buddha of Healing

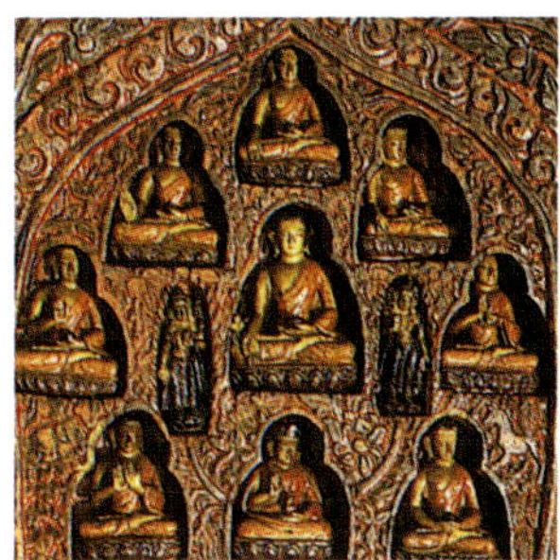

Healing Buddha wards off illnesses and disasters, and bestows longevity. Since illness tends to weaken the mind and causes to lose focus to one's function, proper treatment held a great importance for those who intend to achieve enlightenment. In Pali canon, Shakyamuni Buddha is portrayed as a great healer. The healing methods of the Buddha are two fold: through touch or through miraculous healing. The king of medicines is supposed to be Dharma, the Buddhist teachings in their fundamental and essential form because ignorance is spiritual ailment, which creates hinderances on the way to enlightenment. Devotion to Buddha took material shape in the creation of his images and temples. Paintings and sculptures play an important role in the ritual worship of the Buddha of Healing. The meaning of art is conveyed through the language of symbols, colours, gestures and attributes.

Mahayana texts composed between first century BC and first century AD mention Bhaishajyaraja and Bhaishajyasamudgata as the first major deities possessing the power of healing. Surangama-sutra refers to them as the King of Healing and Supreme Healer respectively. Translated into Chinese several times, Bhaishajyaguru sutra's earliest translation was done by Srimitra in AD 317-22. A monk from Central Asia, Kalayasas translated the sutra spoken by Buddha on the contemplation of Bhaishajyaraja and Bhaisajyasamudgata. Shakyamuni also taught a two stage contemplation on the King of Healing in which the increasing purity and spiritual accomplishment of the devotee qualifies him for more profound revelations.

The cult of Bhaishajyaguru was an important part of the proliferation of north-western ideas and perceptions in the main land of India. Indian tradition speaks of the *bhojakas* who were both healers and saviours. *Bhojakas* do not only mean those who feed the deity, but deduced from

ABOVE: *A carved medicine ritual panel shows Bhaishajyaguru seated in his paradise surrounded by the seven Medicine Buddhas, and the two medicine goddesses who dispel all diseases of cold and heat.*

FACING PAGE: *Bhaishajyaguru holds a medicinal pot in his left hand and performs the mudra of touching the earth with the right.*

the middle Iranian form *'bozak'*, it also means a healer or a saviour. The hygiene and medical skill of people from the northwest were well known since early antiquity.

Veneration to the Sun and Moon was a part of the cult of the Healing Buddha as they are symbols of eternity, nobility, purity and light. Faith in them gained prominence after translation of Sanskrit texts into Chinese. The concept seems to have come from the northwestern region of ancient India. Their first appearance as a pair is found on a dedicating casket offered by the Kushana Emperor Kanishka to the stupa at Shahji ki-dheri monastery built by him. On the side of the receptacle was shown the Buddha flanked in a subordinative way by the solar Mithra and lunar Mao. The pair Miro-Mao, Sun and Moon appear on some coins of Huvishka. The introduction of Iranian motifs in Buddhism seems to have increased during Kushana rule.

Two Bodhisattvas, Suryaprabha and Chandraprabha, acolytes of Bhaishajyaguru are counterparts of Iranian Rasnu (Skt. Rajna) and Sraosa (Skt. Srausa), companions of Mithra. His twelve generals are twelve *adityas* as solar aspects. Although not much is known regarding the origin of Bhaishajyaguru in India, his prototype Bhaishajyaraja bodhisattva plays a significant role in the Lotus-sutra as a healing Buddha. It is quite likely that the idea of Bhaishajyaguru was derived from the concept of historical Buddha as a healer or physician. He does not appear to have enjoyed the extent of popularity in India that he achieved in Japan. Bhaishajyaguru resides in his eastern Buddhaland, which is regarded by his devotees as a type of divine heaven and not as a realm of final liberation. It is Abhirati in the eastern direction where innumerable bodhisattvas dwell with him.

A large number of images of Bhaishajyaguru found from Central Asia are eloquent in their silence that his worship had attained great popularity. But no archaeological evidence could be traced in India to assure its existence. In the earlier phase it was not possible to identify Bhaishajyaguru on the basis of his attributes. Normally all the Buddhas were portrayed with different hand gestures without holding any attributes. Sometimes he sits with both his hands joined, placed in his lap with palms flat and tips of thumbs joined. The mudra is considered as dharmadhatu-dhyana-mudra or the hands can be said to be positioned as if ready to carry the medicinal pot. Another form given to Bhaishajyaguru is seen at the Horyuji temple, where his right hand is in the mudra of granting fearlessness, which brings appeasement and security while the left performs the wish granting mudra. When he performs the abhaya-mudra he might hold a pot with a lid in his left hand. Another mudra associated with Bhaishajyaguru is vitarka-mudra and the mudra of the union of the three worlds, which indicates that he protects the living beings of the three worlds from dangers. In still another form he performs abhaya-mudra with the right hand while the left placed in his lap with fingers turned towards the palm suggest that he is ready to hold a pot.

During the later phase of development a dodecagonal medicine bowl, made of a precious stone, lapiz lazuli found in Afghanistan, was added to the image. The twelve angles of his pot represent twelve vows taken by him to help and save human beings. He gave his parole not to attain Buddhahood before he fulfils these resolutions, for example to enlighten the world by the light radiated from his body, to make the bodies pure like *vaidurya*, to fulfil all the desires of human beings, to inspire and help human beings to attain enlightenment, to save them from hunger and thirst, to cure the poor and the sick by his own power, to help women reborn as men in order to attain salvation, to guide the strayed to the right path, to save everyone without difficulty or mishap, to procure good garments and decorations to the unclothed, to save human beings from misfortunes and difficulties to cure all injuries. The twelve generals standing around the Buddha guard these vows. They stand and watch an hour day and night. Each of the guards command himself seven thousand acolytes.

These twelve generals are: Kumbhira, Vajra, Mihara,

FACING PAGE: *Bhaishajyaguru imparts the knowledge of medicine to the seers, arhats and to Jivaka, his personal physician. He dwells in the innermost palace located on a mountain. Houses of the city are grouped around in concentric circles, surrounded by gardens of medicinal plants, pharmaceutical minerals and hot springs. Shakyamuni's ability to heal the deceased spirit and body was symbolized in the form of Bhaishajyaguru, whose paradise adhirati, is located to the east. According to Bhaishajyaguru-sutra, Bhaishajyaguru and his Buddha brothers are able to provide cures to specific illnesses, both physical or spiritual.*

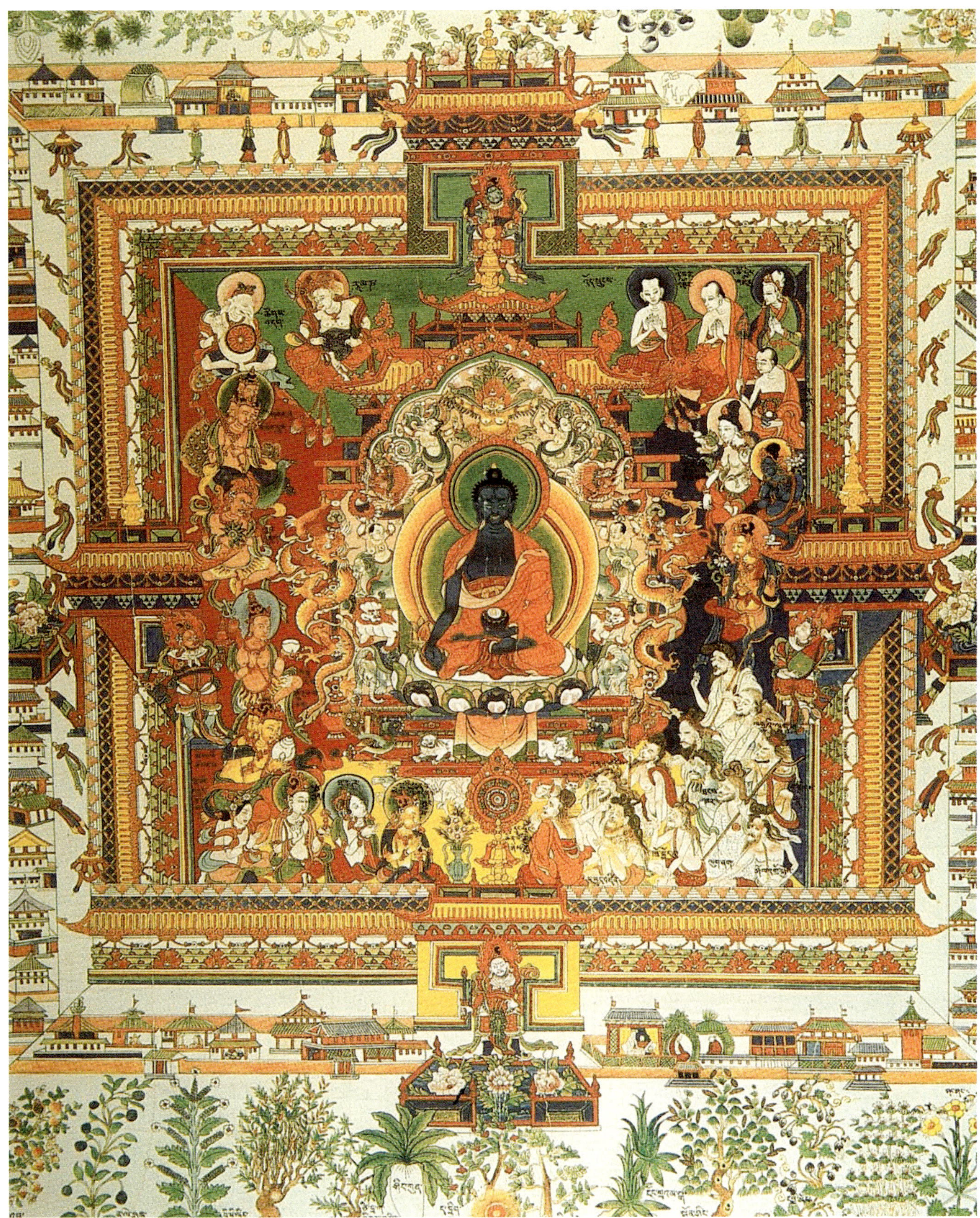

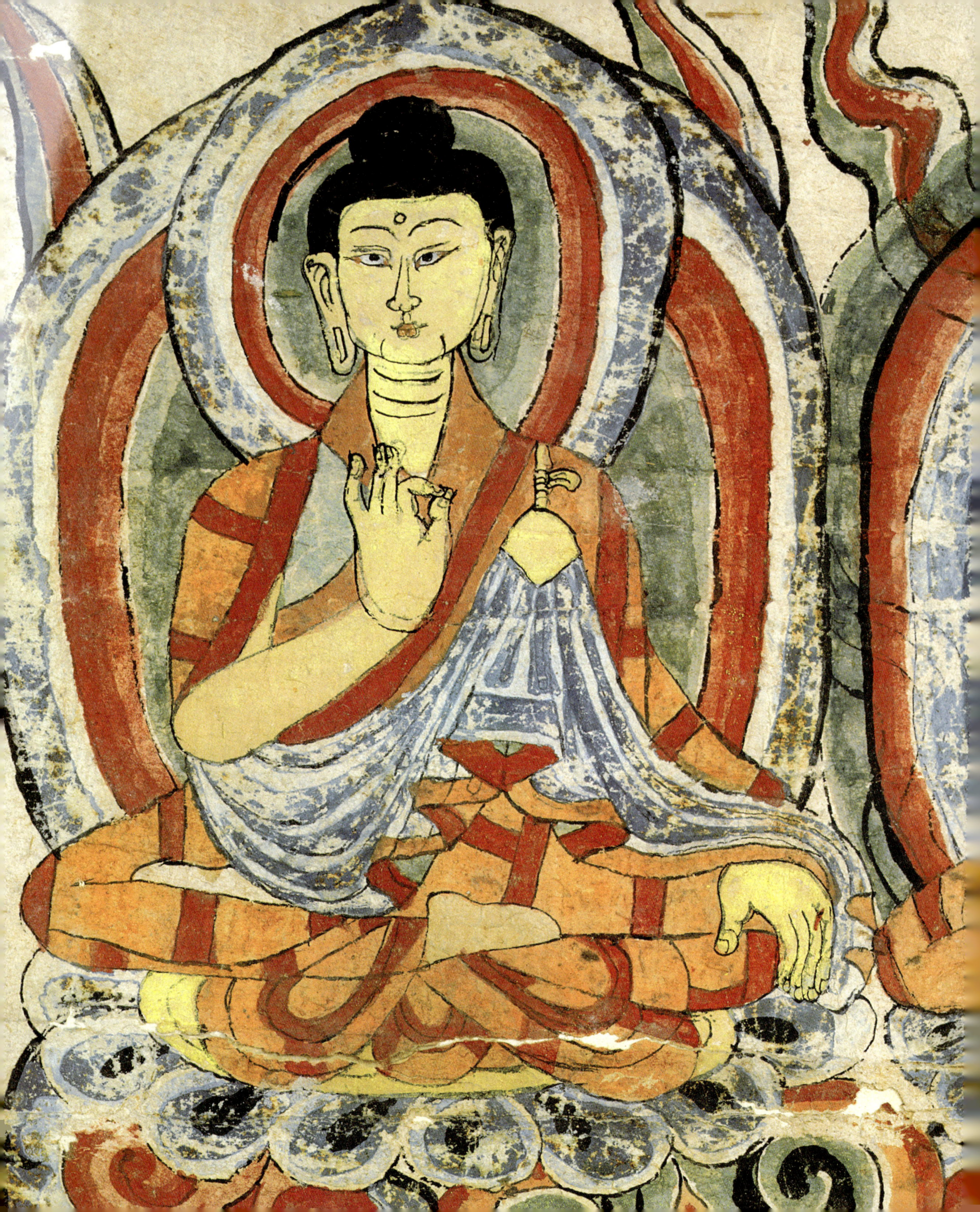

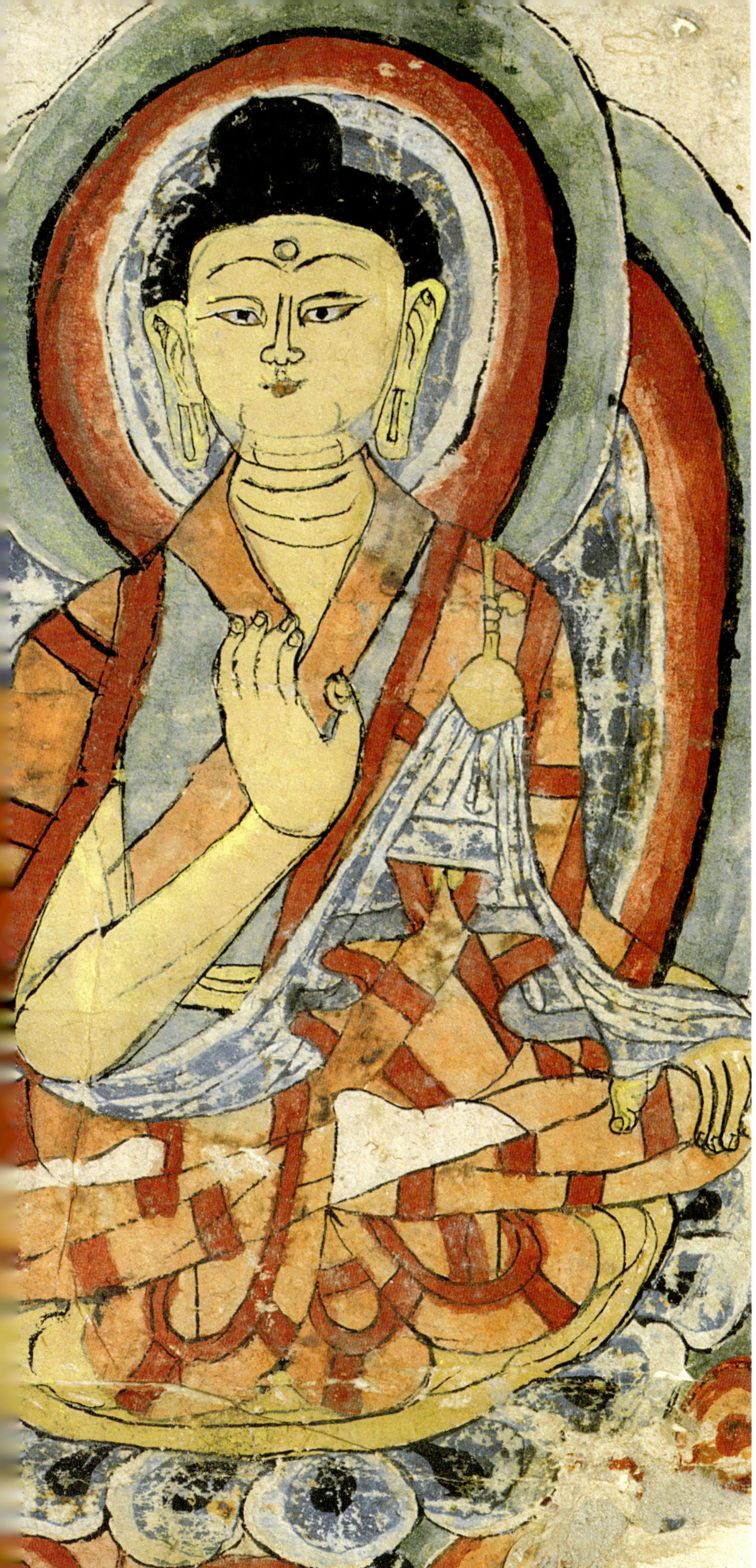

Bhaishajyaguru and his Buddha brothers are able to provide cures to specific illnesses.

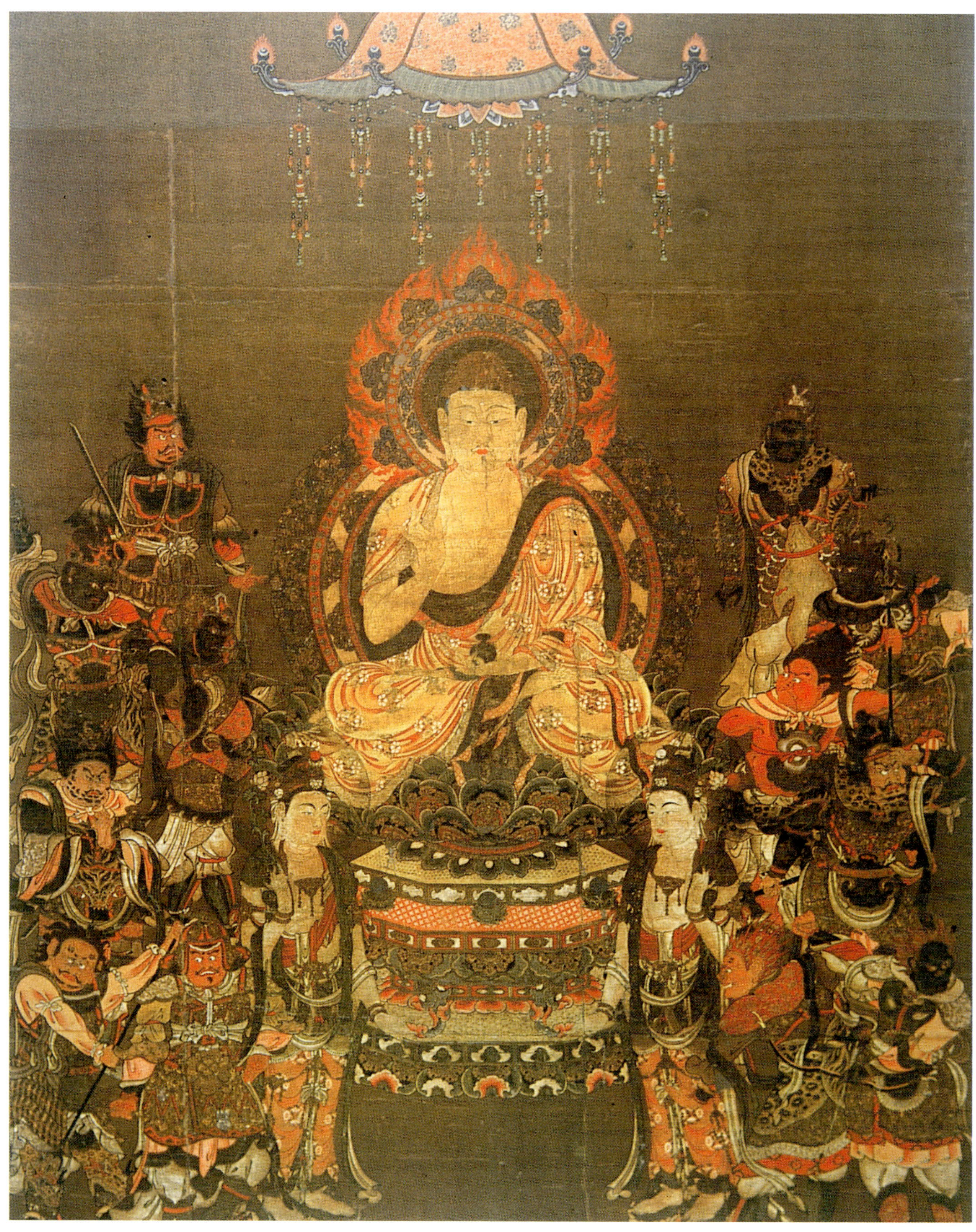

Andira, Majila, Candila, Indra, Makura, Payila, Sindura, Catura, and Vikarala. Each warrior commands himself seven thousand acolytes, which enables them to protect eighty-four thousand pores of skin. They are also called twelve *upasakas* of great virtues.

Bhaishajyaguru can be portrayed alongwith Amitabha and Gautama Buddha or as one of the four deities of Hosso sect – Amitabha, Shakyamuni, Maitreya and Bhaishajyaguru. Bhaishajyaguru is also counted among the five Dhyani Buddhas substituting either Vairocana or Akshobhya. He is also one of the thirteen Buddhas of the Shingon sect in Japan and is believed to look after the departed soul during the seventh week, after death. The finest bronze image of Bhaishajyaguru from the seventh and eighth centuries exists in a fine stage of preservation. During the subsequent epochs, devotion to Bhaishajyaguru continued to exist. Seven Medical Buddhas or Tathagatas were known in Tibet and China as seven emanations of Bhaishajyaguru. Itsing, a Chinese pilgrim explains in his translation of the sutra done in AD 707, that Bhaishajyaguru is the leader of the group of seven Buddhas. Tibetan tradition gives their names also as Vaidurya-prabha-raja, Dharmakirti-sagara, Abhijna-raja, Aksottama, Ratnachandra, Suvarnabhadra-vimala and Sunaman. They are supposed to have created seven medicinal plants to preside over the seven worlds. The farthest among them was of Bhaishajyaguru. In paintings, the seven medical Buddhas are usually grouped around Bhaishajyaguru who is looked upon as their chief. In this case he takes the golden colour. He is known as Manla in Tibet and may be represented as a Buddha or a bodhisattva. When portrayed as a Buddha, he has an *urna*, *ushnisha*, short curls and other characteristics of an ascetic. He wears a five-leaved crown and other usual ornaments when portrayed as a Bodhisattva. In this form he is normally found in paintings and not in bronze sculptures. On the contrary, in China he wears a bodhisattva crown, is dressed like a Buddha and wears very few ornaments. His symbols and mudras are the same as they are when he appears in the form of a Buddha. Painted blue in colour, his altar is decorated with precious things with his statue erected in the middle. All of them bear their symbolic attributes in their crowns.

While venerating Bhaishajyaguru with offerings one should meditate upon the medicinal pot, the twelve mystic remedies and the twelve great resolutions that mitigate sufferings of all human beings. He is prayed for four motives – to invoke protection while in danger, against maladies, at the time of childbirth, and during a journey. Prayers are to be accompanied by the following rites: forty-nine oriflames of five colours are lifted and forty-nine candles are lit.

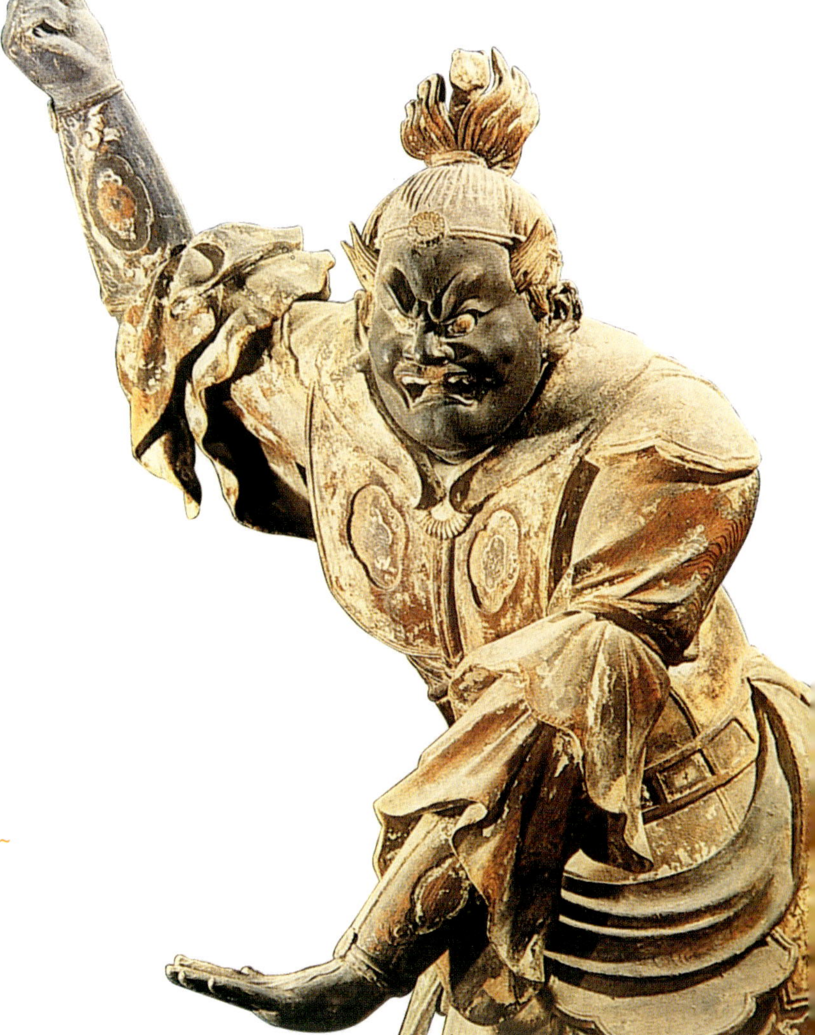

FACING PAGE: *Bhaishajyaguru is accompanied by two bodhisattvas and twelve generals while residing in his paradise. The Yaksa generals watch an hour day and night standing around guarding the vows taken by the Buddha.*

RIGHT: *Basara Taisho, one of the twelve generals, standing around Bhaishajyaguru at the Kofukuji monastery in Japan.*

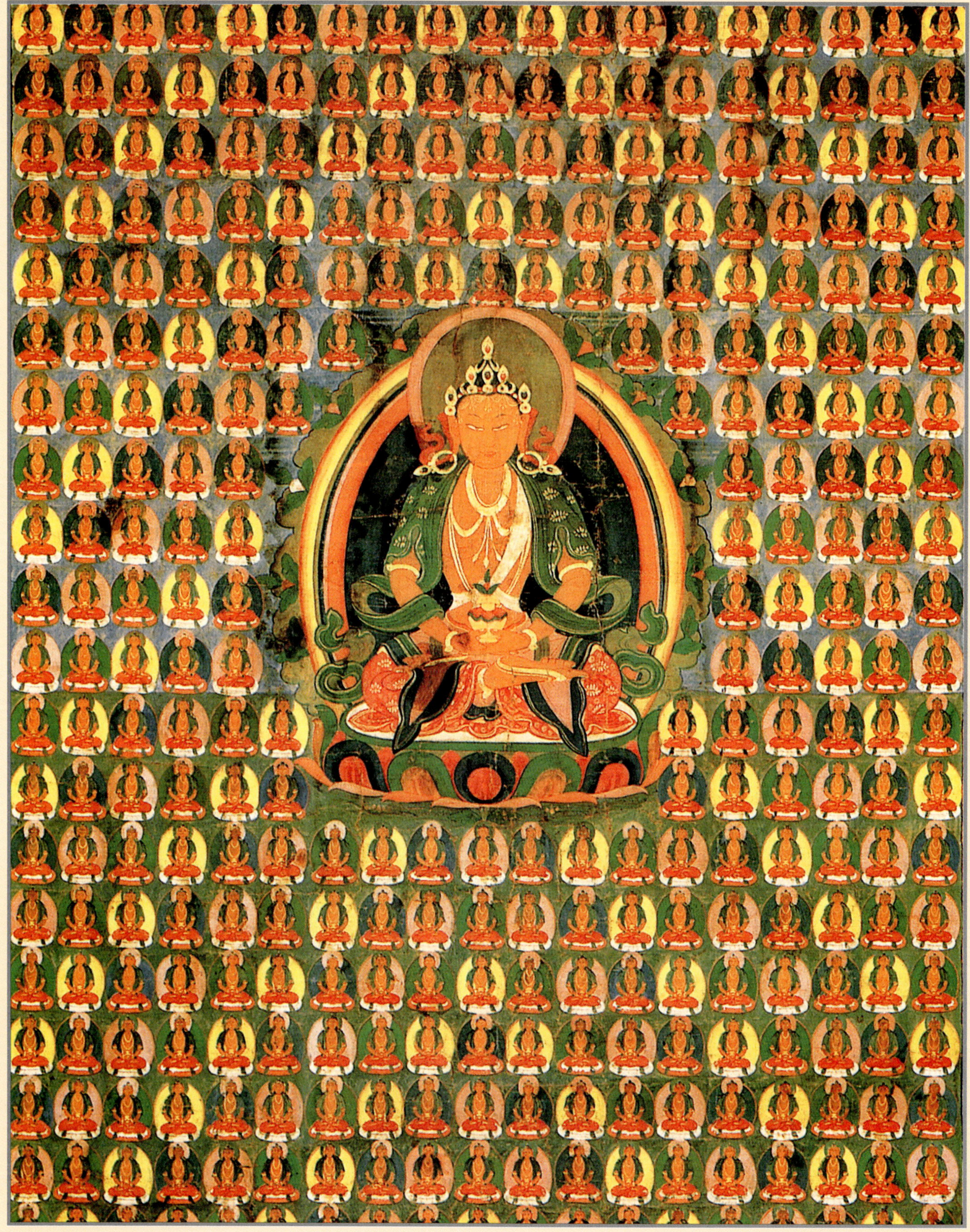

The Buddha of Longevity

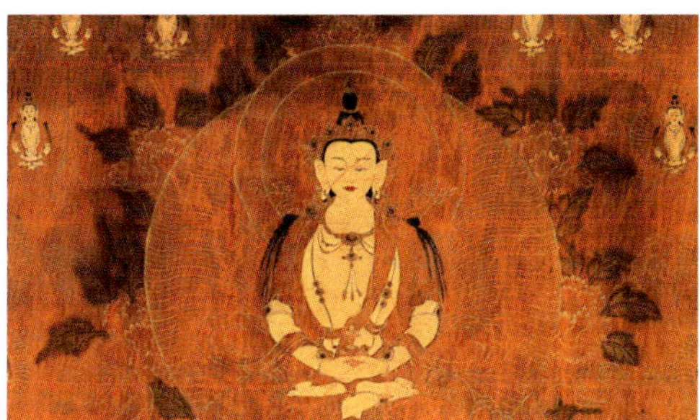

Amitayus is a Buddha parallel to but independent of Amitabha. In Japanese art, Amitabha and Amitayus both are identified as Amida, using the two theonyms synonymously. Both are shown in monastic robes without any ornaments. In Shingon tradition Amitabha occurs in the Vajradhatu-mandala and Amitayus in the Mahakarunagarbha-mandala. In Tibetan tradition he has been clearly distinguished from Amitabha both iconographically and philosophically.

Amitayus bestows long life, heals and sets the devotee free from all sins. He holds a vase of ambrosia in his hands in the dhyana mudra. Leaves of the Ashoka tree (Saraca indica) often sprout from the vase. He wears a diadem and royal ornaments. His colour is deep red and hair is blue.

Amitayus is invoked to cure a person in ill health but on his death he goes to the paradise of Amitabha. Amitayus has no specific heaven. Amitayus is confused with Amitabha in Japanese tradition but in Tibetan Buddhsim the two are clearly distinguished.

Painted scrolls of images of Amitayus are found in abundance in Tibet and Mongolia because of the firm faith of the people in his powers of prolonging life as its absolute symbol. A sacrament to Amitayus is celebrated on an auspicious day. People throng to temples to receive blessings. Mandalas of Amitayus are integral to longevity rites. In these rites, a mandala, a golden or gilded statue, a scripture and a golden or gilded stupa pertaining to Amitayus are placed on the altar as the three mysteries of body, speech and mind. Water is kept in a vase to be consecrated.

Amitayus or infinite life is a deity parallel to but independent of Amitabha. In the Tibetan tradition he has been clearly distinguished from Amitabha both iconographically and philosophically. Amitayus is *sambhogakaya* while Amitabha is *nirmanakaya*.

ABOVE: *Amitayus with immortality nectar vase, seated on a lotus. This special kind of thangka meant for longevity ceremonies is painted with gold on a red-ochre background. Late eighteenth century.*

FACING PAGE: *Amitayus or the Buddha of Limitless Life, seated on a lotus pedestal with a vase of ambrosia. Thangka commissioned to assure longevity. Late eighteenth or early nineteenth century.*

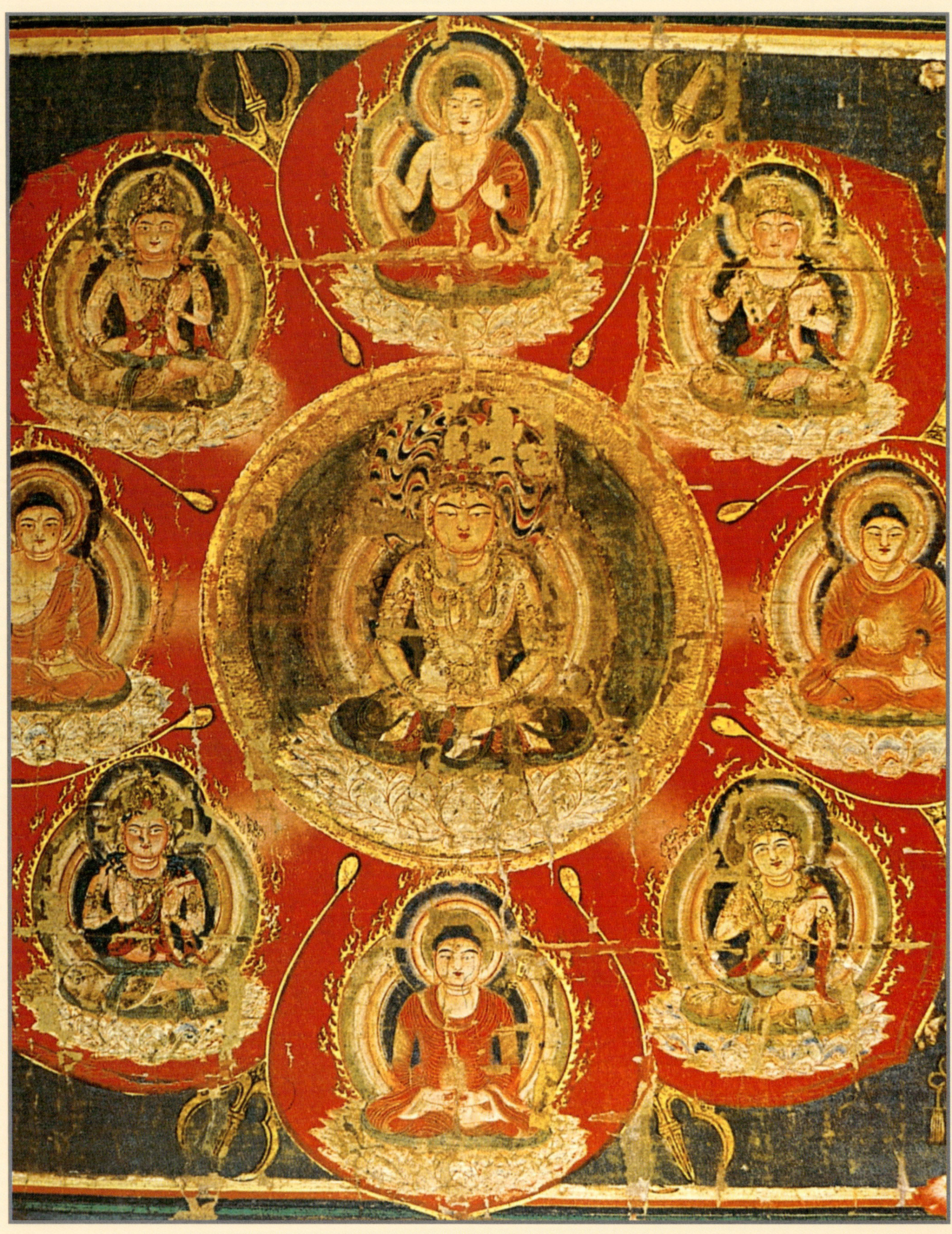

Five Tathagatas

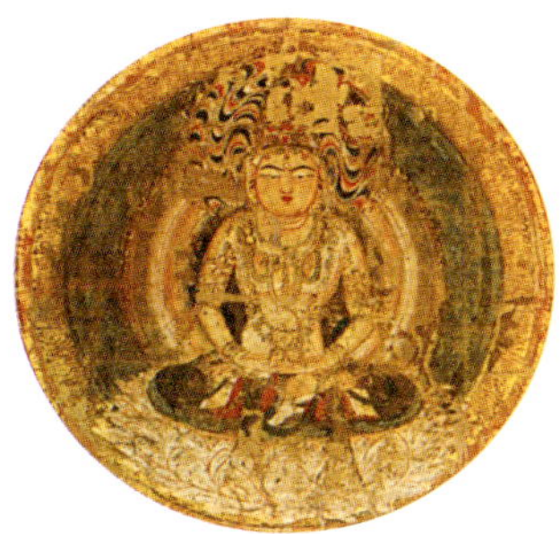

The two mandalas: Mahakarunagarbha-mandala and the Vajradhatu-mandala are pictorial representation of reality – relative and absolute. To the eye of an unenlightened these two are separate and irreconcilable, but to the eye of a Buddha they are inseparable faces of a single truth. Mahakarunagarbha-mandala, or the mandala of birth from the matrix of great compassion, is also known as matrix-, lotus- and the mandala of form. Subhakarasimha, a buddhist teacher, maintains that matrix mandala primarily signifies the progressive stages in the spiritual progress of the being towards buddhahood. There are several forms of this mandala drawn over the centuries but the one that is almost exclusively found in the Shingon temples in Japan today is the Genzu version, modeled on the mandala brought by Kobodaishi from China in the early part of the ninth century.

Garbhadhatu-mandala or the mandala of the Matrix world is constituted of twelve sections. The central section has an eight petaled red or white lotus with a central dais. Mahavairocana Tathagata is seated at the centre, on pericarp of a lotus. Four Tathagatas and four Bodhisattvas sit around him in the four directions and four cardinal points. Ratnaketu is in the east, which is the uppermost petal, Sankusumitaraja in the south, Amitayus to the west, and Divya-dundubhi-nirghosha to the north. The heads of eight golden, three-pronged vajras appear in the interstices between the eight petals. Lotus is the mind of the Buddha and represents compassion; vajra is the diamond thunderbolt, the symbol of knowledge that crushes illusions. The eight petals of lotus and the eight vajras together symbolize perfect union of compassion and knowledge.

The central mansion is the paradigm of the whole mandala and it embodies the *bodhicitta* as cause, great

ABOVE: *Mahavairocana sitting in dharma-dhatu-dhyan-mudra, the posture of dharma world meditation as the central figure in the Mahakarunagarbha-mandala.*

FACING PAGE: *Five Tathagatas of the mandala of the matrix world or Mahakarunagarbha-mandala, popularly known as Garbhadhatu-mandala form the central sanctum with Mahavairocana in dhyana mudra sitting at the centre with four Buddhas in the four directions and four bodhisattvas in the cardinal points.*

compassion as root, and method as the supreme end. These three *padas* expand to give a five-fold order of progress: quickening of mind, practice, awakening, entry into *nirvana* and method as the supreme end. Mahavairocana embodies quickening of *bodhicitta*, Ratnaketu embodies practice, Sankusumitaraja is awakening, Amitayus is entry into *nirvana*, and Divya-dundubhi-nirghosha embodies method as the final end. This schema of correlation is given in descending order.

MAHAVAIROCANA

Mahavairocana is the infinite, unbounded and supreme Tathagata. He is the origin of all the Buddhas whence they arise. He is non-dual container of both Buddhas and the phenomena of Buddhas and beings. Mahavairocana Tathagata, translated into Japanese as *Dainichi Nyorai*, means Great Sun Tathagata. He transcends all limitations. Whereas the light of the physical sun comes and goes, the light of the sun of wisdom shines brilliantly at all times and in all places. The light of the Tathagata of Great Sun shines throughout the *dharma* world and causes the root of virtue in all beings to quicken and grow.

Mahavairocana sutra describes Mahavairocana in the matrix world as sitting on a white lotus and crowned with a brilliantly white hair-knot crown. He wears a silk lion cloth; has a gold coloured body encircled by flames and sits in the dharma world meditation (dharmadhatu-dhyana-mudra), indicating that he is free from heat of passions. His whole body radiates a light of many hues. The right hand is held by the left hand and the thumbs are joined forming a triangle. The triangle is the female sexual organ, since this is the seal of the Matrix that gives birth to Buddhas.

RATNAKETU

Ratnaketu is the Tathagata of Jewel Pennant. He sits on the eastern petal of the lotus in the central mansion of Mahakaruna-garbha-mandala. He has a ruddy appearance, the colour of newly risen sun. His pennant symbolizes quickening of the *bodhicitta*. It is like a pennant of a general who uses it to rally various sections of his great army hosts, when leading them into a battle, thus defeating the enemy and winning great renown. When the Tathagata showed the pennant of his vows of total wisdom beneath the bodhi tree, he defeated the four demons.

In the mandala of the Matrix World he is shown with a light yellow body and wearing a dark red *kashaya* (silk) with right shoulder bare, which is a mark of respect paid to the teacher and to the Buddha at the time of the first quickening of the *bodhicitta*. His right hand makes *varada* or a vow-granting mudra with the arm bent at the elbow so that the hand is at chest level, palm upward and with the fingers extended and pointing outwards away from the body. This signifies bestowing of the compassionate vow of the *bodhicitta* upon beings. The left hand is held in front of the chest and holds the two corners of his robe, which represents the Dharma: the gesture shows his grasp over it. He sits in lotus posture on a jewel lotus.

SANKUSUMITARAJA

Opening flower king Tathagata, sits on the southern petal of the lotus in the central mansion of Mahakaruna-garbha-mandala. In the schema of descending conversions he represents awakening and in the older forms of the mandala he makes the mudra of vow granting which symbolizes bestowing of vows and the gift of the Truth of the Dharma. Open hand and extended fingers signify flowering of this truth and the consequent awakening. His body is of the colour of gold, shining with an all-illuminating light symbolizing that he abides in the *samadhi* of freedom from defilements. He wears a dark red *kashaya* (silk) with both shoulders covered. This is the form taken by the Buddhas when they undertake the work of cleansing – removing the attachments of beings of inferior spiritual capacity.

Beginning with the seed of the *bodhicitta* at the centre he long cultivated the ten thousand practices of Great Compassion and has now attained the universal awakening and reveals his ten thousand virtues. This is the reason why he is called Opening Flower Tathagata. Freedom from defilement means the Great Void and his awakening to the Great Void is like gold that has been purified. This is why his body is golden. In the schema of the Mahakaruna-garbha-mandala he represents practice.

FACING PAGE: *The qualities of Amitayus are symbolized by his crown and jewels, the ornaments worn by a complete enjoyment body. He is sitting in lotus posture with hands joined in his lap in the gesture of contemplation, holding the vase.*

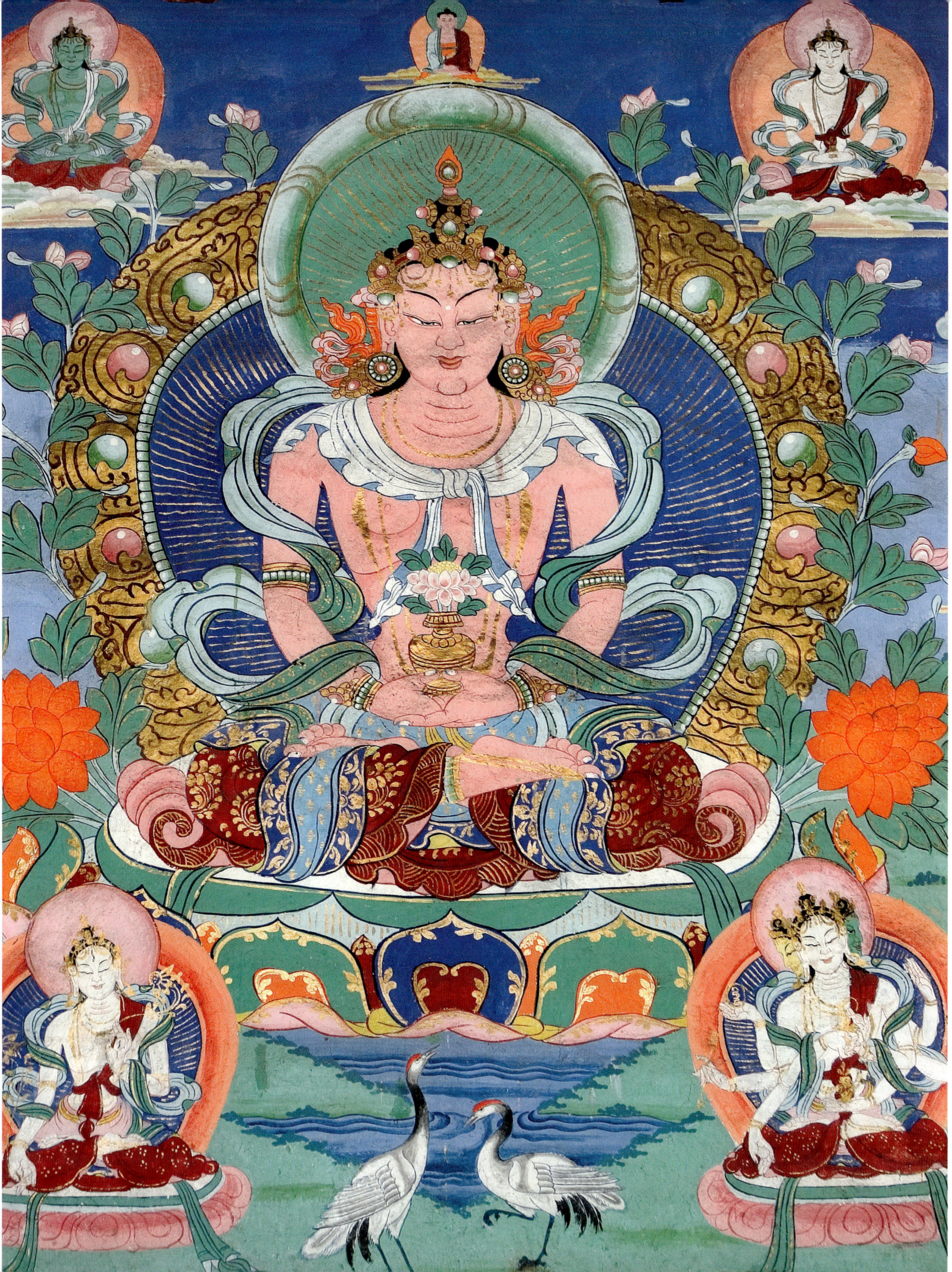

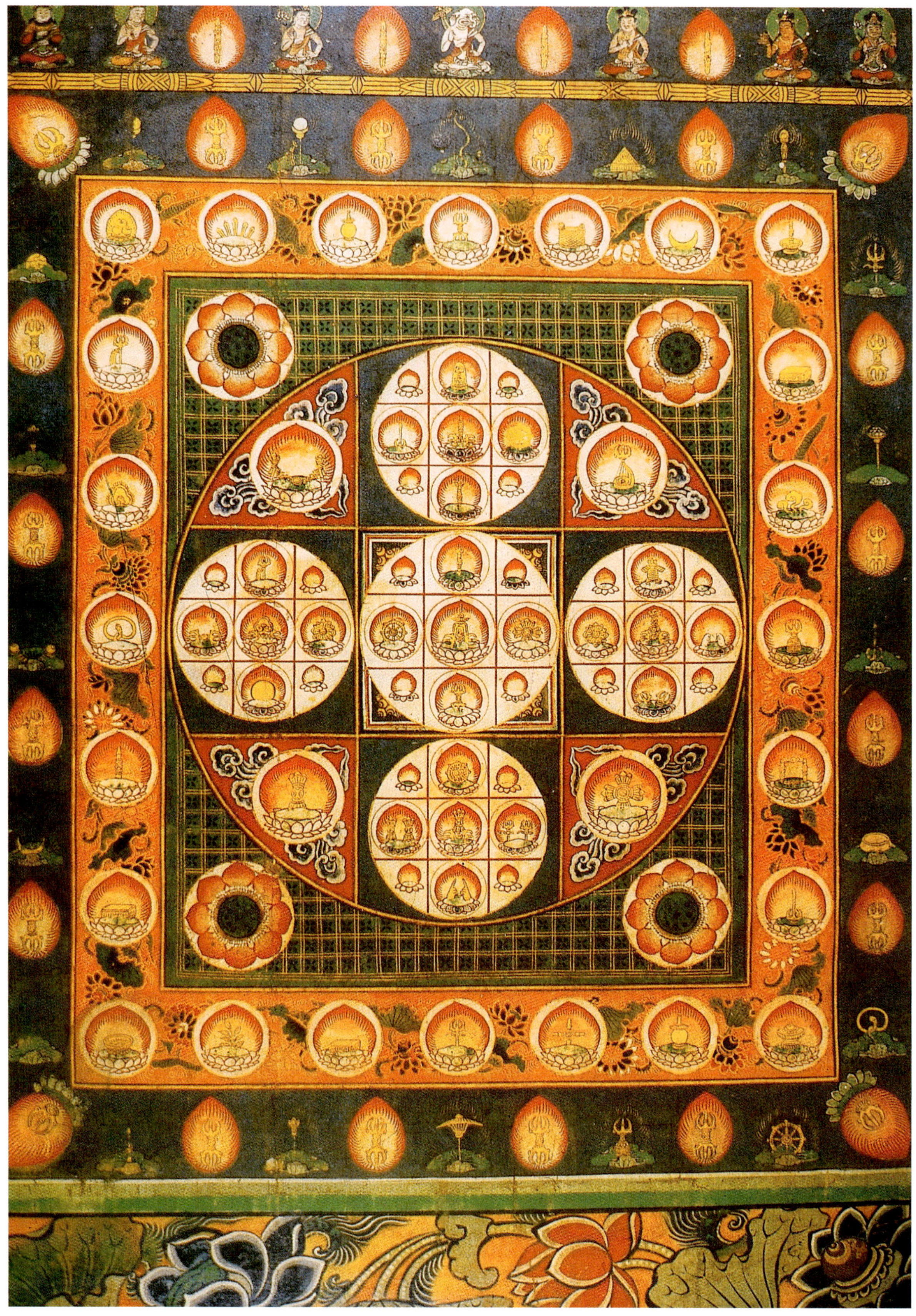

AMITAYUS

Amitayus is the Tathagata of immeasurable or infinite life. He occupies the western petal of the central mansion of Mahakaruna-garbha-mandala. According to the sutra he does not relinquish his vow of compassion. When his immeasurable light shines upon the *sadhaka*, all his grave sins and hindrances of *karma* are nullified. He is said to be the Tathagata of the knowledge of method. He is called 'Immeasurable Life' because just as the worlds of beings are inexhaustible so likewise is the method of great compassion of all the Buddhas. He represents entry into *nirvana* in the five descending conversions and awakening in the ascending conversions. Exoteric sutras describe his previous births as King Aranemi and a monk called Dharmakara. Dharmakara had a vision of twenty-one millions of Buddha lands.

Amitayus embodies Mahavairocana's knowledge of subtle perception, which contemplates the subtle distinctions of various spiritual capacities of beings. He preaches the dharma, cutting away doubts and revealing to devotees the lotus like principle and the purity of their fundamental nature. In the form of Buddha, he is shown seated in a lotus posture on a jewel lotus. He wears red *kashaya* with both shoulders covered, which signifies that he embodies the virtue of method, the functioning of the Buddha in the world of beings. He tucks up his robes to work among the unenlightened.

He performs dhyana mudra with his hands placed in the lap. The two hands represent the two worlds, the left being the world of beings, the matrix world and the right being the world of Buddhas, the daimond world. The right hand supports the left hand, showing that the world of Buddhas sustains the world of phenomena. Two phalanges of the index fingers are vertical and touch back to back. The thumbs come together to the tips of index fingers forming two circles. The circles symbolize perfection of the dharma in the two worlds.

DIVYADUNDUBHI-MEGHA-NIRGHOSHA

Tathagata of the Sound of the Celestial Drum sits on the northern petal of lotus in the central mansion of the Matrix World. He is formless and without location and yet able to give out the sound of the Dharma for the quick understanding of sentient beings. He resides in serene meditation in the north, embodies the virtue of *nirvana*, for which Buddha acts by preaching the Dharma. This activity is compared to the sounding of a celestial drum, whose thunderous reverberations throb through all the worlds. Because of this resonance he is called 'Thunderous Sound of the Celestial Drum'.

He is represented with golden colour body, wearing a dark red *kashaya*, with the right shoulder uncovered, as a sign that he has attained the *nirvana* of no fixed abode. He sits in full lotus posture upon a jewel lotus. He holds his left hand palm upward and below the navel. His right hand makes bhumi-sparsha mudra.

FACING PAGE: *Samaya mandala, second among the nine sections of Vajradhatu mandala visualizes Buddhas and Bodhisattvas in their symbolic form in place of anthropomorphic images, such as vajras, jewels and lotuses.*

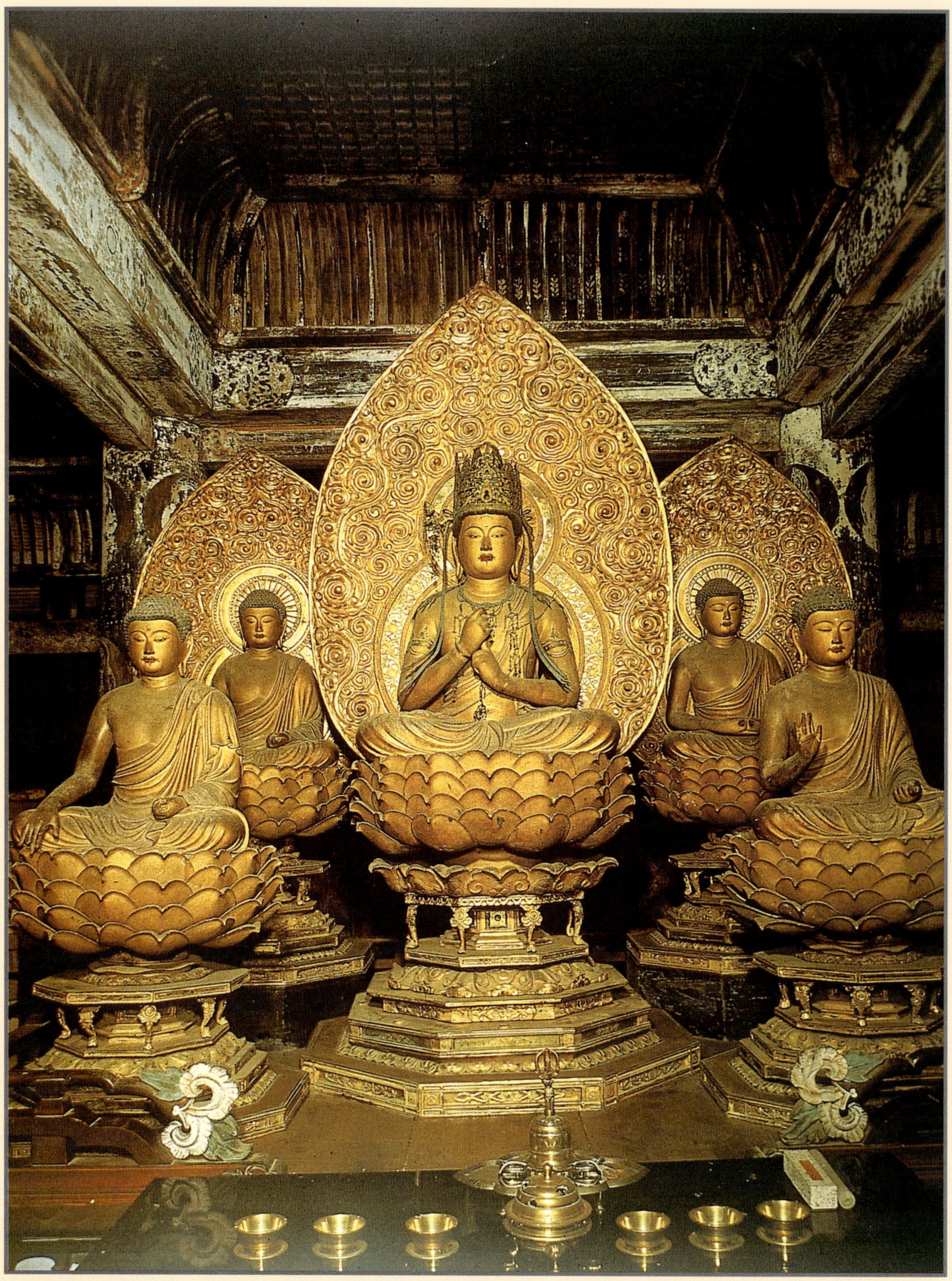

Five Transcendental Buddhas

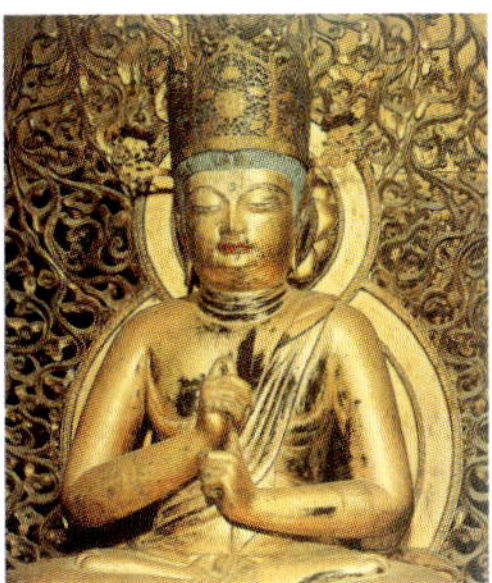

MAHAVAIROCANA: Mahavairocana sits at the centre in the Vajradhatu-mandala, as the first among the Five Transcendental Buddhas divided into nine parts, surrounded by Four Paramitas: Vajra-paramita, Ratna-paramita, Dharma-paramita, and Karma-paramita. He wears a crown of Five Tathagatas and ornaments in the first three sections and in the fourth, wears monastic garments. His ride in the first section is seven lions in the central mandala and in the other three he sits on lotus seats. It symbolizes that Vairocana has the power to manifest himself without obstruction, as lion is the king of beasts, who roams everywhere fearlessly.

He represents the light of supreme wisdom making the mudra of supreme enlightenment, called *bodhyagri* or *jnanamushti,* which symbolizes his capability of destroying ignorance and errors of heart attached to desire. He attains perfect illumination in the palace of Akanishtha heaven and is white like pure moon. His mandala is encircled by thousand buddhas of Bhadrakalpa, thirty-three deities form his entourage and the wisdom that destroys illusions, the feminine symbolism, introduced in the form of deities of transcendental perfection.

This particular form ofVairocana can be further seen in three different manifestations – *sambhogakaya, dharmakaya* and *nirmanakaya.* In *sambhogakaya* form he wears a crown and ornaments, sits on a seat of single or seven lions or on a lotus seat and dwells in the Akanishtha heaven. As the *dharmakaya* manifestation, he may be crowned or adorned by vajras and sits on a lotus seat. In the *nirmanakaya* form he is dressed in monk's garments and sits on a lotus. He has four faces. According to Nishpannyogavali, Vairocana sits on a lion in a pavilion atop Mount Sumeru. The pavilion rises within a vajra enclosure, towering over the seven seas, continents and their sub-continents.

ABOVE: *Vairocana, the first among the five transcendental Buddhas in the Vajradhatu-mandala is the central deity.*

FACING PAGE: *Mahavairocana performing the mudra of supreme enlightenment, bodhyagri mudra, wearing ornaments and crown, is surrounded by other four transcendental Buddhas of the Vajradhatu-maha-mandala: Akshobhya, Ratnasambhava, Amitabha and Amoghasiddhi.*

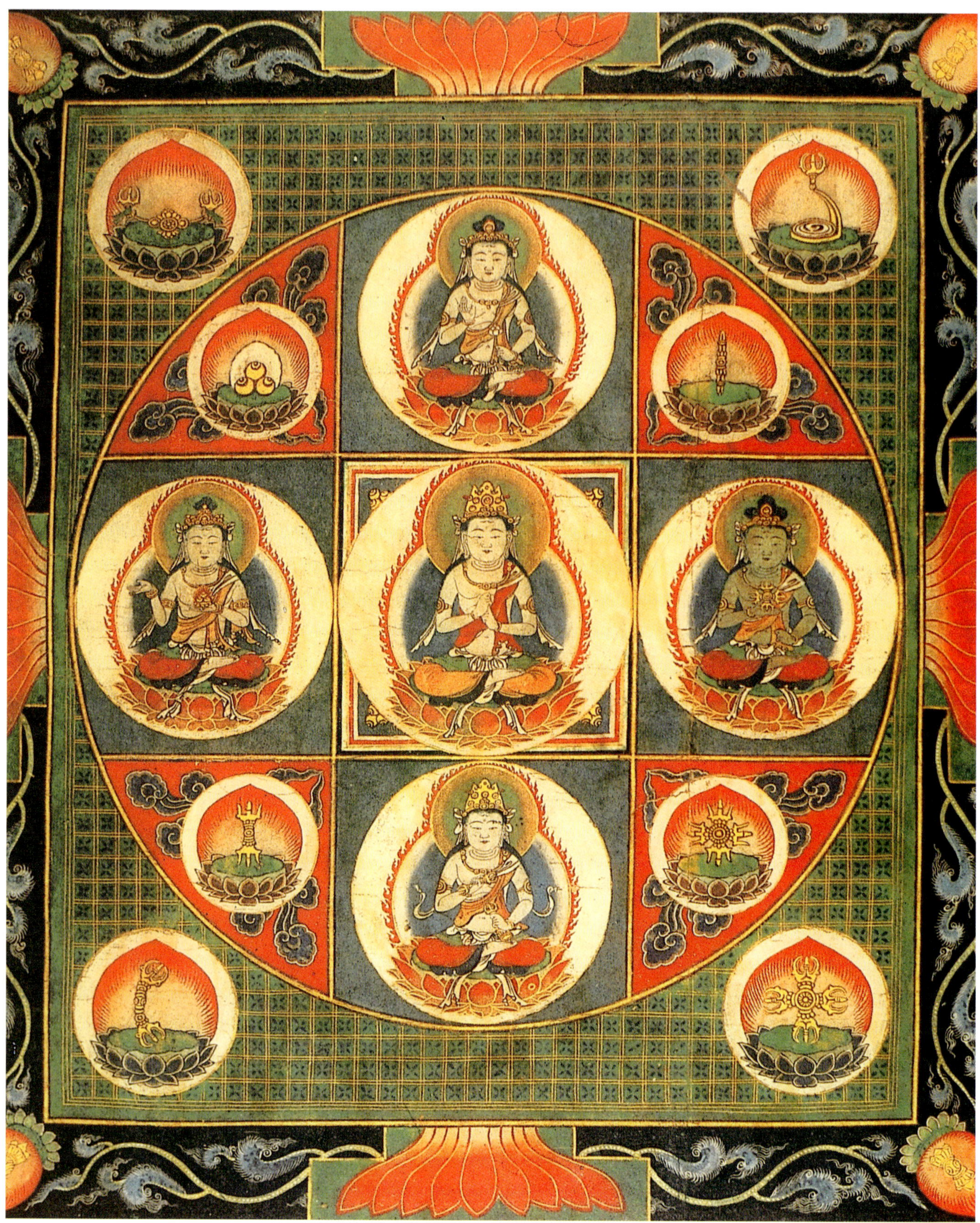

AKSHOBHYA

Akshobhya is one of the five Buddhas representing five stages of enlightenment. The name Akshobhya means one who is without anger, a Buddha who is firm, unshakable, namely the adamantine state of being, its quintessential nature, beyond all becoming. He is a depersonalized substitute of Shakyamuni, like Amitabha. His abode is called Abhirati, situated in the eastern direction. Whoever is born there, attains the degree of 'without regression'. According to a sutra dedicated to Akshobhya, women play an essential role in his paradise where he preaches the dharma to them; their jewels are talked about with frequent allusions, and childbirth is described with a profusion of unusual details.

He performs the mudra of calling the earth to witness because he originated as a symbol of the unchangeableness of a Buddha's condition. When supreme enlightenment has been achieved, he who sought it can never leave possession of it. His name symbolizes immutable firmness of the mind of *bodhi*, a firmity equal to that of vajra. Akshobhya is also one of the five manifestations of cosmic consciousness in its creative principle as he holds a vajra as a symbol. His vehicle is an elephant, a symbol of strength. His strength is that he cannot be swayed by defilement or constructive thought as said in the sutra.

Akshobhya is the symbol of purification, in the meditative process, namely the visual perception and corresponds to the second of the five mystic knowledges, the knowledge that lets us see all things not as self-existent but as a subjective reflection almost as an image on the mirror. This is called 'the great, perfect mirror wisdom' which resembles the great mirror that reflects all things in their true state. Absorbed in the contemplation of great round mirror, he destroys demons and passions and presides over the deities who symbolize the pure mind.

Akshobhya is the embodiment of vajra family and represents winter season, noon time, pungent taste, faculty of hearing, the element of ether and sound, and the palatal group of letters. He is of blue colour because of being 'the paradigm of the Dharma's ability to transmute all the hate of all beings into blue ultimate-reality-wisdom'.

Akshobhya portrayed through sculpture, drawings and paintings from India, Tibet, Indonesia, Japan, Nepal, Mongolia and China attains a variety of forms. In his two armed to ten armed forms he is given single to five faces. He may sit in the meditative posture of touching the earth, bhumisparsha mudra with the right hand, while his left hand forms a clenched fist, holding the robe or alms bowl or a flower, a noose, or a vajra bell or it can be placed in the posture of meditation, the dhyana mudra. He holds attributes of war when he is represented in his six or eight armed forms, like vajra, chakra, wheel, sword, banner, bow and arrow etc. He is embraced by Mother Mamaki in his yabyum forms.

RATNASAMBHAVA

Ratnasambhava, the 'Jewel Born' is the third among the Five Transcendental Buddhas or Jinas. He, with his four Bodhisattvas – Vajraratna, Vajratejas, Vajraketu and Vajrahasa, forms the jewel section of the mandala. The jewel bestows felicities and initiation, that is entry to the way that ascends to the station of the Dharma King of the three worlds. Ratnasambhava possesses the knowledge of equality of essences, the knowledge that does not differentiate the ignorant and the awakened, or the humble or the world honoured ones, but knows that they are essentially equal. Sitting in the south of Vairocana in the Daimond World mandala he embodies the virtue of practice. As a result of practice the *sadhaka* gains innumerable felicities, so Ratnasambhava is the anthropomorphic equivalent of the wish-granting jewel that gives birth to all felicities. He represents knowledge of fundamental identity of things in which all are fleeting images emanated from the depth. A yellow or golden colour Buddha, he suppresses pride and greed, and is located in the south. He often keeps his right hand in varada mudra or holds a jewel while the left hand rests in his lap in dhyana mudra. He sits in vajrasana on a lotus or a seat, which can be comprised of a single or four horses.

Giving details of his qualities a sutra comments that from the space in between his separated fingers he drops a shower of jewels that fulfils all desires, namely of heavenly garments, of heavenly nectar, divine music, of divine palaces, of heaven that satisfy all desires of sentient beings.

FACING PAGE: *Mahavairocana Tathagata at the centre, making the diamond fist mudra is surrounded by four great Bodhisattvas – Vajrasattva, Vajraratna, Vajradharma and Vajrakarma.*

A single or a group of three jewels is drawn in Japanese Buddhist pantheons as his major characteristic feature and symbol.

In a stone image of Ratnasambhava from Udyagiri stupa from the period of mid-eighth century, Samantabhadra and Akashagarbha are shown flanking him. A polychrome clay image in the assembly hall of the main temple of Tabo, constitute a part of the Vajradhatu mandala. He is in full splendour, joined by eight Bodhisattvas in a thirteenth century painting from Nepal. There are two horses painted on the base of his throne. His horse throne is described in a Javanese text, San hyan Nagabayu sutra. According to Dharmakoshasangraha, his abode is Ratnavati-bhuvana and he has a brilliant jewel-like body. In the monasteries and cave temples in Tibet, China, Japan, Mongolia and other countries he can be seen painted on scrolls, murals, drawn in pantheons and sculpted in bronze. One of the finest bronzes is by the famous Mongol sculptor Zanabazar who lived from 1635 to 1723. On a silk scroll from Dun-huan caves he is painted as one of the Five Tathagatas where his body is of blue colour.

Ratnasambhava is also a symbol of elimination of sensation in the meditative process. This condition is necessary in order to spur our spiritual ascension and to acquire the trust to realize in ourselves the status of a Buddha. The horses on the throne symbolize the impetus. There are ninety-two images of Ratnasambhava at Borobudur, built in around AD 800. In Tibetan and Nepalese art he may have three faces with six arms and four faces with eight arms. In such manifestations he holds attributes like emerald, sword, jewels, vajra, cakra, chopper, fire-arrows, vajra-goad, vajra bell, *cintamani* banner and *damaru*.

AMITABHA

Fourth among the Five Transcendental Buddhas in the Vajradhatu or the Daimond World mandala, Amitabha embodies virtues of awakening and sits in the west. The virtue of awakening is the Paramita of the great wisdom samadhi of all the Tathagatas. He possesses the knowledge of subtle perception, which perceives the spiritual capacities of human beings so that the *dharma* may be preached to them in modes appropriate to their understanding. Amitabha rules over the lotus section of the mandala, where preaching the *dharma* causes the lotus mind of the being to open revealing its pure and original nature. The four attending Bodhisattvas sitting around Amitabha are – Vajradharma, Vajratikshna, Vajrahetu and Vajrabhasha.

AMOGHASIDDHI

Amoghasiddhi is Shakyamuni, who abides in the world of transforming action in the north. He embodies the virtue of entry into *nirvana*, which is the stage wherein all the passions have been cut away and the practices of benefit-for-self and benefit-for-others have been completed. He symbolizes completion of all rituals and actions. Amoghasiddhi with his attending Bodhisattvas constitute the action section of the Daimond World mandala. He embodies knowledge that arises as a result of completing all rites, the knowledge of the perfection of action. He is the fifth among the Five Transcendental Buddhas. The four Bodhisattvas attending him are the four aspects of virtue for an entry into *nirvana*, which is the completion of all actions, attained as a result of the perfection of Paramita of exertion.

Often painted green in colour, as *nirmanakaya* he wears monastic robes and sits in *vajrasana* with right hand in the mudra of fearlessness and the left in *dhyana mudra* placed in the lap. The name of his paradise is Amoghavati. According to a sutra the absolute knowledge that is most effective in the realization of the aims and cannot be fettered, is called Amoghasiddhi.

One of the best examples of the images of Amoghasiddhi is from Borobudur in Indonesia where ninety-two sculptures adorn the northern niches. He is a symbol of knowledge through which power is expressed as act and spreads out from it. In the Japanese *Vajradhatu-mandala*, he is the intermediary of *vajra-karma-paramita* and presides over the virtues of Vairocana, which are perseverance in the conversion of beings and *nirvana*. He presides over the *karma* class. The mudra of fearlessness of his right hand symbolizes his great compassion and

FACING PAGE: *Amitabha is sitting in Sukhavati performing dhyana mudra, the posture of contemplation. Behind him are twenty-five Bodhisattvas joining him when he descends from his paradise to receive the soul of the deceased. All of them are in a joyous mood holding banners, dancing, singing or playing musical instruments.*

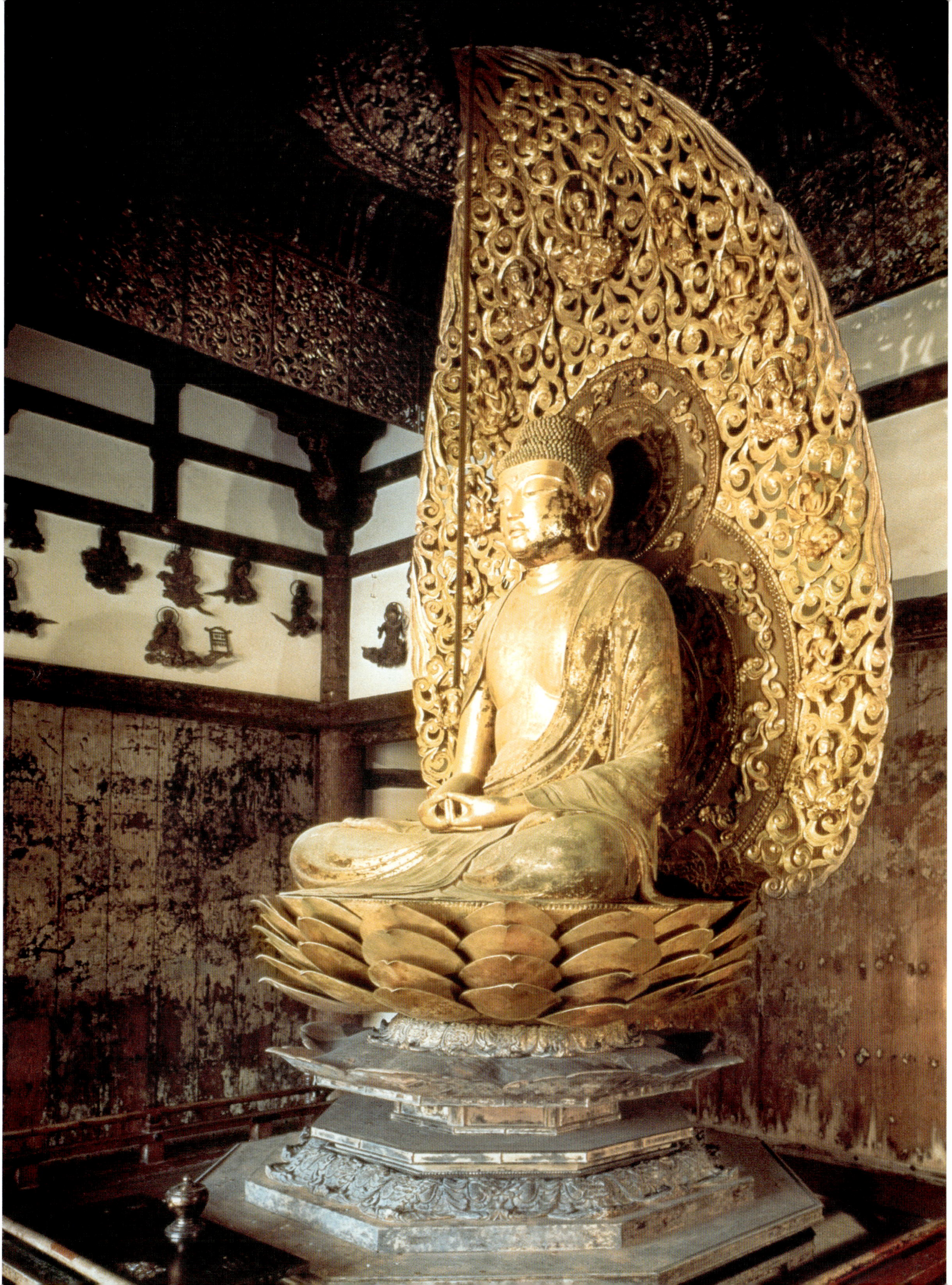

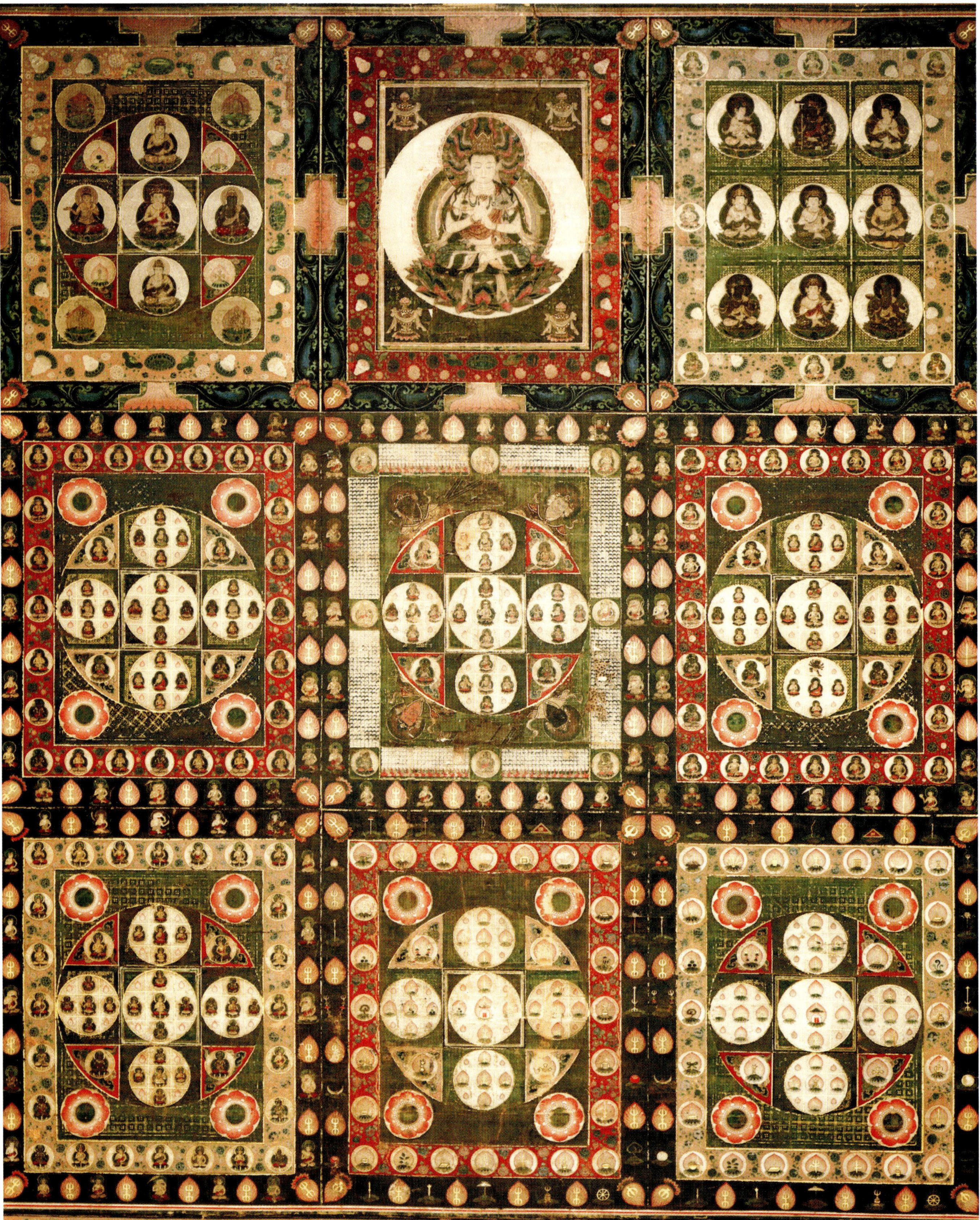

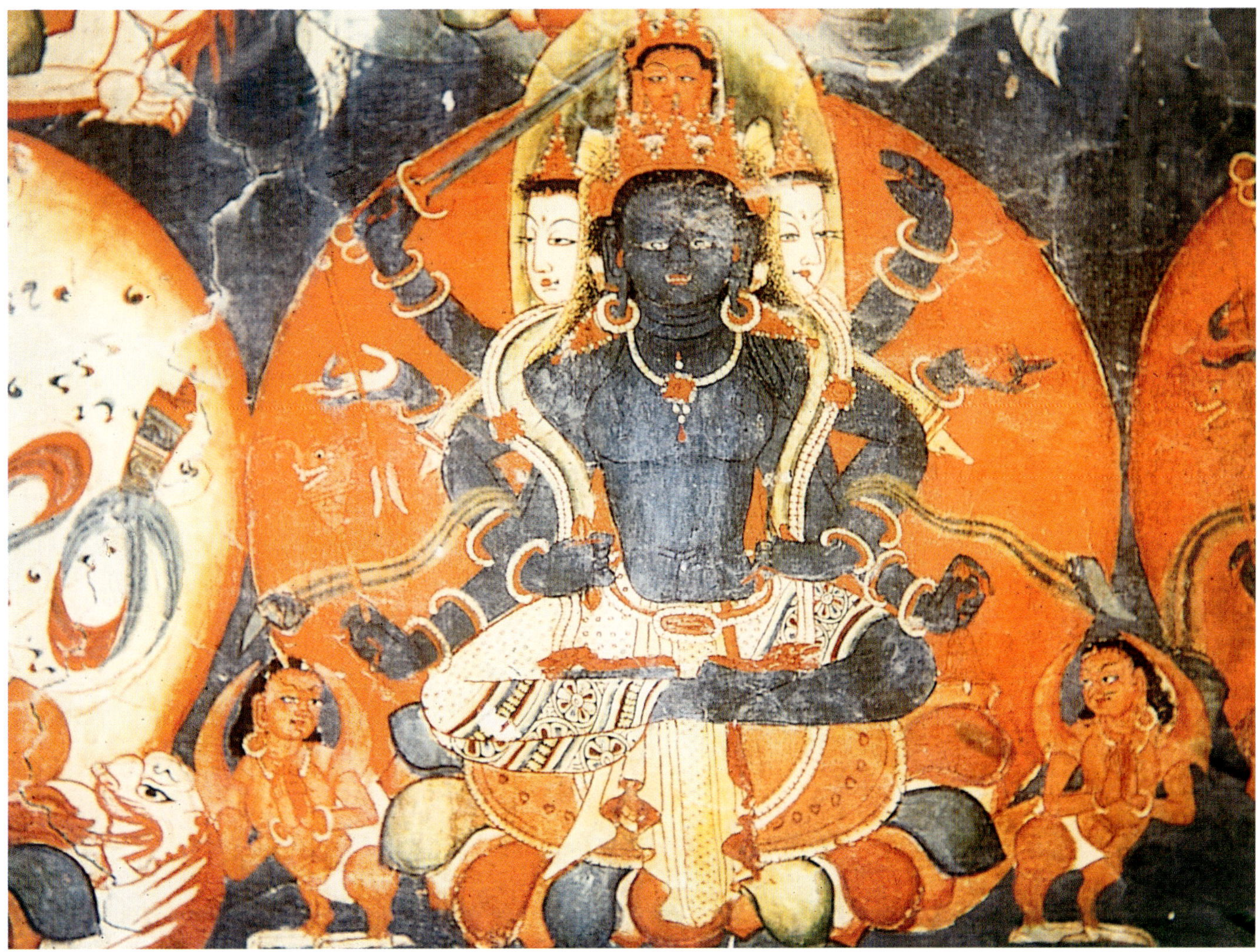

removal of sufferings. His complexion is bright green, the colour of *nirvana*.

Tibet produced a number of his images from early eleventh to fifteenth century. In a scroll discovered from Kharakhoto in Central Asia, he is the Tathagata of north who transmutes envy into green all-accomplishing wisdom. Nepalese manuscripts depict him in miniature size. In a scroll, Gobu-shingan, drawn in seventh-eighth century he assumes various type of forms. With a body in the hues of yellow, he rides seven *garudas* in its maha-mandala. In the *sukshma-mandala* he holds a vishva-vajra by both his hands. In the *Karma-mandala* he is represented in *sambhogakaya* form wearing a crown, ornaments and royal robes. A *vishva-vajra* is placed on a lotus held in his left hand. Tibetan pantheon represent him in yab-yum form in various manifestations in which he embraces his consort and holds attributes like vajra-bell, sword and cranium. He assumes forms with multi arms and multi faces also. In a Nepalese drawing he is seen with three faces and six arms. According to Nishpannayogavali, he has four faces and eight arms holding attributes of war.

ABOVE: *Amoghasiddhi painted on the upper section of the west wall of assembly hall of the main temple at Tabo.*

FACING PAGE: *Vajradhatu-mandala from Japan, divided into nine sections – eight peripheral and one central. In the central section are the five Tathagatas each sitting at the centre of the circle surrounded by four bodhisattvas.*

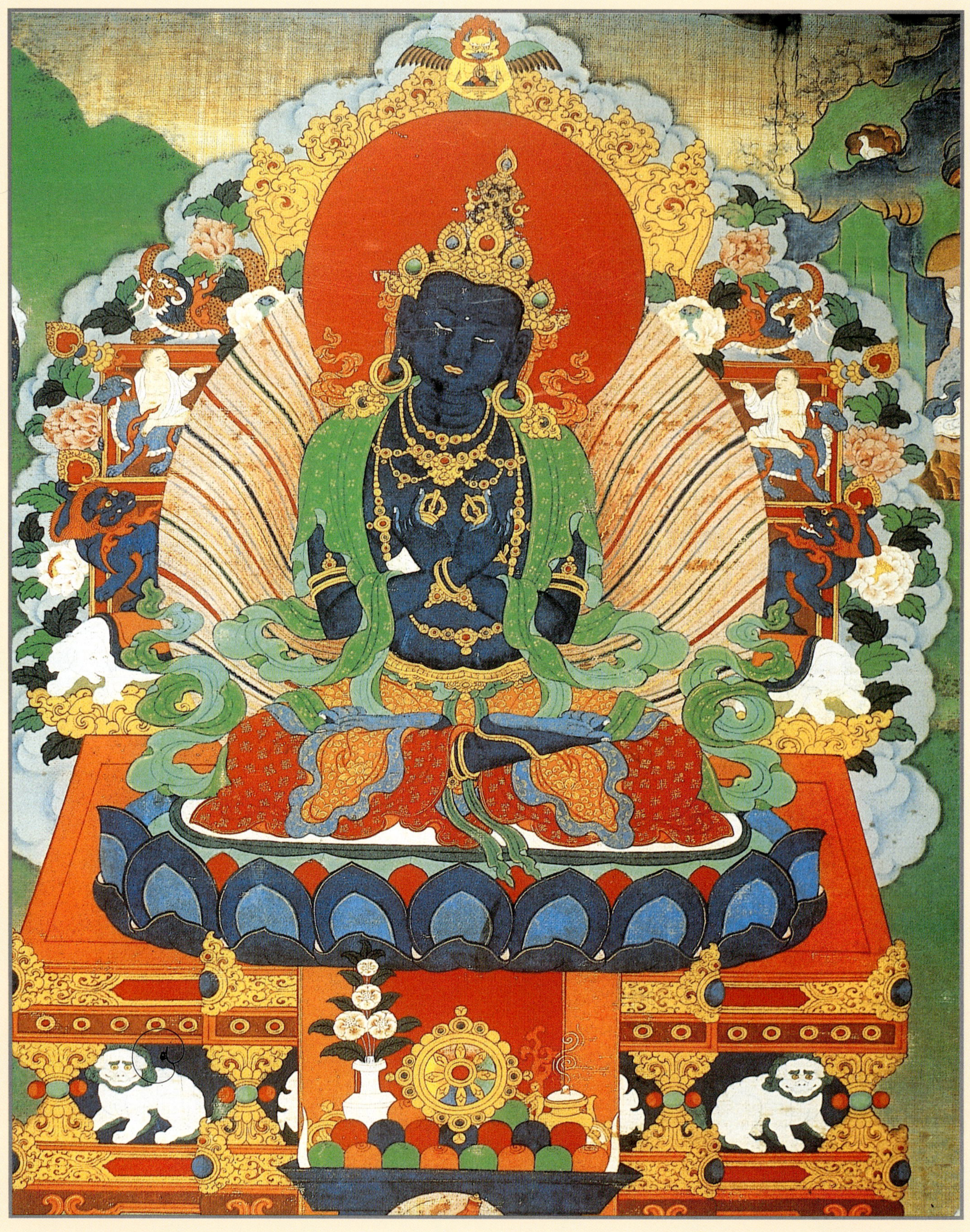

Adibuddhas

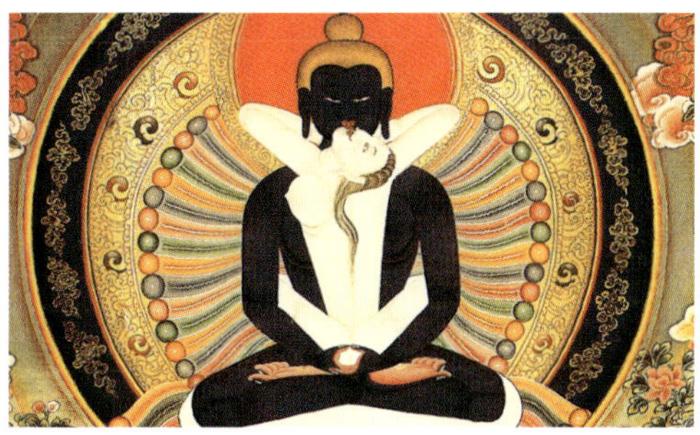

The term Adibuddha does not refer to a theistic God the Creator, or to a Primordial Buddha in a universal theistic sense, but is a generic appellation applied to the Supreme *(adi)* Enlightened Being (Buddha) of a specific school or system. Understanding Adibuddha as the primordial monotheistic god has been conditioned by the biblical conception of creation. Because Buddhism believes in plurality of all things, there is no supreme god, or creator. Every sentient being is a potential Buddha. Buddha does not offer any commandments. Buddhists do not worship one supreme god but they have identified with the Adibuddha some particular deities, varying according to different sects. Thus Samantabhadra was selected as an Adibuddha by some. Manjushri is called Adibuddha in the Nama-sangiti. Shakyamuni is the Adibuddha in *Mahakaruna-garbha-mandala.* The tantras have an Adibuddha in Vajrasattva-vajradhara. Tibetans accept their own Adibuddhas. In Vajrayana, Adibuddha is the primeval cause. He is specially proper to the Kalacakra system. It represents a new aspect of the first principle.

Adibuddhas are originating Buddhas in mandalas. They are found at the top of the thangkas, e.g. Amitabha on the top of Padmasambhava, Vajradhara over Buston, yab-yum Samantabhadra over Chemchok Heruka. Amitabha at the top of four faced Vajradhatu Vairocana. Adibuddha explained as the self-born, mahabuddha, adinath, is a later addition to the Karandavyuhasutra. Scholars have accepted that those not initiated into the teachings regard Adibuddha as the supreme deity, which is apparently erroneous. G.P. Malasekera, in the *Dictionary of Pali Proper Names* suggests that the concept arose as a part of the development of theistic Buddhism, which was prevalent in Nepal and Java. But it would be a misconception to consider the Adibuddha as just another version of God Creator.

Answering the questions put by Hodgeson, Pundit Amritananda propounded the theory of a primordial, or Adibuddha in the nineteenth century. Pundit Amritananda fused Hindu and Buddhist elements and provided his own interpretation of the Buddha. All the later works on Buddhist iconography are based on the interpretations by Hodgeson and fabrication by Amritananda.

ABOVE: *The Adibuddha Samantabhadra with his consort. Late nineteenth century.*

FACING PAGE: *Adibuddha Vajradhara, dressed in royal attire is the Buddha from beginless beginning. He is absolute and wears a Five Tathagata crown to demonstrate from where they originate.*

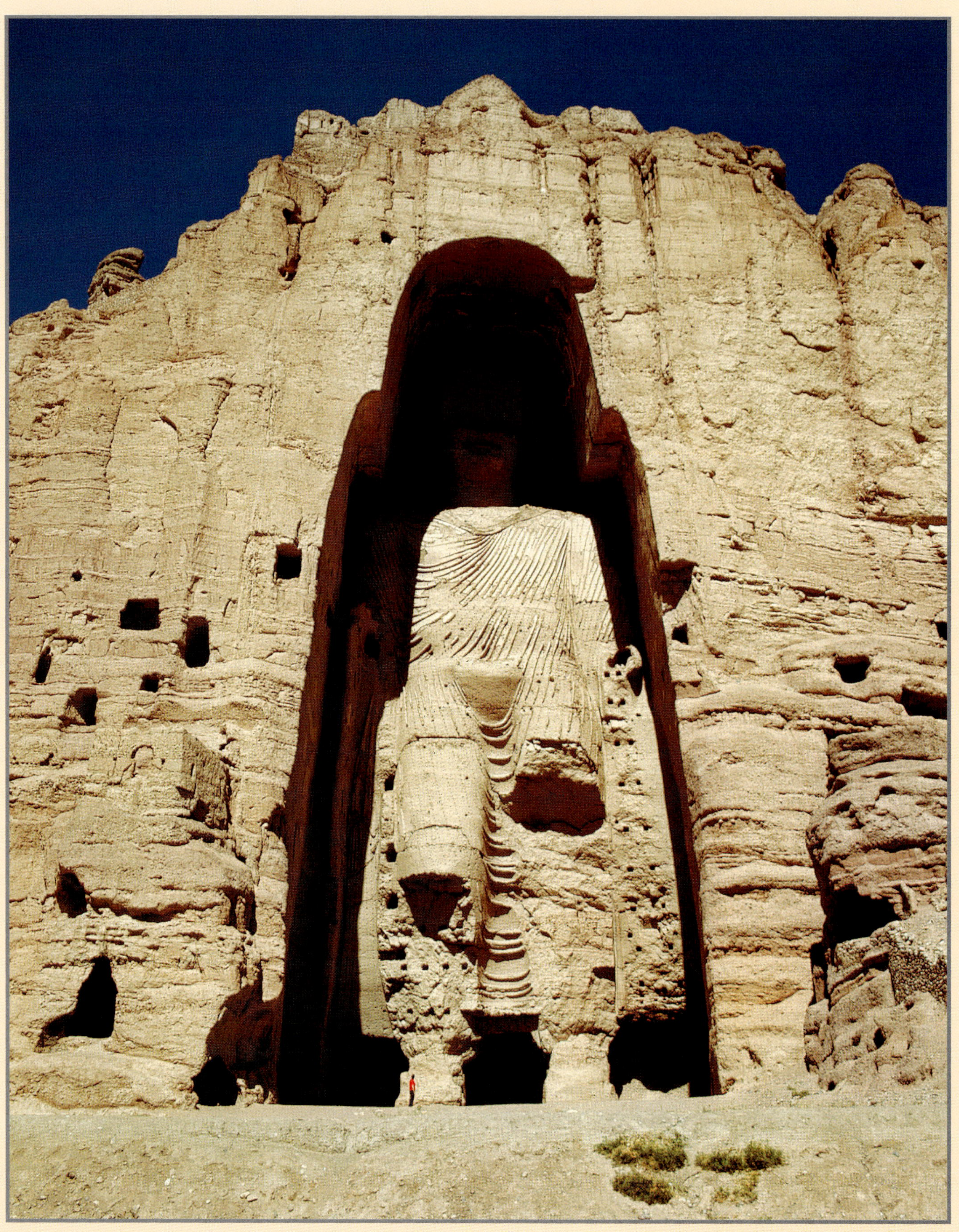

Colossal Buddhas

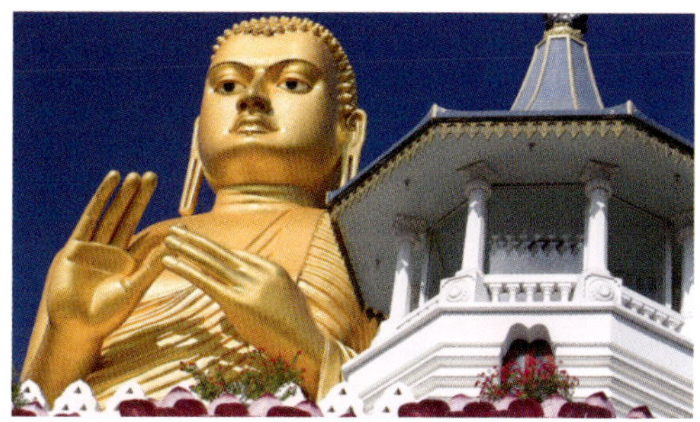

Over the ages colossal images were made by rulers all over the world to exhibit their power, their political or religious strength and will. In the Buddhist world they were meant to inspire the devotee by the grand personality of Shakyamuni who was so majestic, overwhelming and strong yet serene and humane. In the northwest, enormous images of the Buddhas suggested supra-terrestrial power. Beauty was joined to magnitude, and size became a symbol of status, the bigger the image the higher was the position. So the highest in rank are made the largest in size. Colossus does not only mean huge, extremely large, gigantic or titanic but also great, grand, spectacular, extravagant, overwhelming, awe inspiring, imposing, and monumental, evincing the importance of size.

Buddhism introduced the philosophy of grandeur in image making. Overwhelming size of images awed the devotees in Buddhist temples. Only major divinities were sculpted large in size, i.e. Shakyamuni, Bhaishajyaguru, Maitreya, Avalokiteshvara, Amitabha and Vairocana/Rocana.

Life-size images often correspond to the measurements of donors or sponsors. In China many stone sculptures were made to the likeness of the emperors. To arrive at colossal statues measurements were raised to their multiples. Five meters was accepted as the traditional height for statues of Buddhas and Bodhisattvas from base to forehead hairline.

The massive statue of Apollo Helios made from the melted down weapons of defeated enemies, one of the Seven Wonders of the World, symbolized victory. The Roman Empire erected colossal statues to impress the world with its might. In the Buddhist world, however, the statues were meant to inspire the devotee by the grand personality of Shakyamuni who was so majestic,

ABOVE: *A colossal Buddha setting the Wheel of Law in motion 100 feet in height, at the Golden temple of Dambulla, a sacred pilgrimage site, was completed in 1998.*

FACING PAGE: *One of the two colossal images of the Buddhas that stood at Bamiyan in Afghanistan. The smaller statue 127 feet in height was Maitreya, the Future Buddha and the other known as Surkha. But in Iranian was Rocana. Their grandeur lingers on in memories. The Persian sources record grand ceremonies of the two colossi when they were living statues, when the stone structures were sanctified by plastering, gilding, draping and adornments.*

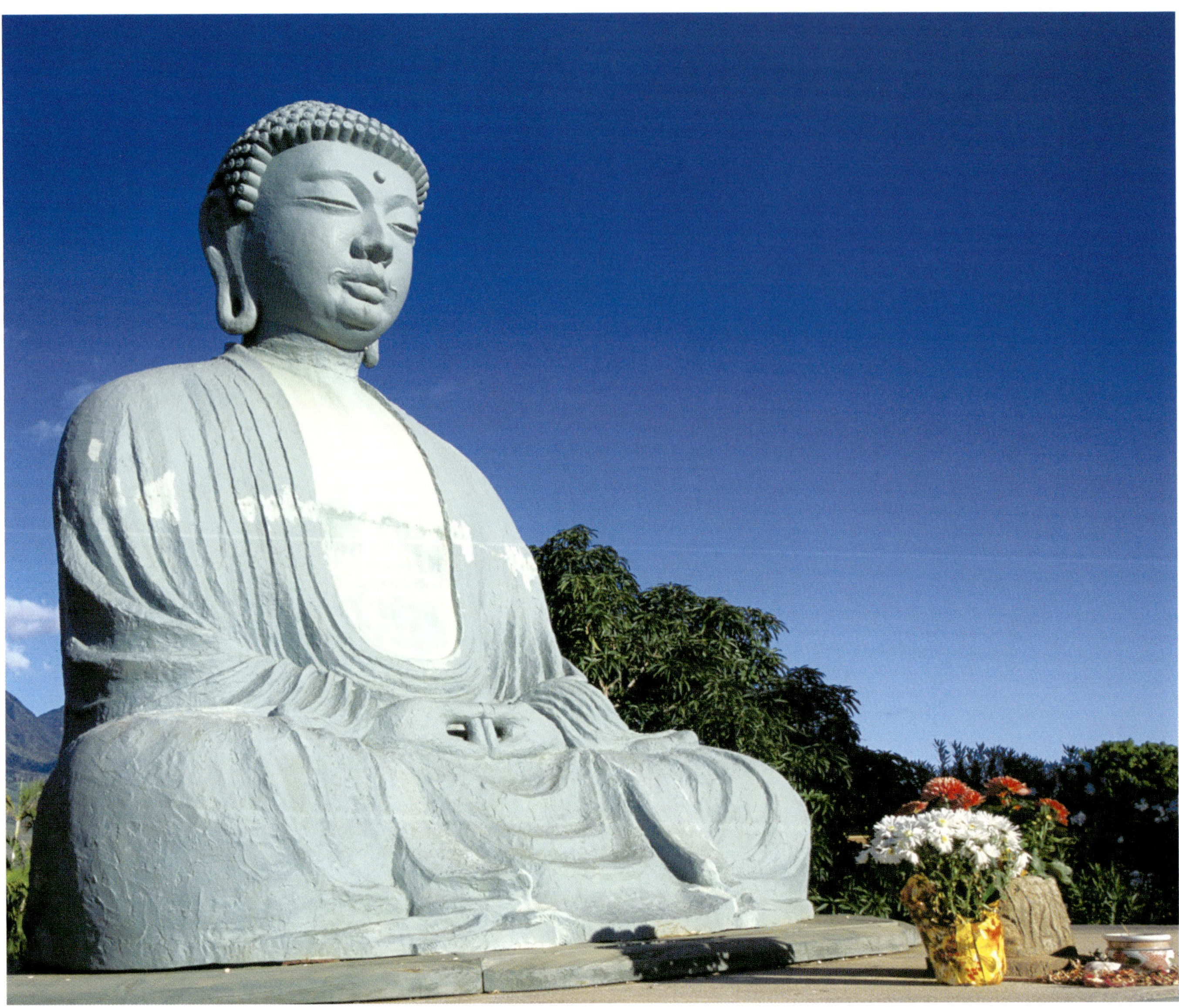

ovepowering, strong yet serene and humane. In Japan, Emperor Shomu tried to establish himself as the counterpart of Vairocana through Nara Daibutsu. Popularity of various sutras at different times led to a variety of images made on a grand scale.

In Afghanistan at Bamiyan, colossal statues espoused admiration mingled with reverence and devotion to the transcendental power. For centuries pilgrims and merchants, monks and scholars, kings and nobles were attracted to the place. The images were carved out of a cliff. The details, folds of drapery, and other fillings were modeled from a thick layer of clay covered with a veneer of lime plaster on which the final coating was given with lime. Then the statues were painted, as suggested by the traces of blue paint left at some places. Hsuan-tsang had described the images as made of metallic stone. Its pieces were cast separately and welded together later. Probably,

ABOVE: *A colossal statue of Amitabha sitting in meditative posture with both hands placed in his lap and down-cast eyes, a creation of the Jodo mission. Jodo sect is devoted to the worship of Amitabha.*

when he had paid a visit, the images were covered with gold leaf or some other resplendent metal or were painted in metallic colour. The images were carved and wooden pegs were fixed to hold the robes for modeling the folds and then covered with a thick coat of mud mixed with chopped straw. Finally, they were plastered and then coloured. Stylistically, the images were associated with the Gandhara tradition. Brocades and precious jewels were hung on the Buddhas during the ceremonial adorning. The larger image was red and the smaller was moon-white in colour. They glittered with gold and precious ornaments. A Persian poet, moved by the splendour of the adorned Buddhas sang of their pure beauty. The Persian poets in the early eleventh century seem to echo Hsuan-tsang's vision of the Bamiyan Buddhas. In the middle ages, the bigger statue was known as '*surkh but*', the red statue and the smaller as '*khink but*'. A gigantic painting of the Sun in his chariot was done on the soffit of the niche.

The idea of making colossal images spread from the northwest of ancient India to as far as Sri Lanka. *Mahavamsha*, a Sri Lankan chronicle notes that monastic dignitaries came from Gandhara at the crowning ceremony of Mahasaya stupa completed by King Dutthagamani around 161-37 BC. The famous colossal in Sri Lanka is the Avukana Buddha, which has features similar to those of the colossal Buddhas at Bamiyan. It is approximately 43 feet in height. A statue resembling Avukana colossus has been found from Matara in southern Sri Lanka. It is a 5.5 feet tall granite statue, most probably from the ninth century.

In China stone sculptures were made to the likeness of emperors. To arrive at colossal statues, measurements were raised to multiples. Colossal statues of Buddhas, 13-16 metres in height, were carved in five caves of Yun-kang, to honour the five emperors. Smiling faces, elongated ears, strongly chiseled noses and lips cannot fail to impress. Folds of drapery modeled in flat bands are close to Kizil in Kucha and not to the Gandharan or Khotanese figures. Khotan was a famous centre of Buddhist art and learning. Shakyamuni in grotto no. 5 at Yun-kang caves is 17 metre in height, his foot being 4.5-metre and the toe is bigger than an average person's height. It bends slightly forward; its head and eyebrows are lowered; facial expression is rich and gives a feeling of warmth and kindness. Lokesvararaja in China is a masterpiece at the Lung-men caves. Its height is 17.14 metres, the head alone measures over 4 metres, and the ears are 1.9-metre long.

The first colossal bronze statue of Shakyamuni in Japan is popularly known as Asuka Daibutsu. The Japanese were impressed by the teachings of Lord Buddha who was seen as the epitome of the Six Perfections and the eight-fold path. He was the enlightened one who taught the four noble truths, the doctrine of impermanence, the Twelve Chains of Causation, nirvana, spiritual insight, the doctrine of karma, and the transmigration of soul. The Dai Butsu at Nara or the Great Buddha at the Todaiji monastery is 53 feet high. It is a symbol of political will and visualizes the vision of Emperor Shomu who commissioned the grand image of Rocana as an apt symbol of unification of the country under him as the controlling head of the state. He saw himself as an earthly counterpart of Rocana. Vairocana at the Toshodaiji monastery resembles Rocana at Todaiji. Hundreds of Transformation Buddhas on the mandorla of Vairocana are the Thousand Buddhas of the Vajradhatu-mandala, carved in thirty-three clusters.

Colossal images of Amitabha were created for meditation and contemplation, to eventually gain a total intellectual identity. The famous colossal statue of Amitabha sitting in open in Kamakura, the first warrior capital of Japan is a 42 feet high statue (49 feet in height including dais) and was cast in AD 1252 for the Kotokuin monastery. Dimensions heighten the calm majesty of Amitabha. Kamakura Buddha is heroic in scale, imperturbable in expression, looks downward and is full of compassion. He is the enlightened one sitting cross-legged in dhyana mudra, wearing monk's robes. The statue is an expression of the appeal of Buddhism to the masses. Production of Buddhist colossi does not cease with the classical age. The Buddhist world still has a fancy for the concept. Many of the Buddhist countries are still producing such images displaying a grand view of totality.

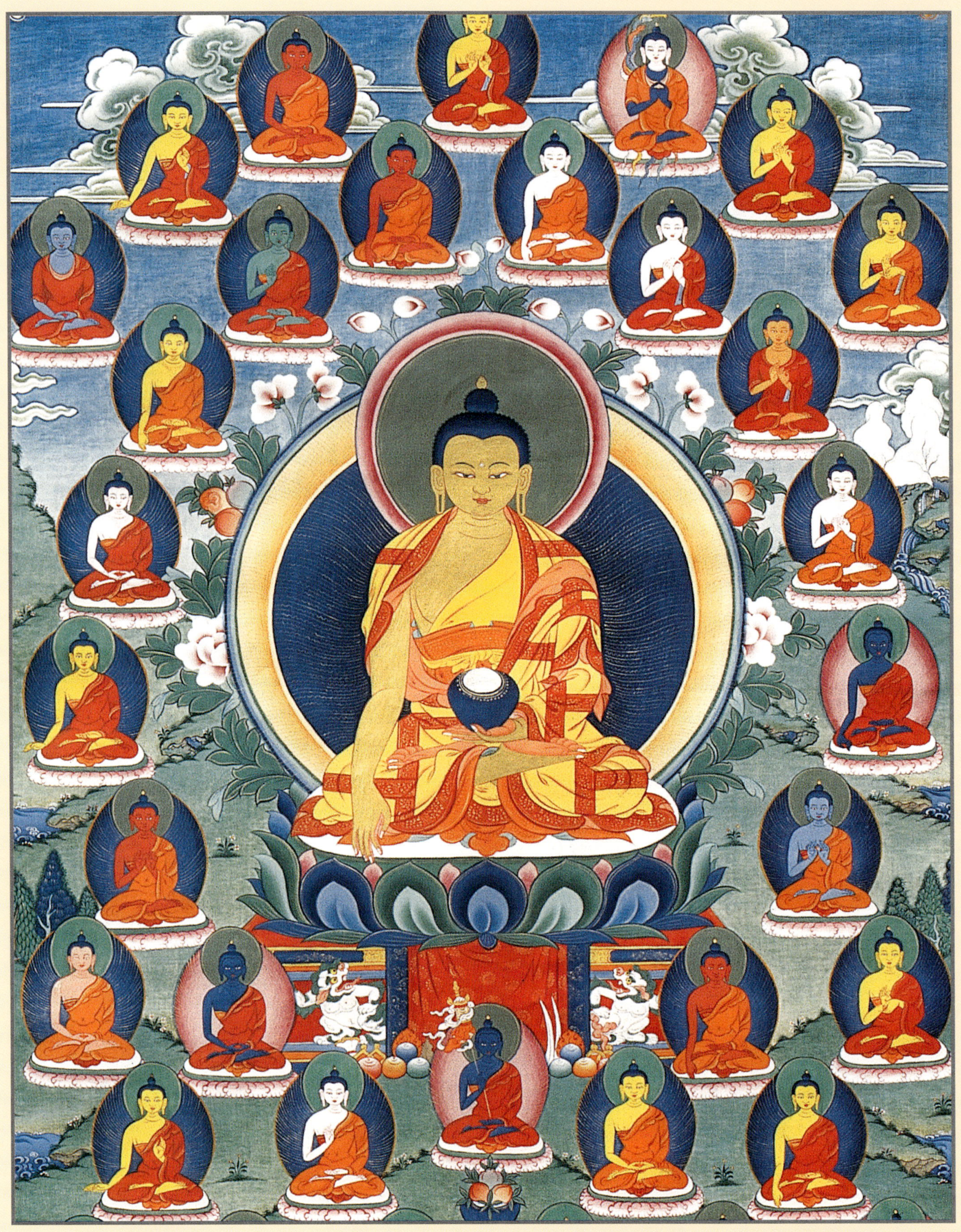

Buddhas of Confession

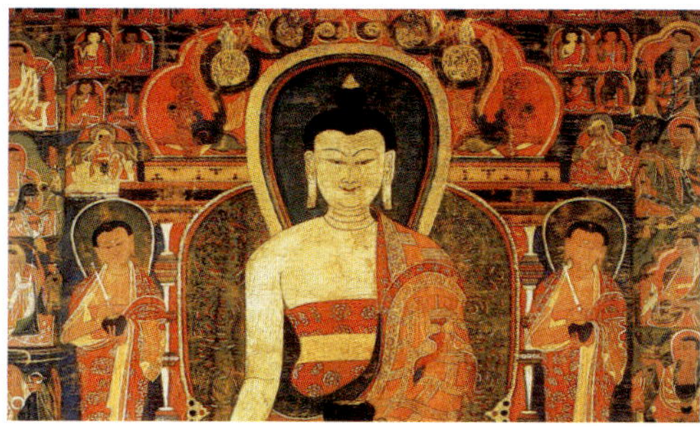

Thirty-five Buddhas of Confession are invoked during the rite of confession to liberate from sin or defilement. In the Dharmasangraha it developed into a seven-item rite – praise, worship, confession of sins, joy, solicitation for the Buddha to instruct, generating the mind of enlightenment and transferring one's merit to others. The oldest textual source enumerating their names is the sutra on meditation of Akasagarbha Bodhisattva. Upalipariprіccha comes next translated into Chinese by Amoghavajra in the eighth century. In Tibet Tson.kha.pa and his disciple Rgyal.tshab wrote on their liturgy and iconography.

The number thirty-five is reached by the spatial diagram of four directions, four secondary directions, twenty-four intermediate points, centre, zenith and nadir. It is a synthesis of space in the Upalipariprіccha and connects the thirty-five to twenty-eight constellations and four lokapalas with sun, moon and Pole star. All of them are invoked to live in all the spheres of existence and protect the devotees. They are drawn, printed and painted on manuscripts and painted scrolls, or engraved on wood or stone. For a comprehensive study of their iconography the most important sources are the collections – Derge edition of Kanjur and Tanjur from Tibet, Kanjur from Mongolia, 300 Icons drawn in AD c.1715, and 360 Icons drawn in AD c.1761. A votive stele from the end of the T'ang period depicts five rows of seven Buddhas each kept at the Museum Rietberg in Zurich. A set of these Buddhas was carved on the outer side of the wooden cover of a Prajnaparamita manuscript of the thirteenth century, now in the British Museum.

Their iconography is different in different collections. For example, the third buddha in the list of thirty-five, Ratnarcis holds a vajra in the right hand and an alms bowl in the left in the Mongolian Kanjur but both of his hands are in dharmacakra-pravartana-mudra in the Tibetan Derga Kanjur and Tanjur. He is painted as one of the Buddhas of Ten Directions on the north wall of the assembly hall of Tabo monastery. There he is red in colour and his hands are in the gesture of blessing.

ABOVE: *Thirty-five Buddhas of Confession painted on the upper section of a thangka painting with Shakyamuni Buddha sitting at the centre.*

FACING PAGE: *Thirty-four Buddhas of Confession painted around Shakyamuni, being thirty-fifth, encompass all directions of space.*

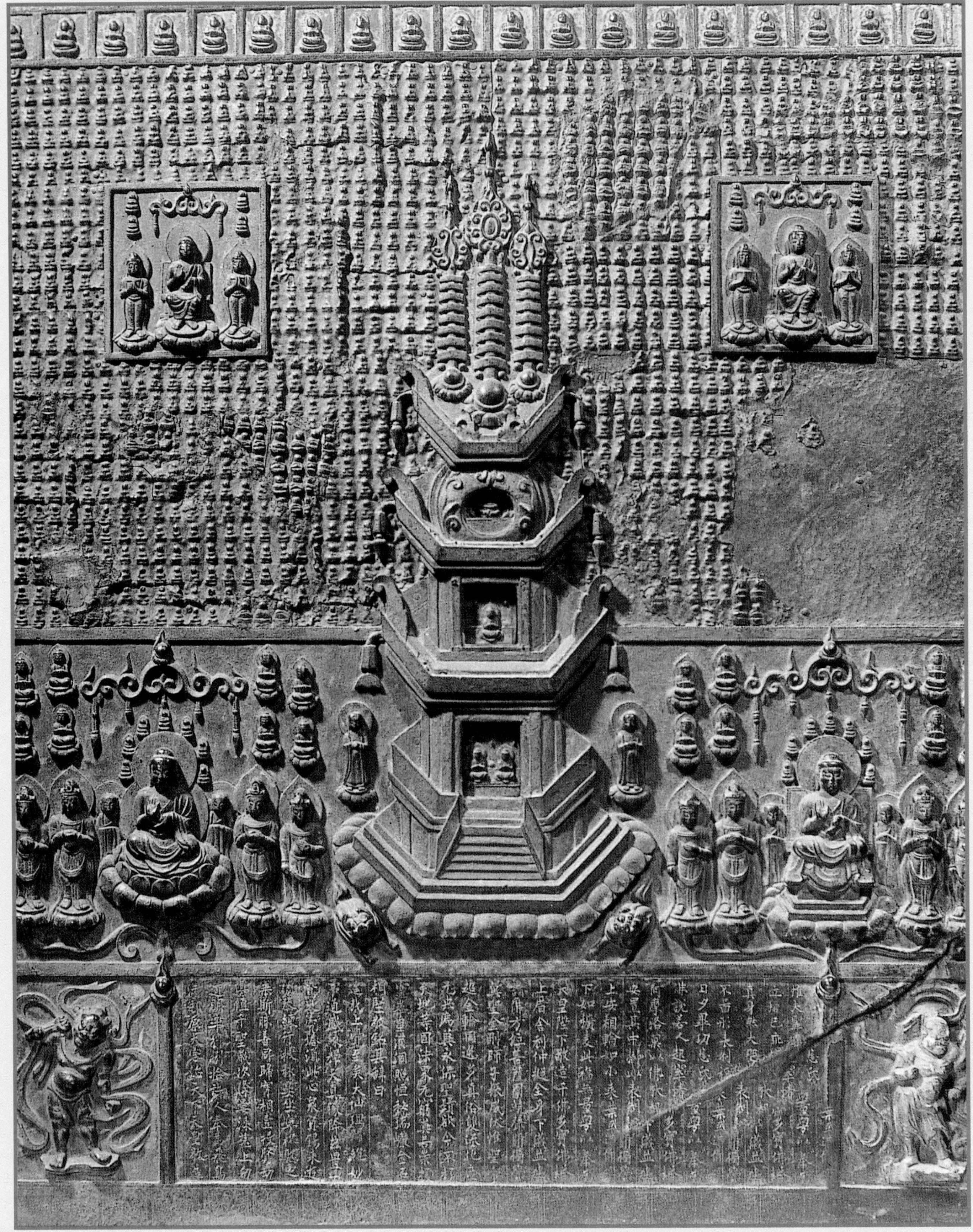

Prabhutaratna

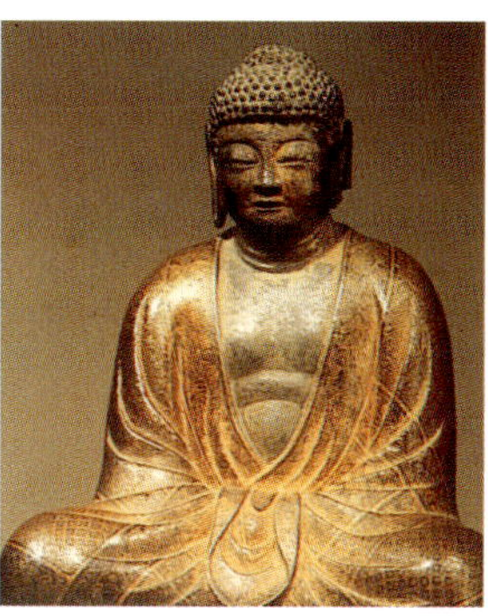

Prabhutaratna, protector of Lotus Sutra, the Buddha of immense treasures forms a pair with Shakyamuni representing the event of meeting of the two Buddhas. He belongs to the distant past and is so remote that he does not figure among the predecessors of the Buddha. He is sacred to the third day of the month. According to the story relating the meeting of the two Buddhas, when Shakyamuni was sitting on the Vulture Peak expounding the Lotus Law, a stupa had appeared in the sky. He arose, stood in the sky, opened the stupa and saw that a Buddha of the past, Prabhutaratna, who had come to hear the Law, was sitting inside. Shakyamuni sat beside him and continued his discourse.

The legend says that his funerary stupa has been preserved through immeasurable ages, to appear whenever the True Law is preached, and thus it emerges out of the ground, is immense and covered with jewels. It hovers in the air before the astonished eyes of Shakyamuni's audience on the Vulture peak. Hosts of Buddhas and Bodhisattvas come to honour the occasion. When Shakyamuni rises into air, touches the door of the stupa with his fingers of the right hand, the gate is opened and Tathagata of manifold treasures, Prabhutaratna appears, seated on lion throne. He says: 'Excellent, excellent, O Shakyamuni Buddha; make haste to preach the Lotus Sutra, for it is to hear the sutra that I have come.' The audience rejoices and showers flowers. And then Shakyamuni shares the throne with him.

The stupa in which Prabhutaratna appeared is identified as Treasure Tower. According to the eleventh chapter of the Lotus Sutra on Treasure Tower, Prabhutaratna lived in the Treasure Land in an eastern part of the universe. While engaged in the Bodhisattva practice, he vowed that after attaining Buddhahood he would

ABOVE: *Prabhutaratna, the Buddha of abundant treasures, a late eighth century statue is from the Todaiji monastery in Nara, Japan.*

FACING PAGE: *The bronze plaque from the Hasedera temple in Japan is the earliest representation of the eleventh chapter of the Lotus Sutra. It was commissioned in AD 686 for longevity and prosperity for Emperor Temmu.*

appear in the Treasure Tower and attest the validity of the lotus sutra. When Shakyamuni had preached the first ten chapters of the sutra, he appeared and praised Shakyamuni.

The single storey stupa in which Prabhutaratna appears, adorned with seven kinds of precious substances including gold and silver, is portrayed through images, drawings, paintings, mandalas and plaques, found from China and Japan. One of the best-known examples is the bronze plaque from Hasedera monastery in Nara prefecture. In the central stupa on the plaque Shakyamuni and Prabutaratna sit on the same throne smiling at each other. The stupa arises from the earth supported by a lotus and four vajra lions as mentioned in the inscription below. Two guardians stand on the sides of the inscription. On the left of the stupas is Shakyamuni in the posture of teaching, attended by Ananda and Rahula and four Bodhisattvas and on the other side is Maitreya. The rest of the plaque is filled with figures of Thousand Buddhas.

A number of images in pairs, portraying the two Buddhas have been found from various monasteries in China and Japan. A painting on silk from the ninth-tenth century is kept at Musee Guimet museum in France. A variety of mandalas based on the Lotus Sutra served as main objects of worship for well being, for averting disasters, for rooting out crime, for longevity and rapid realization of Enlightenment. They were often constituted of three enclosures and the deities were represented in image or in seed syllable form.

In the eleventh chapter of the Lotus Sutra, Tathagata Prabhutaratna sees that the sutra has been well expounded by Lord Shakyamuni. He himself had preached this sutra in a previous age and had vowed that wherever and whenever it would be preached he would appear . He presides in the distant land Ratnavishuddha. The stupa is called Ratna stupa. The Lotus Sutra was also popular in Khotan which was itself called Ratnajanapada. The royal dynasties of Khotan considered Prabhutaratna to be the guardian of their kingdom and to be the giver of abundance (prabhuta) of jade (ratna) which was the main stay of their prosperity.

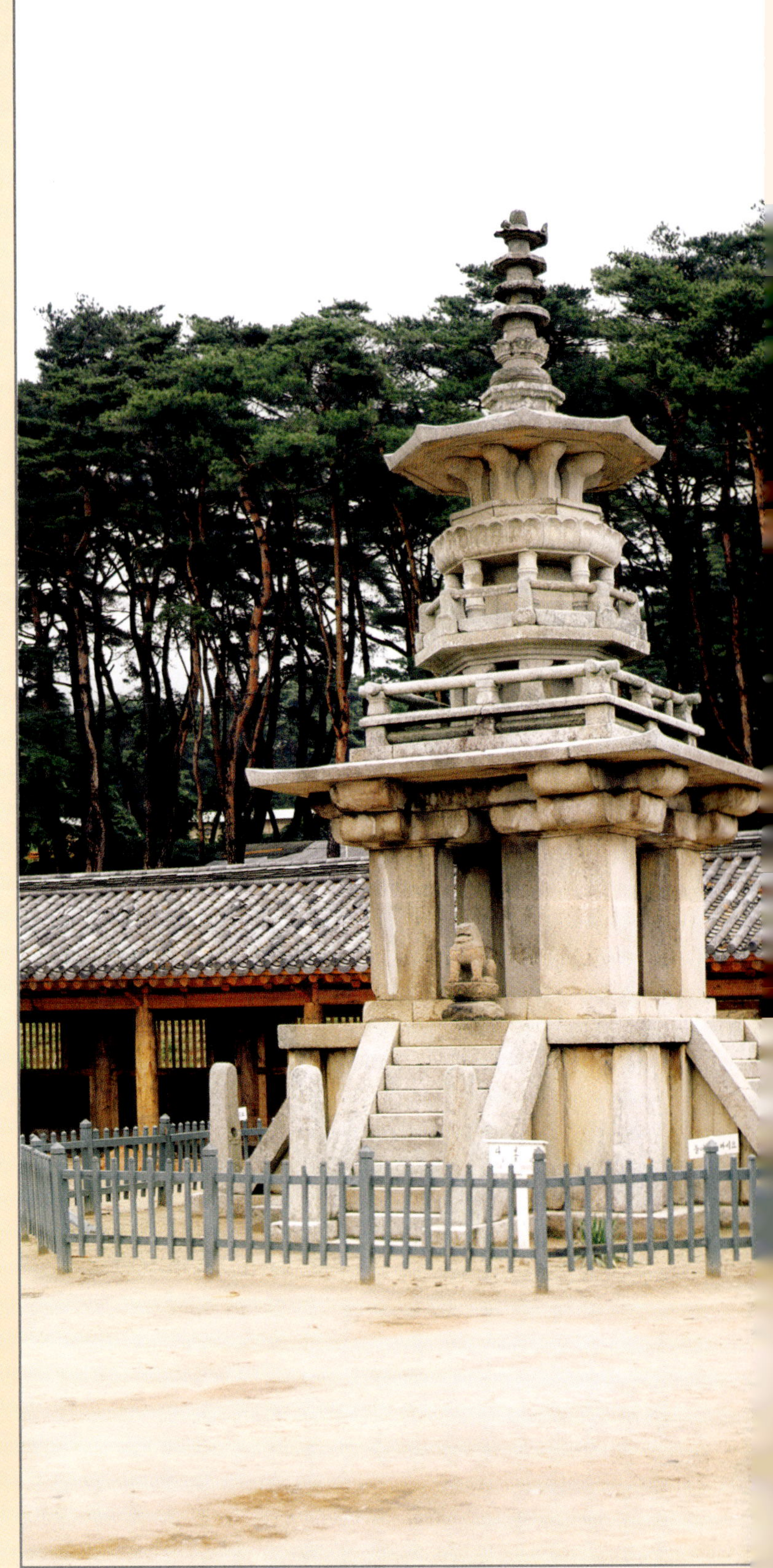

Seokgatap Pagoda

Pagodas at Pulguksa Temple

A pair of pagodas stand in the Pulguksa temple site in South Korea – the Sakyamuni Pagoda is three-storey called Seokgatap and stands at 8.2 meters built in a traditional Korean-style with simple lines and minimal detailing. It is over thirteen centuries old. The other – Prabhutaratna or Many Treasure Pagoda called Dabotap is 10.4 meters tall. It is a highly ornate structure. Its image is reproduced on the South Korean 10 won coin. Both the pagodas are Korean National Treasures nos. 20 and 21, respectively. The three-storey pagoda was built in an ornate style not seen in other Buddhist countries. The techniques used are unique for its time and include delicate features. It has a staircase on each of the four sides. Four stone square pillars support the pagoda's first roof, where is build a square stone railing. Inside the railing is the body of the pagoda, and above it, standing on the second octagonal-shaped roof surrounded by an octagonal stone railing, are eight bamboo-shaped stone pillars support the octagonal-shaped lotus stone carved with sixteen petals. Above it eight stone pillars support the third octagonal-shaped roof. Of the four stone lions guarding the top of the staircases only one remains.

No pairs of pagodas in the world could be so different from one another and yet in harmony than the ones at Pulguksa. The two pagodas reflect a story in the Lotus sutra. Prabhutaratna, a Buddha who had already achieved enlightenment, riding the Tower of Many Treasures, appeared to attest to the validity of Sakyamuni's sermons at Vulture Peak. Prabhutaratna and Sakyamuni then sat side by side within the tower. This pagoda represents the Prabhutaratna Buddha, while the other pagoda represents Sakyamuni. It represents the objective truth, while Sakyamuni represents the subjective wisdom to realize it. Ptabhutaratna pagoda is highly decorative and looks feminine, whereas Sakyamuni pagopda is highly simplified and symbolizes the brevity of spiritual ascent and looks more masculine. The other looks sophisticated and symbolizes the complexity of the world.

The pagodas were said to have been built by the stone mason, Asadal of Baekje. He left his young wife at home while he went to direct the long project of building the pagodas and soon became so immersed in his work that he neglected his wife. When she went to see him, she was turned away from the temple because women were not allowed on the grounds at the time. Asadal's wife was directed to Shadow Pond where she would be able to see her husband's reflection in water. When she looked into the water, all she could see was the completed Prabhutaratna pagoda with no one in sight on the temple grounds. In anguish, Asadal's wife threw herself into the pond and drowned. Unknown to her, though, was that Asadal had finally finished it and was working on Shakyamuni pagoda. This is why it is known as the Shadowless Pagoda because Asadal's wife did not see the pagoda in the pond. In 1966, the monks of the temple were awakened by sounds of exploding dynamite. They discovered that thieves had attempted to blast the pagoda and steal what was hidden inside. The thieves ran away before they could steal any of the treasures but the Buddhist monks discovered precious reliquaries, sariras, and the oldest extant example of printed material from a wood block in the world.

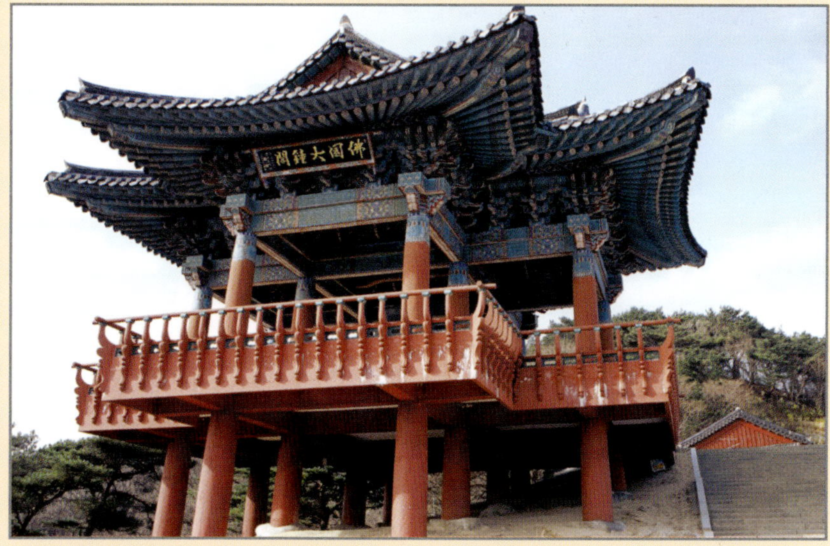

Dabotap Pagoda

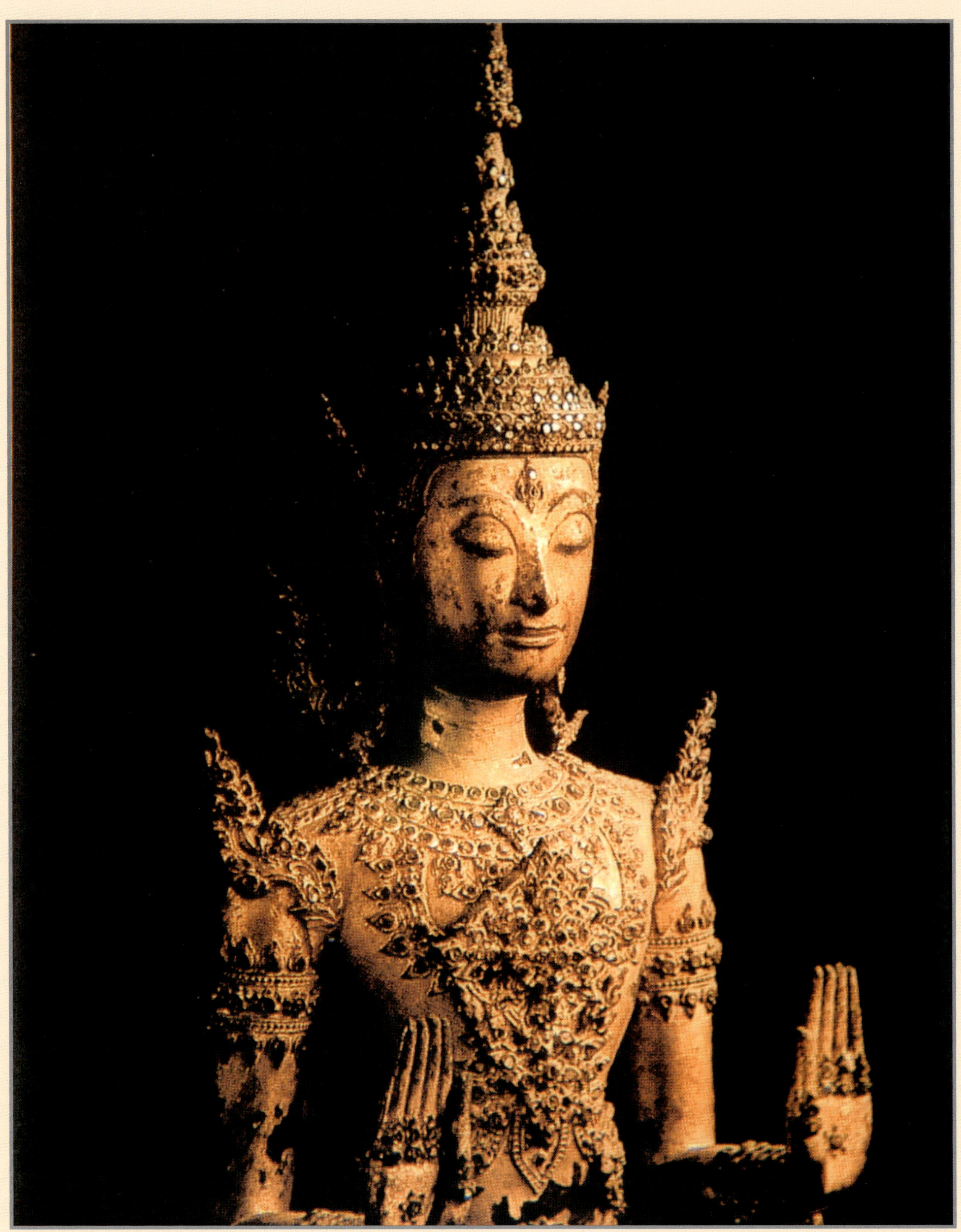

Bejewelled and Crowned Buddhas

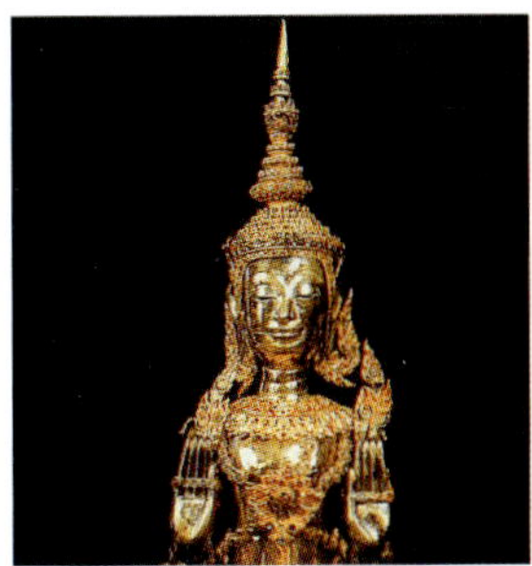

In Theravada countries, links between secular and religious authorities go back into history. Kings themselves have been servants of the Buddha and Buddha has shared with the ruler the function of protecting the state assuming attributes of kingship. Such sculptures stand out throughout the Theravada world, ranging in size from colossal images to tiny amulets. Crowned and bejewelled Buddha is seen as a ruler of the world reflecting identification of Buddhahood and ideal kingship. 'Buddha pare' 'Buddha in princely attire' began to appear in the sixteenth century in Thailand but can be traced back to an earlier date in Cambodia and in India in late Mahayana art, such a manifestation of the Buddha is found during the Pala period. From there it had spread to other countries like Burma, Nepal and Tibet, etc.

Jewelled Buddha images in Theravada countries sit in lotus posture with the right hand making the bhumi-sparsha mudra. The ornaments they wear include a crown, ear pendants, necklace with body chains attached to it, armlets, bracelets, anklets, rings, and elbow ornaments. The finial in the shape of a lotus bud protrudes over the crown. These images represent Buddha as *rajadhiraj*, king of the kings. According to the legend of Jambupati, a certain king of that name had such high esteem of himself that he would not listen to the teachings of the master. So the Buddha manifested himself as *rajadhiraj* and summoned Jambupati to visit him. The latter, awestruck by the splendour of the scene before him, paid obeisance to the Buddha, especially when he saw the chasm, open before him issuing fire. He was converted to Buddhism and became a disciple. An imperious yet approachable mien is a characteristic of such images, which are distinguished by cool nobility.

Crowned Buddhas wearing jewellery from the Pagan period in Burma are also associated to royalty. They wear bands crossing over the chest similar to those worn by the

ABOVE: *Adorned Buddha from Thailand in bronze alloy with red and green enamel ornaments, gems and pendants typical of early nineteenth century image.*

FACING PAGE: *Bejeweled and crowned Buddha representing Buddha as universal monarch (cakravarti) and as king of the kings (rajadhiraj).*

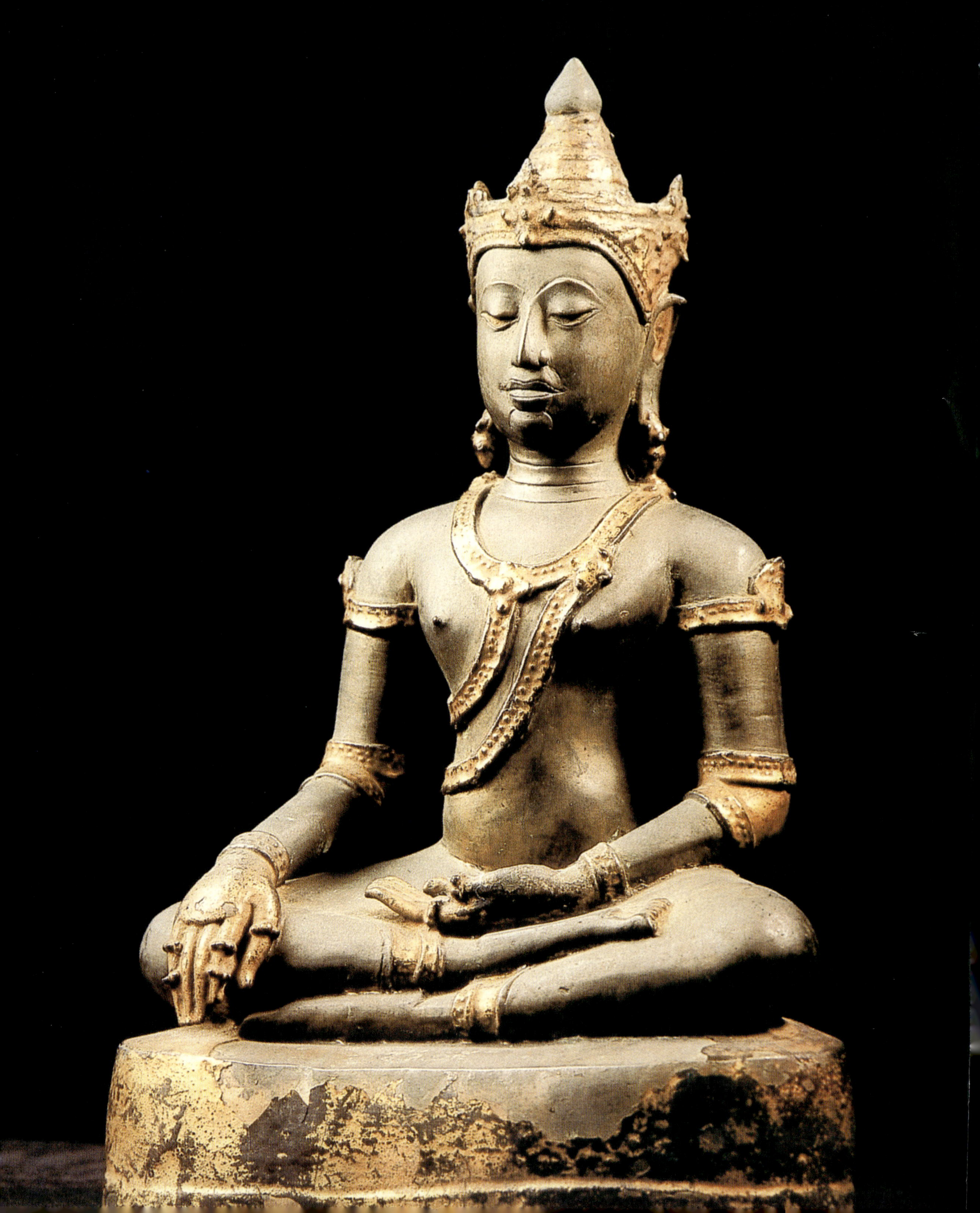

Burmese kings. Such images were found in Shrikshetra, Pagan and Pegu. According to the Pali commentaries, the Buddha took on the form of a king to preach the kings. The flame shaped *ketumala* is a conspicuous hallmark of the Sukhothai images from Thailand, as well as those from south India and Sri Lanka.

Buddha pare in Theravada and Vajrayana or Mahayana traditions are found in completely different religious systems. Buddha appears richly bejeweled, in the glory and brilliance of a transcendental being, when he manifests himself in *sambhogakaya*. In eastern Asia Buddha wears crown and jewellery but there he manifests as Vairocana. Buddha as a world ruler embracing within himself the entire world and indeed the entire universe, and making them manifest; the role entitles him to wear princely jewellery. In this form he appears as the central figure in the twin mandalas of the esoteric tradition.

Buddhas at Bamiyan were also covered with jewellery and ornamental chains. The Musee Guimet in Paris owns a fragmentary clay figure from Fondukistan from the seventh century with a jewel studded shoulder cap worn over the monk's habit. This style of caps are long coming down to shoulders. A gilded bronze statue of Shakyamuni as a crowned Buddha, from the sixteenth century, from Tibet is kept at the Tibet House Museum in New Delhi.

Some of the crowned and bejeweled Buddhas may be identified as portrait images in Southeast Asia. The grand temples and the images housed there, represent the dual principal of religion and politics, the apotheosis of kings, a symbiosis of royalty and religion, humanity and divinity. At the time of political instability, ambitious dynasts sought transmission of divine grace unto them through the evocation of transcendental powers. They resorted to religious activities to consolidate their political power.

A variety of explanations have been given by scholars on jeweled Buddhas. In the first place from the stand point of the doctrine of trikaya, the three bodies, the Buddha appears richly bejewelled in the glory and brilliance of a transcendental being, when he manifests himself as sambhogakaya. Another concept relavent in this connection is that the Buddha as world ruler, *cakravarti* or as cosmocrator, embracing within himself the entire world and indeed the entire universe and making them manifest. This role entitles him to wear princely jewellery. The idea of cakravarti merged with that of the Adibuddhas, the absolute original, or all-embracing Buddha, whose true self is invisible but who manifests himself as ruler of the universe to those who meditate upon him or to Bodhisattvas. It is in this form that the jeweled Buddha appears in Vajrayana notably as Vairocana, the central figure of the two mandalas as Vajradhatu and Garbhadhatu.

FACING PAGE: *Buddha in royal attire, bronze.*

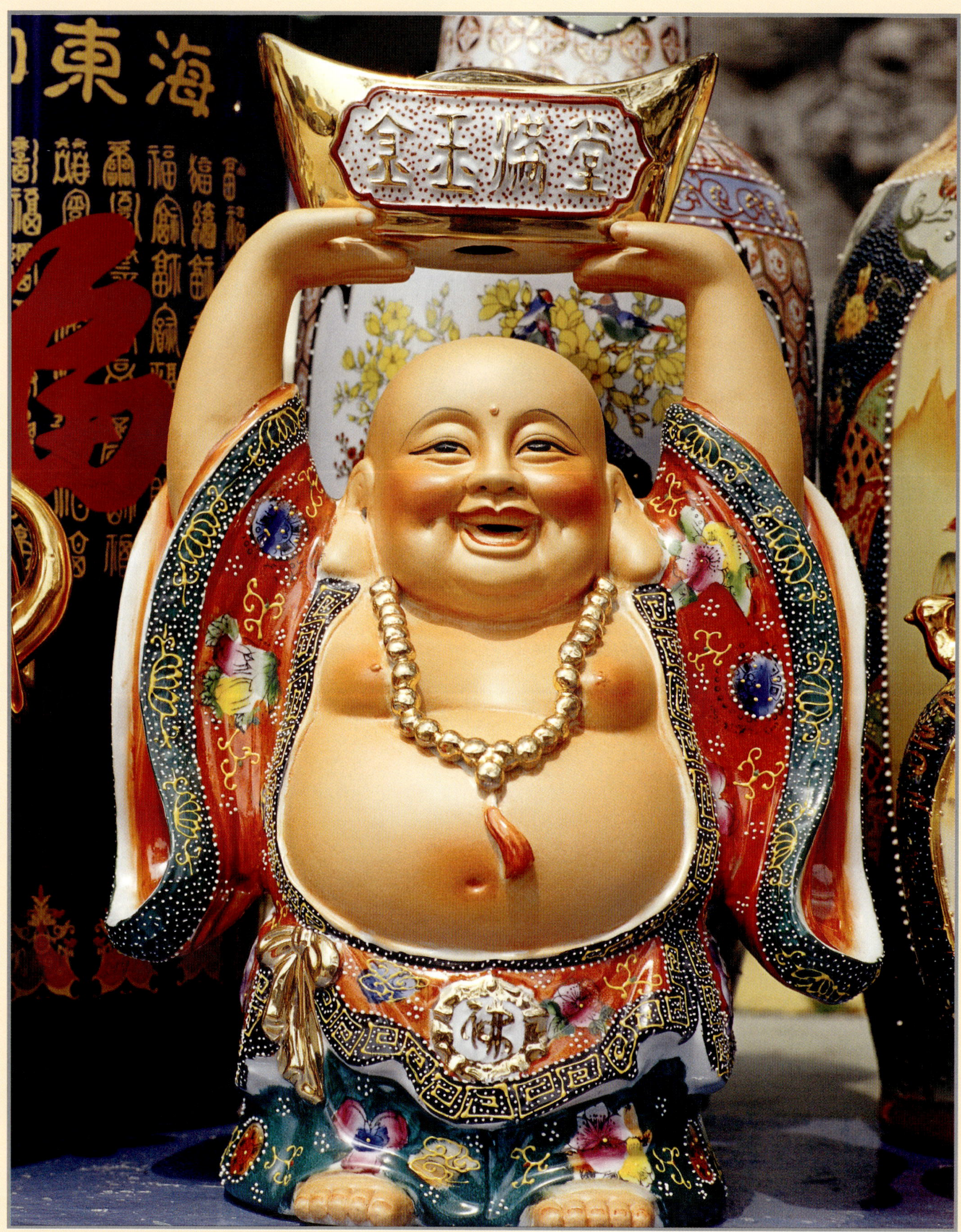
東海
金玉滿堂
佛

Laughing Buddha

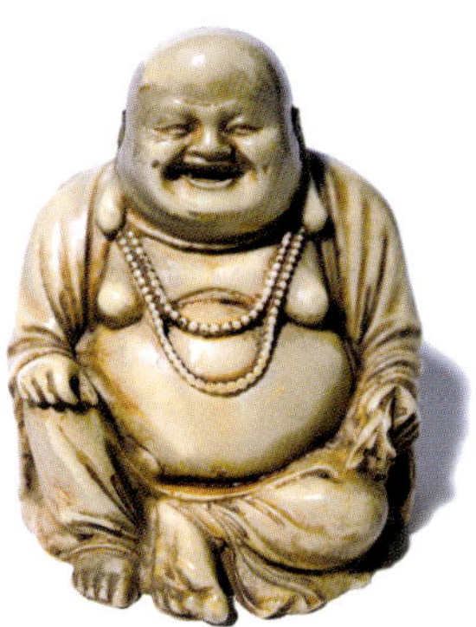

The Buddhist saviour, Maitreya underwent an amazing transformation in China. In popuplar imagination he was identified with a tenth century eccentric monk called Pu-tai, 'Hemp Sack', who in his time had posed as a manifestation of Maitreya. As a result, the slender and majestic figure that we know from so many early sculptures, changed into the familiar 'Laughing Buddha', a pot bellied representation with a broad grin. Such images have assumed a typically Chinese form.

Maitreya, known as Mi-lo-fu in China, acts as a tutelary god. At the very entrance to a temple one meets his plump image with a broad, good-natured smile on his lips, a flower in the right hand and with the left grasping the mouth of the sack in which the future's gifts of happiness are hidden. His cloak is thrown aside so that the enormous chest and fat stomach are exposed. His image is so strange and in a way so comic and appealing that it has found its way into the homes and shops. Actually deepest thoughts and loveliest hopes of Buddhism are bound up with this figure because Mi-lo-fu is believed to descend in future. It is also believed that he once let himself be born an arhat because there is actually a counterpart of Mi-lo-fu in the group of eighteen arhats.

Images of Laughing Buddhas grace many temples, restaurants, and amulets, as he has became a deity of contentment and abundance. Often seen carring a cloth or linen sack filled with precious items, including rice plants (indicating wealth), candy for children, food, or the woes of the world, he is patron of the weak, poor and children.

ABOVE: *Laughing Buddha, loving and caring, is portrayed with a large protruding stomach and jolly smile. He is a symbol of contentment and abundance.*

FACING PAGE: *One of the Laughing Buddhas used as Feng shui images which can be often seen in homes, offices, restaurants or in cars. He carries wishing fan that was at one time used by aristocracy to tell vassals their request would be granted. Travelling Buddhas walk with belongings in pack on a stick.*

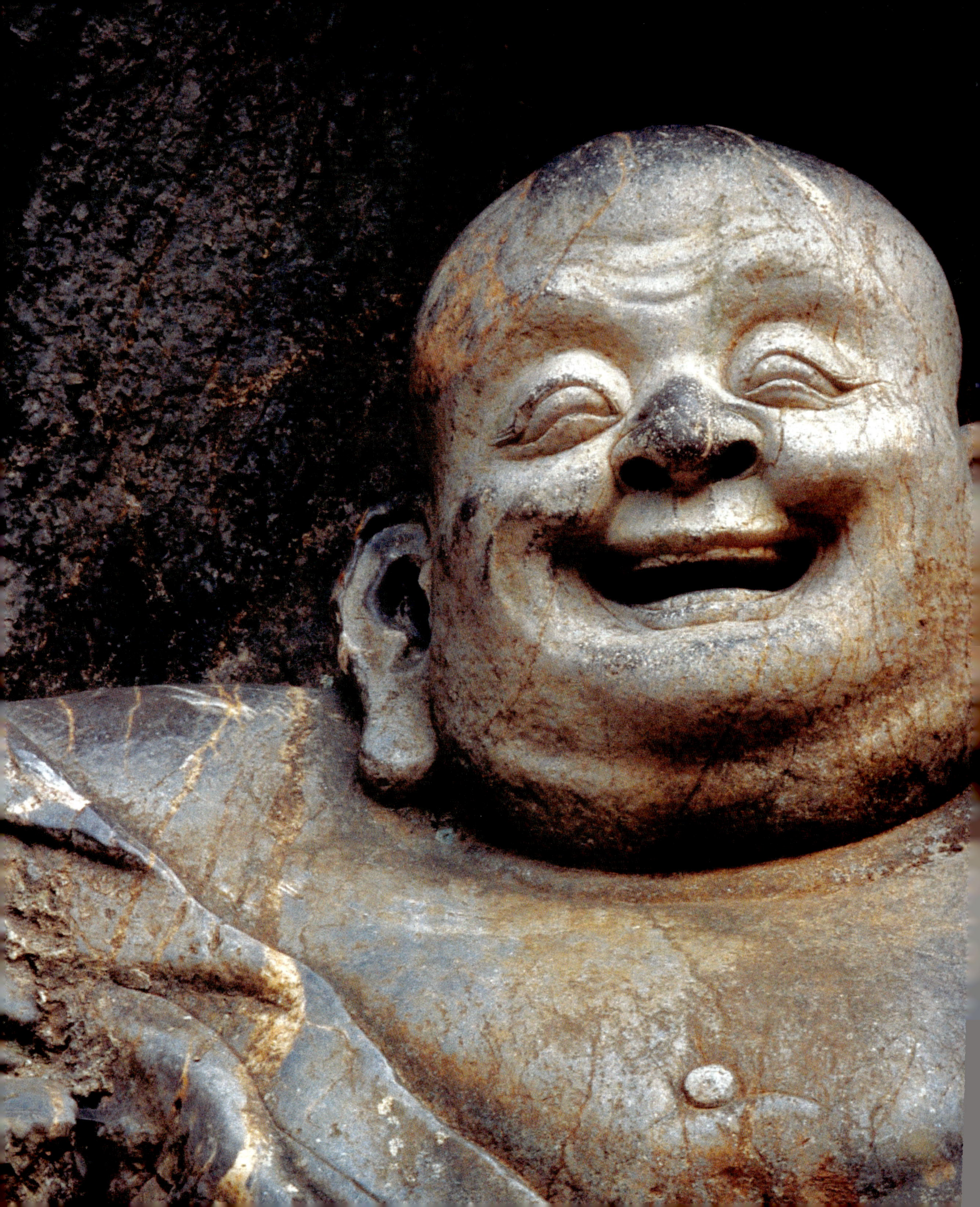

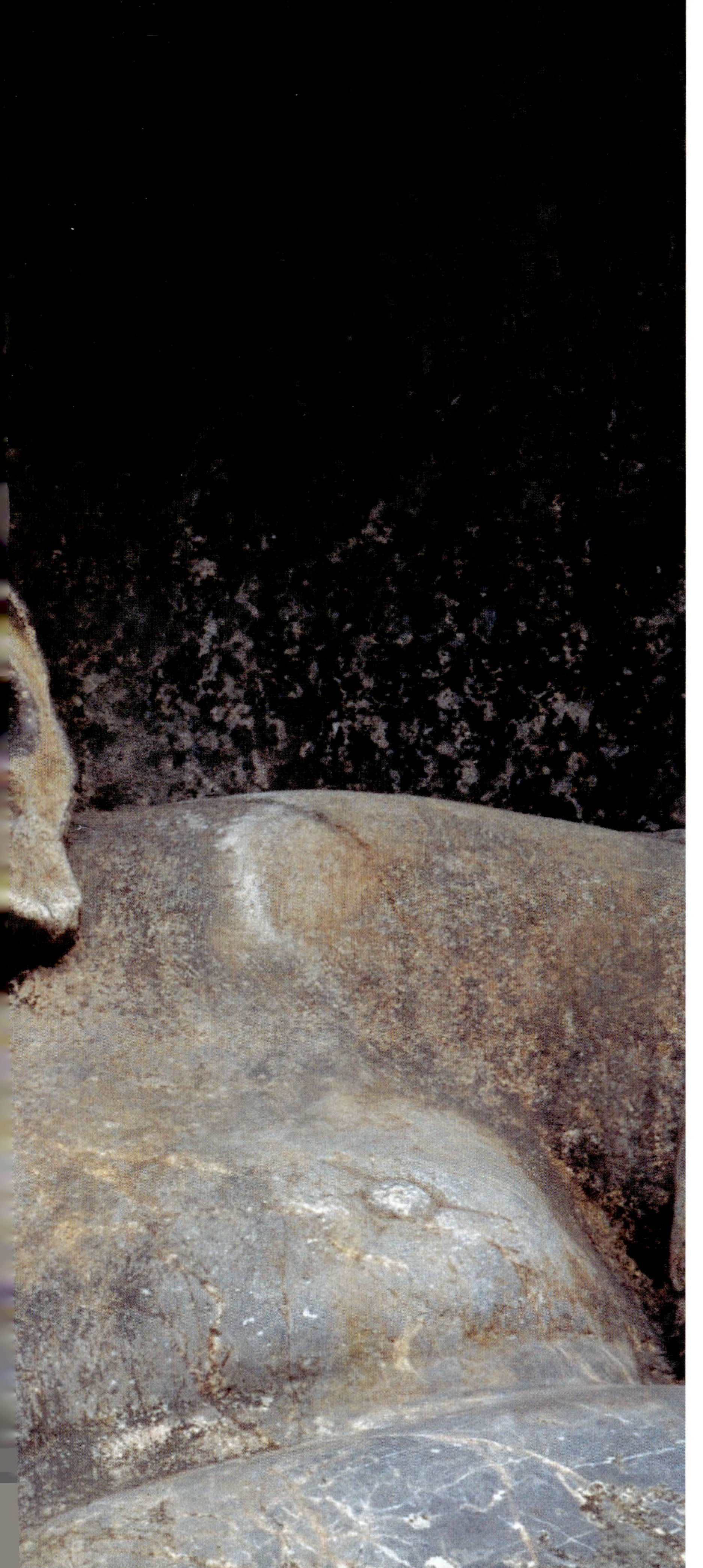

The Buddha holds court in the cave of Laughing Buddha situated on the Liying mountain in China.

Photo credits

CORBIS

Pgs 20, 22-23, 30, 31, 32 (right),
38, 39, 40-41, 42, 44-45, 48, 56, 60, 65, 74,
80-81, 92, 100, 113, 121, 122, 126, 127, 128,
140, 141, 142-43, Cover

GETTY IMAGES

Pgs 26-27, 62-63, 78-79, 104-05, 134, 135

SHASHIBALA

Pgs 2-3, 4-5, 12, 13, 14, 15, 16, 18, 19, 21, 24, 28-29, 32 (left)
33, 34, 35, 37, 43, 47, 49, 50, 52-53, 54, 55, 57, 58, 59, 61, 64, 66, 67, 68, 69, 70
71, 72-73, 77, 82, 83, 84-85, 86, 87, 88, 90, 91, 94, 95, 97, 98-99, 103, 106, 107, 110, 111
114, 116, 117, 118, 123, 124, 131, 132, 133, 136, 137, 138

ROLI COLLECTION

Pgs 75, 101, 108, 109, 125, 130